NARRATIVE APPROACHES
IN SOCIAL WORK PRACTICE

NARRATIVE APPROACHES IN SOCIAL WORK PRACTICE

A Life Span, Culturally Centered, Strengths Perspective

By

EDITH M. FREEMAN, Ph.D., M.S.W.

*Professor Emerita
School of Social Welfare
The University of Kansas
Lawrence, Kansas*

CHARLES C THOMAS • PUBLISHER, LTD.
Springfield • Illinois • U.S.A.

Published and Distributed Throughout the World by

CHARLES C THOMAS • PUBLISHER, LTD.
2600 South First Street
Springfield, Illinois 62704

This book is protected by copyright. No part of
it may be reproduced in any manner without
written permission from the publisher.
All rights reserved.

©2011 by CHARLES C THOMAS • PUBLISHER, LTD.

ISBN 978-0-398-08654-1 (hard)
ISBN 978-0-398-08655-8 (paper)
ISBN 978-0-398-08651-0 (Ebook)

Library of Congress Catalog Card Number: 2011004022

With THOMAS BOOKS *careful attention is given to all details of manufacturing and design. It is the Publisher's desire to present books that are satisfactory as to their physical qualities and artistic possibilities and appropriate for their particular use.* THOMAS BOOKS *will be true to those laws of quality that assure a good name and good will.*

Printed in the United States of America
CR-R-3

Library of Congress Cataloging-in-Publication Data

Freeman, Edith M.
  Narrative approaches in social work practice : a life span, culturally centered, strengths perspective / by Edith M. Freeman.
    p. cm.
  Includes bibliographical references and index.
  ISBN 978-0-398-08654-1 (hbk.) -- ISBN 978-0-398-08655-8 (pbk.) -- ISBN 978-0-398-08651-0 (ebook)
  1. Social service--Psychological aspects. 2. Narrative therapy. I. Title..

HV41.F66 2011
361.3'2--dc22

2011004022

Narratives

A narrative is like clear water
seeking its' own level;
reflecting the sun's healing glow
as it tumbles downhill to natural resting places—
where its musical splashing yields to silence.
There water reflects on its journey,
on its way of meandering around
yesterday's rocks and thorns
and leaving unexpected gemstones in its wake.
For tomorrow.

                        Edith M. Freeman

PREFACE

Freedman and Combs (1996) indicate that narratives define a sequence of experiences or events, as well as relationships, which individuals tend to remember as an often emotionally-charged and complex whole. The purpose of this book is to explain the process in which individuals tell and retell their narratives, especially during developmental and other transitions in order to create meaning and continuity in their lives. The life span framework assumes that such transitions are opportunistic because they allow individuals and families to examine and revise their life narratives during critical times within their natural environments.

Another purpose of the book is to clarify the nature and types of narratives that emerge in people's natural environments during such transitions and during counseling sessions with social workers, psychologists, psychiatrists, counselors, nurses, and other service providers. The book's discussions on postmodern and social construction theories help to expand the conceptual framework that explains clients' narratives and their unique realities, as well as the narrative helping process itself.

The book's purpose is also to describe practical narrative approaches and skills. It includes relevant case examples to illustrate how those approaches have been applied effectively in social work and other helping professions. For example, these narrative practice applications have been effective in a range of practice settings in which time limitations, the nature of clients' challenges, environmental constraints, and helpers' preferred practice approaches often vary. Individual, family, community, organizational, and cultural narratives are included in the book, along with other story forms such as poetry, metaphors, proverbs, parables, letters, personal journals, art, and music.

The book's discussions demonstrate respect for clients' resilience and other natural resources, consistent with the values and orientation of social work and with the strengths perspective. The narrative approaches included in the book build on clients' valuable local knowledge about their experiences, as one source of their self-empowerment and self-healing. Empowerment also occurs because of the collaborative nature of narrative work in which practitioners acknowledge clients as experts and partners in their work together.

The book's social construction framework draws attention to the cultural context in which clients' narratives emerge naturally. This framework is used to analyze how social justice barriers can impact upon clients' lived experiences and upon their efforts to narrate and heal from those experiences. The framework also helps practitioners to elicit exception narratives in which clients have successfully coped with and overcome these and other challenges.

The cultural context of such narratives may involve a combination of significant cultural factors, such as a client's race and ethnicity, language, religion and spirituality, gender, age, sexual orientation, disabling conditions, social class, and/or location. Moreover, the book suggests that effective practitioners should focus on this expanded cultural context related to all clients' narratives, including the narratives of African Americans, Asian Americans and Pacific Islanders, European Americans, Latinos, Native Americans, and Middle Eastern people.

The discussions on the cultural context of clients' narratives encourage helping professionals to reexamine and redefine the concept of cultural competence. Some of the current practice literature defines cultural competence narrowly, that is, as effective practice with clients of color. This book, however takes a broader perspective. It analyzes the effects of cultural factors such as location and spirituality on cultural groups such as white ethnic groups and African immigrants, which are seldom addressed in the literature. The book defines cultural competence as a practitioner's ability to understand, support, and help clients and other providers to consider a broad combination of cultural and other factors during assessment and intervention. This broader and more positive view of culture builds on the strengths perspective literature. It demonstrates how attention to the intersection between culture and narratives helps practitioners to build on and enhance clients' individual skills and abilities, cultural resources, and other strengths.

The book's life span framework enables practitioners to help clients normalize life course transitions and their efforts to narrate those transitions, while challenging their beliefs that the expert knowledge of professionals is more valuable than their own local knowledge. Moreover, this normalization and power-sharing process helps clients to clarify how narratives that emerge during transitions are an opportunity for managing those transitions.

For example, such narratives may reveal clients' strengths and other resources, unfinished issues, or developmental skill gaps from previous transitions that can be addressed during the current transition. Family system problems identified in those narratives may support or inhibit clients' abilities to narrate their transitions, explore the meaning of their narratives, normalize those experiences, or continue their self-healing process. Large systems barriers and supports may also be revealed in clients' narratives which practitioners can help clients to address during current transitions or to anticipate during future transitions.

Based on those multisystem analyses, the book describes strategies that can be used at the micro or direct practice level with clients, the mezzo or community level, and the macro or large systems-institutions level. In the process, the book addresses the effects of the community context, organizational policy and administration, and social policy on clients' narratives. The discussions include analyses of the narrative strategies used by practitioners in specific client, organizational, and community vignettes as well as examples of clients' narratives that are part of those vignettes.

Those analyses and the tables and figures included in each chapter illustrate specifically how particular narrative strategies can be used with clients, while the book includes examples of effective as well as ineffective applications by providers. The book also clarifies how to use those approaches in combination with other practice frameworks, including family systems, task-centered, crisis, solution-focused, group mutual aid, cognitive behavioral, and brief theoretical approaches.

This practice text is organized into two sections. Part One is focused on the theoretical foundations of narrative practice and on five basic principles. Chapter 1 sets the stage by describing the book's first basic principle on the natural emergence of narratives over the life course, and the timing and context in which such narratives surface. Explanatory conceptual and theoretical frameworks presented in that discussion include life span, social construction, spirituality, and cultural perspectives. The sharing of narratives by clients is viewed as part of their ongoing development over the life course. Factors that affect how they experience those transitions and their ability to narrate and heal from them are also highlighted.

The other four chapters in Part One address four other basic principles. Those principles clarify the shared experience and transformation from sharing and listening to narratives, naming and unpacking narratives for assessment and intervention, exploring the meaning making nature of narratives, and implementing socio-political-cultural interventions. Fully developed practice examples and clients' narratives are used in each of the four chapters to illustrate the relevant principle. The chapters in Part One are written in a "how to" format to address basic questions that many practitioners typically ask about the use of narrative approaches.

Although those chapters are organized separately and sequentially for learning purposes, the book encourages practitioners to draw upon the principles in a more organic and integrated manner. Hence, narrative work with a particular client may include combined and simultaneous applications of one or more of these principles, based on a practitioner's judgment about what is required in the situation. Part One can stand alone as a resource for enhancing the professional development and learning curves of beginning practitioners. However, Part One can also be used as a resource by more experienced practitioners who wish to integrate narrative approaches with other practice frameworks they are already using.

The six chapters in Part Two demonstrate the application of advanced narrative skills in practice with clients who are challenged by various life span transitions. The focus is also on systems issues, such as the practices and policies of service organizations and other large institutions. Clients' narratives are included in each chapter to illustrate particular advanced narrative skills and major discussion points. While the focus is on advanced narrative skills in Part Two, those discussions explain how each chapter builds upon principles and narrative strategies from Part One.

The chapters demonstrate the use of narrative strategies and skills with individuals, groups, couples, and families across the life span, for example, with children, adolescents, young and middle adults, and older adults. The discussions in those chapters also include narrative strategies involving communities and large institutions. Many cutting edge practice issues are discussed related to narrative work with clients in different modalities and at different developmental stages. The narrative practice illustrations in both Parts One and Two can be applied by practitioners incrementally in order to monitor and evaluate client outcomes more effectively.

Edith M. Freeman

References

Freedman, J., & Combs, G. (1996). *Narrative therapy: The social construction of preferred realities.* New York: W. W. Norton.

ACKNOWLEDGMENTS

The development of this book is based on my many years of teaching courses on narrative practice, and providing consultation and training to various practice organizations that implemented narrative approaches with their clients. I would like therefore to acknowledge the rich and incredibly gifted contributions of those graduate students and the agency staff and administrators whose paths crossed mine. I am also thankful to the anonymous clients whose life experiences and narratives students and agency personnel shared with me as part of our narrative learning communities over the years. I hope I have captured in this book the essence of what I learned from them, as well as what they concluded they learned from me about narrative practice. Therefore, I am forever grateful to them.

I am also most grateful to family members for their support and the sharing of their narratives over the years, which has enriched all of our lives. They also helped me to integrate the personal and professional understanding I developed about narratives and meaning making. My thanks to those who are no longer with us, Mom and Dad, Ted N, and David N.; along with Gloria, David F, Meredith, Karen, David L, Ted L, and Olivia. This book could not have been written without their contributions about our jointly narrated and lived experiences.

Edith M. Freeman

CONTENTS

Preface vii

PART ONE: BASIC PRINCIPLES AND THEORETICAL FOUNDATIONS OF NARRATIVE PRACTICE APPROACHES

Chapter 1: OBSERVING AND ANALYZING HOW CLIENTS' NARRATIVES EMERGE OVER THE LIFE COURSE: THE NARRATIVE KNOWLEDGE, TIMING, AND CONTEXT PRINCIPLE 5

Chapter 2: LISTENING TO CLIENTS' SPONTANEOUS NARRATIVES: THE SHARED EXPERIENCE AND TRANSFORMATION PRINCIPLE 25

Chapter 3: RESPONDING TO CLIENTS' SPONTANEOUS NARRATIVES: THE NAMING AND UNPACKING ASSESSMENT AND INTERVENTION PRINCIPLE 46

Chapter 4: USING NARRATIVE QUESTIONS TO CONNECT CLIENTS' SINGLE EVENT NARRATIVES AND LIFE NARRATIVES: THE MEANING-MAKING PRINCIPLE 68

Chapter 5: HELPING MARGINALIZED CLIENTS TO SHARE AND ADVOCATE FOR THEIR NARRATED AND UNNARRATED EXPERIENCES: THE SOCIAL JUSTICE-SYSTEMS CHANGE INTERVENTION PRINCIPLE 97

PART TWO: ADVANCED NARRATIVE APPROACHES AND SKILLS WITH INDIVIDUALS, MULTIPLE CLIENT SYSTEMS, AND LARGE SYSTEMS ACROSS THE LIFE SPAN

Chapter 6: USING PLAY, INTERPRETIVE, AND IMPROVISATIONAL NARRATIVE STRATEGIES WITH CHILDREN: PREVENTION, EARLY INTERVENTION, AND TREATMENT 125

Chapter 7: ASSISTING YOUTHS IN EXPLORING CHOICES AND CONSEQUENCES AT CRITICAL MOMENTS THROUGH THEIR LIFE STORIES AND TRANSITION NARRATIVES 146

Chapter 8: HELPING CLIENTS TO REAUTHOR CHALLENGING NARRATIVES ABOUT GENDER AND OTHER ADULT DEVELOPMENT ISSUES 164

Chapter 9: FACILITATING OLDER ADULTS' USE OF LIFE NARRATIVES FOR PERSONAL WELL-BEING, PEER SUPPORT, AND MENTORING 177

Chapter 10: HELPING FAMILIES AND COUPLES TO MANAGE CONFLICTS THROUGH RESOLUTION-BASED METAPHORS AND OTHER NARRATIVE RITUALS 195

Chapter 11: UTILIZING COMMON MARGINALIZED AND EXCEPTION NARRATIVES WITH MULTIPLE CLIENT SYSTEMS TO FACILITATE INDIVIDUAL AND STRUCTURAL CHANGES 208

EPILOGUE:
Lessons Learned and Future Directions for Narrative Practice 225

Author Index 235
Subject Index 239

NARRATIVE APPROACHES
IN SOCIAL WORK PRACTICE

Part One

BASIC PRINCIPLES AND THEORETICAL FOUNDATIONS OF NARRATIVE PRACTICE APPROACHES

Chapter 1

OBSERVING AND ANALYZING HOW CLIENTS' NARRATIVES EMERGE OVER THE LIFE COURSE: THE NARRATIVE KNOWLEDGE, TIMING, AND CONTEXT PRINCIPLE

*What should you do if you find you are
riding a dead horse? Dismount!*

—Native American Proverb

A social worker was concerned about an elderly hospitalized client who told the same story every time she met with him. His story involved a recent house fire that destroyed all of his possessions and led to his heart attack and hospitalization. Her goal was to encourage the client to participate in discharge planning since his cardiac condition had improved. Possibly, the client's goal was to renarrate his loss experience in order to explore its meaning, provide some continuity in his life, and also, help him to heal from several traumatic losses and life transitions (Bahyham, 2003; Thornton, 2003). Those losses included physical functioning, the family home and possessions, and the family's relocation from a familiar rural area. Such impasses are missed narrative opportunities because, in this situation, the practitioner's efforts to maintain focus prevented her from hearing the client's narrative and understanding the conditions that affected the timing and context in which it emerged spontaneously (Freeman & Couchonnal, 2006).

This chapter's epigraph suggests such impasses can be resolved when practitioners reevaluate their preassumptions about how a situation should be handled. In fact, dismounting is a metaphor for practitioners stepping outside their personal cultural paradigms to a space where they can better understand clients' cultural narratives. The epigraph also recommends using a different and often paradoxical strategy in place of an ineffective one (i.e., trying to persuade a dead horse to gallop). In this case, eliminating the persuasion strategy (participation in discharge planning) means the social worker is free to consider explanations of the client's behavior other than resistance, and to use solutions such as observation and listening. Moreover, Freedman and Combs (1996) believe when practitioners give up their predetermined assumptions, they can assume a "not knowing" attitude, which implies that clients rather than practitioners are the experts on their own narratives.

This chapter introduces five basic principles of effective narrative practice that are consistent with a not knowing attitude. It then describes the main elements of the first principle. Next, a narrative conceptual framework is presented along with a case example to explain theoretical assumptions about how this principle works. The discussion illustrates the skill of understanding and applying the identified knowledge base to practice. Finally, another section demonstrates how practitioners can use the skill of asking timing and context questions related to that knowledge base. Principles 2 through 5 are discussed in more detail in subsequent chapters in this section of the book.

Five Principles of Effective Narrative Practice

Table 1.1 illustrates how the five basic principles of effective narrative practice are related synergistically rather than linearly (Freeman, 2004). For example, in this chapter's introduction, the social worker could have drawn upon Principles 1 and 2 simultaneously in response to her client's narrative. Principle 1 clarifies how her elderly client's recent losses and life course transition into the old-old age range probably influenced the timing and retelling of his loss narrative in the hospital. The context for the client's narrative includes both his current losses and past situations where he felt vulnerable, such as during his military service. Understanding these timing and context issues could

Table 1.1
FIVE BASIC PRINCIPLES OF EFFECTIVE NARRATIVE PRACTICE

Basic Principles	Main Elements of Principles	Significance of Each Principle	Narrative Practice Skills
Principle I: The Timing and Context of Narratives Principle	*Timing:* The right narrative emerges at the right time/context. *Context:* Narratives are retold as a way of coping with understanding-controlling key life situations.	Understanding the natural narrative process is the foundation for understanding how narrative practice works.	Understanding and applying the narrative knowledge base. Using timing and context questions.
Principle II: The Shared Experience & Transformation Principle	*Narrative Indicators:* Bench marks for a shared transformation process between teller/listener. *Narrative Challenges:* Helper, client, system barriers to process.	The shared process supports the practitioner in maintaining a not knowing attitude, and the role of clients as experts on their narratives.	Identifying narrative forms and functions. Listening for and acknowledging clients' spontaneous narratives, and the transformative process.
Principle III: Naming and Unpacking: The Assessment-Intervention Principle	*Naming Process:* Clients' power to voice unacknowledged-unidentified aspects of narratives. *Unpacking Process:* Clients' expertise in adding more detailed thicker descriptions of narratives.	Responding effectively to clients' spontaneous narratives facilitates the assessment-intervention process. It identifies and draws upon clients' local knowledge and other strengths.	Using naming questions. Using unpacking questions. Clarifying where clients are in the narrative space. Using solution-focused narrative questions.
Principle IV: The Meaning Making Principle	Narratives people chose to tell have personal meanings central to their *world views and life narratives. Single event narratives* emerge when they conflict with peoples' life narratives.	Helping clients find thematic links between their single event and life narratives provides coherence and continuity, which leads to meaning making in a life review or whole life context.	Using coherence questions focused on narrative themes from single event narratives. Using continuity questions to construct, review, revise, or maintain life narratives.

Continued on next page

Table 1.1 *(continued)*
FIVE BASIC PRINCIPLES OF EFFECTIVE NARRATIVE PRACTICE

Basic Principles	Main Elements of Principles	Significance of Each Principle	Narrative Practice Skills
Principle V: Social-Political-Cultural Intervention Principle	Clients *low currency narratives* can be *externalized* and *deconstructed* to help them separate themselves from their problem situations (*marginalization* analysis)	Encouraging clients to share unnarrated oppressed narratives provides them with new opportunities for voice and agency; to address universal social justice issues through system change.	Eliciting low currency narratives/facilitating policy reform groups. Eliciting exception narratives. Using marginalization analysis. Eliciting decision-makers' dilemma and resolution narratives.

help the practitioner anticipate and value the clients' loss narrative. In addition, Principle 2 could have prepared her to listen for specific indicators of the client's shift from simply recounting the facts of the event to his beginning and ongoing efforts to narrate his loss experience. This principle also explains that storytelling is a shared transformative process that only works if both the listener (the social worker) and the narrator (the client) participate by actively living and reliving the narrative.

Table 1.1 shows also how the other three principles can guide narrative practice. They are focused on responding to clients' narratives by using naming and unpacking questions (for assessment and initial interventions), exploring the meaning of clients' single event narratives and connections between those narratives and their life narratives, and eliciting clients' low currency narratives involving social justice issues (for ongoing interventions at micro, mezzo, and macro levels) (Freeman, 2004).

Overview of the Narrative Timing and Context Principle

Main Elements of Principle One

Principle 1 explains that clients' narratives emerge spontaneously during their life course transitions that are universal and normative (Thornton, 2003). This process occurs naturally in clients' environments and within their significant relationships. However, the process is sometimes inhibited by the manner in which professional services are provided. For instance, paper work requirements and inflexible methods of information gathering can discourage clients from narrating experiences of importance to them related to their past and current situations. Consequently, some clients may assume they should describe only the facts of their situations in a linear sequence.

In contrast, the following main elements of Principle 1 encourage practitioners to support clients in fully narrating their key experiences (Dixon & Gould, 1996; Freeman, 2004):

- Narratives are a mechanism for clients to manage their current life transitions and their recurring unresolved issues.
- Consequently, both current and past transitions are often embedded in clients' narratives.
- The right narrative always emerges when it is supposed to and in the right contexts or situations (the reason a particular narrative was told on a given day and where it was told).

Significance of Principle 1 to Narrative Practice

Clients share narratives spontaneously in their natural family-social-cultural networks that include current and past transitions, so their narratives may include high priority unresolved issues related to those transitions. Effective narrative practice requires an understanding of this natural narrative process (see Table 1.1). The previous hospital social worker with an elderly client had observed her own family members work through issues connected to their narratives. When others listened and acknowledged the value of that process to the teller and listeners, family members sometimes integrated insights and meanings from those discussions into the next retelling of their narratives. If she had applied this family lesson to her work with the elderly client, she would have encouraged him to retell his narrative as a way of working through and coping with his losses.

Definition of Narratives Related to Narrative Practice

The importance of utilizing lessons from practice is reinforced by the definition of narratives, which clarifies their significance to clients and to effective narrative practice. Dart and Davies (2003) believe that clients' narratives "... define relationships, a sequence of events, cause and effect, and a priority among items—and those elements likely to be remembered as a complex whole" (pp. 140-141). This definition emphasizes the importance of what a narrative contains as well as how the parts are related in terms of the meanings and priorities clients infer from their narratives. Furthermore, people's narratives vary in type and purpose, including family, cultural, individual or personal, community, organizational, and life narratives.

Components of the Knowledge Base for the Timing and Context Principle

Table 1.2 includes four theories and perspectives that clarify the knowledge base for the narrative timing and context principle. This knowledge base includes life span development, social construction, spirituality, and cultural theories and perspectives, although other theories are also relevant to an understanding of how narratives work. Examples include empowerment, strengths, postmodern, feminist, and cognitive theories and perspectives, which are integrated into other chapters of this book. Table 1.2 provides examples of the four theories/perspective's assumptions about when narratives emerge and the context of those narratives. The table also describes how narrative approaches work and how they benefit clients according to each perspective and theory. While there is some overlap between each set of assumptions and the operational explanations in Table 1.2, each theory adds some distinct knowledge areas about narratives and narrative practice.

Skill: Understanding and Applying the Knowledge Base

This section includes a discussion about how practitioners can develop an understanding and begin to apply the knowledge base summarized in Table 1.2. A case example is included in this discussion to illustrate how this skill can be operationalized. All four theories and perspectives are applied to the same case example sequentially to illustrate how each adds similar and different knowledge about the individual's narrative. Typically, however, practitioners should identify the

Table 1.2
PRINCIPLE 1: THE NARRATIVE KNOWLEDGE, TIMING,
AND CONTEXT PRINCIPLE
THE SKILL: UNDERSTANDING AND APPLYING THE KNOWLEDGE BASE

The Conceptual Framework's Theories	*Key Assumptions of Each Theory About the Timing and Context of Narratives*	*How Narrative Approaches Work According to Each Theory*
Life Span Development	• Narratives surface at critical transition points in clients' life spans. • The context of clients' narratives involves their past, current, and future challenges.	Narrative approaches allow clients to relive narrated or unarrated experiences at the emotional age when those experiences occurred. They allow clients to work through/resolve those experiences.
Social Construction	• Clients' narratives emerge when they have unique lived experiences/local knowledge. • Those narratives reflect multiple realities or contexts; e.g., oppression or privilege.	These approaches help clients to voice unnarrated experiences that have been silenced, oppressed, and marginalized by the dominant discourse. They give clients opportunities for voice and agency.
Spirituality	• People's narratives emerge during spiritual crises (conflicts in morals, values, beliefs). • Narratives reflect their relationships with a higher power and others which are contextually consistent across situations.	Narrative approaches provide opportunities for clients to act on, question, or explore the meaning of their spirituality; and to stabilize their spiritual values, identity, beliefs, power, and resources.
Cultural	• Individual's narratives surface when they experience significant events related to their cultural values, beliefs, and traditions. • They narrate their experiences to maintain those values, beliefs, traditions across multiple cultural contexts.	Narrative strategies help clients identify cultural themes that reveal their cultural conflicts, solutions, and successes. These strategies allow them to apply cultural lessons from those themes to current difficult life events (to remain culturally centered).

combination of theories that might be most useful for understanding a particular client's narrative and life situation, including these four theories and others.

Background Information on the Case Example

The narrator is an eight-year-old caucasian boy, David, whose narrative is about a previously unstoried loss experience. His narrative was elicited by his mother as part of his natural family support network. David's family consisted of his parents, Mr. and Ms. Wainwright, and his 12- year-old brother Kevin. This white, working class family lived in a rural area of approximately 3,500 residents until the previous year. They moved to an urban area with a population of 500,000. The family lived on the same street as this author, to whom they often waved or made small talk. Kevin had died the previous summer from leukemia. His death seemed sudden to the family; and although they acknowledged the seriousness of his illness, they believed he had been getting better for several months. David attended Kevin's funeral with the family but did not have an opportunity to say goodbye to him in the hospital.

Prior to his death, Ms. Wainwright asked for this author's advice about a conflict the parents had with Kevin about not following his medical regimen and restrictions. A month after Kevin's death, Ms. Wainwright sought this author's advice again about how she had handled David's reaction to Kevin's death. At first, David did not talk much about Kevin's death. Then one day he asked her, "Where is Kevin right now?" When she told him Kevin was in heaven, David said he wanted to talk to him. Ms. Wainwright suggested he write Kevin a letter, and assured him that Kevin would know and understand what David wrote in his letter. Although David seemed satisfied after writing the letter, his mother wondered if she had done the right thing and what she should do if David asked about Kevin again.

David's Letter Narrative

Ms. Wainwright shared the following letter that David wrote with her support:

Dear Kevin,
Mommy said I can write you. I think about you at night in bed. Your room is quiet. I was in there one time. Brown boy had puppies. I got one. Grandpa painted your room. I want to see you soon. Mommy said maybe you can see me from heaven. I made a wish for my birthday. Maybe you can come to my party.

Your little brother David

Questions Raised by David's Narrative

First, is David's letter an actual narrative? Considering the previous definition of narratives, this letter is a first person account of David's life since Kevin died. Moreover, it includes meanings he inferred from different parts of the narrative, his relationships, and his priorities among several concerns. Therefore, David's letter meets the definition of narratives. Second, to what extent is this narrative form appropriate for David's age? Given his stage of cognitive and emotional development, letters are one of several action-oriented tools appropriate for narrating David's experiences, including puppets, action figures or dolls, sand trays, and artwork. A letter narrative is appropriate also for the issues David was struggling with because it helped to normalize his loss and allowed him to express and externalize his reactions safely in the face of societal taboos against expressing feelings about loss.

Life Span Theory

UNDERSTANDING THE THEORY'S ASSUMPTIONS AND EXPLANATORY SYSTEM. This theory provides a normative perspective about developmental strengths and needs across the life span (Freeman, 2000), such as those David expressed. It is consistent with narrative approaches in its view of clients as experts and of client-centered services as essential. Most authors assume change is an implicit aspect of life span theory. Some current thinking has clarified the role of change by suggesting that learning is a bridge between experiencing an event, narrating it, and subsequent growth or change (Dixon & Gould, 1996; Thornton, 2003). This assumption applies to both children and adults, even though the amount and type of learning differs for individuals in the two age groups.

Table 1.2 includes an assumption about life span transitions, which represent periods of tremendous upheaval and change and involve both risks and opportunities for growth. Current transitions present opportunities to master new life course demands through narratives that emerge during those transitions. Individuals can be confronted with unfinished issues from previous transitions that are part of the context of current narratives. According to this theory, narrative approaches work by helping people relive past transitions and clarify where they are stuck. Narratives may reveal how a person's past and current situations are related and can be resolved (Table 1.2).

APPLYING LIFE SPAN THEORY TO DAVID'S NARRATIVE. In David's situation, this theory assumes his narrative emerges when it does (its timing) because it allows him to name and externalize the transition or great upheaval he is experiencing (the narrative's context or the quietness since Kevin died). David's current and future challenges are also part of this context. For example, his current loneliness for his brother is expressed by his statement, "I think about you at night in bed"; while his future hopes are apparent in his plea, "Maybe you can come to my party." Life span theory clarifies how David's narrative works for him (see Table 1.2). For example, the tone and content of his narrative indicate David relived his loss experience at his current emotional age, which is very sensory oriented according to his comment, "Maybe you can see me from heaven." Moreover, this theory indicates that David's narrative helped him to begin to work through his loss experience. He has a new companion ("Brown boy had puppies. I got one"), he has located Kevin in a specific place called heaven, and he realizes Kevin is no longer in his room because it is now quiet compared to when Kevin was alive.

Social Construction Theory

UNDERSTANDING THE THEORETICAL ASSUMPTIONS AND EXPLANATIONS. This theory explains how culture in its broadest sense, as society, structures and interprets individual experience through a dominant rather than multiple reality discourse (Crossley, 2003). It is important to understand that people whose narratives are silenced, oppressed, or marginalized because they threaten those in power, often experience a "shattered sense of identity and meaning" (Crossley, 2003, p. 287). McLeod (1997) believes people who are able to narrate their lived experiences can reconstruct themselves and their identities through their narratives, especially when they are confronted with unexpected events. The theory assumes people's narrative contexts can reveal their status as oppressed or privileged individuals, and the challenges associated with their status. Operationally, social construction indicates that narrating unstoried experiences allows clients to name their interpretive systems (to voice previously hidden meanings) and to act on behalf of change (to experience agency) (see Table 1.2).

APPLYING SOCIAL CONSTRUCTION THEORY TO DAVID'S NARRATIVE. David's narrative illustrates this theory's assumption about how society interprets and limits people's opportunities to narrate certain devalued experiences. His narrative, like those of many children, has been silenced by society's general taboos about expressing reactions to a death, and by taboos specifically focused on not acknowledging children's losses. Adults may believe they should protect children by denying or underrating the intensity of their losses. The adults in David's situation have moved on by engaging in rituals designed specifically by and for adults (funerals), and by eliminating several signs of Kevin's previous existence such as repainting his room.

David's request to ". . . know where Kevin is right now," is an effort to construct meaning out of the unexpected event of his brother's death, according to another social construction assumption. David's experience demonstrates how his narrative works for him based on this theory. For instance, his narrative allows him to exercise voice or the power to initiate dialogue about his recent loss in his own language (his letter). The narrative is also an example of agency or taking positive action; it recounts how David went into Kevin's room once and made a birthday wish.

The Spiritual Perspective or Spirituality

UNDERSTANDING THE PERSPECTIVE'S ASSUMPTIONS AND EXPLANATORY SYSTEM. To understand this perspective requires clarity about how it is defined and how it is different from religion. Spirituality consists of the internalization and consistent expression of positive values, life meaning, and an effort to manifest goodness in daily life (Potts, 1991; Zinnbauer, Pargament, Cole, Rye, Butter, Belavich, Hipp, Scott, & Kadar, 1997). Mattis (2000) defines spirituality as a belief in the existence and presence of a higher power and spirits, and in abilities and experiences that are consistent with the nonmaterial aspects of people's lives. This perspective differs from but is often compared to religion, which is, ". . . an individual's level of adherence to the doctrines, beliefs, and ritual practices of religious institutions and level of organizational religious involvement (e.g., church attendance)" (Mattis, 2000).

The spiritual perspective assumes that people's narratives emerge when they experience spiritual crises. Not only is the timing of narratives linked to such crises, but those crises are the narrative context in which individuals either apply their spiritual values to new aspects of their lives or refine those values (see Table 1.2). Spirituality allows individuals to maintain contextually consistent values and beliefs across different situations and times when crises are not occurring. According to spirituality, narratives allow people to address meaning in their lives and relationships to themselves and others. Those relationships include both transcendent connections (ancestors, a higher power) and nontranscendent ones (current family, social, or cultural relationships) (see Table 1.2).

APPLYING SPIRITUALITY TO DAVID'S NARRATIVE. From this perspective, David's narrative clearly emerged from his questions about how to maintain his relationship and connection to Kevin after death. Although he is in a spiritual crisis, David's narrative radiated hope for maintaining this relationship as part of the spirituality he had been taught by his parents ("Mommy said maybe you can see me from heaven"). In fact, his mother placed this hopeful narrative in her "spirit bowl" where it could receive special attention from her higher power. This act implied she was David's spiritual guide, and that he did not have to face his life crisis alone. However, David may have experienced a conflict between being hopeful that he could stay connected to Kevin (via the spirit bowl's benefits) and accepting his mother's belief that Kevin's death happened for a reason and was a matter of fate.

David's narrative seemed to work for him because it reflected his effort to question and then create consistent beliefs about his connection with Kevin across two situations, when Kevin was alive and the period since his death. David inferred meaning from his narrative and his loss based on a spiritual perspective. For instance he wrote, "Your room is quiet" (so this must be what death is like), and "I was in there (in your room) once" (something must have changed or he would not be allowed to go in there). In addition, connecting with Kevin through the narrative may have allayed some of David's natural anxiety about his own mortality, a common reaction to death by children.

Adults who share their spiritual crisis narratives benefit from challenging their conflicting values and beliefs and from refining them as needed. They also can do a spiritual self-examination for increased self-knowledge. For children at David's stage of cognitive development, this self-knowledge aspect of spirituality may not be possible although they can make their spiritual and narrative experiences a part of their lives.

Cultural Theory

UNDERSTANDING THE THEORY'S ASSUMPTIONS AND EXPLANATIONS. This theory assumes that people's culture impacts their significant lived experiences over time and across multiple contexts (see Table 1.2). Moreover, McGill (1992) suggests an understanding of cultural theory and narratives involves a belief that all cultural groups story or narrate such experiences. Those narratives are central to their cultural and personal identities. The meanings they infer from such narratives are expressed as cultural themes. These stated or unstated themes highlight a group's cultural beliefs, traditions, values, transitions, and strengths and challenges. The themes also reflect a cultural group's relationships with and understanding of dominant society. Moreover, they illustrate a group's ways of coping with, surviving, or thriving in spite of oppression from society's practices and policies. Although these assumptions about oppression have been applied primarily to groups of color, they have been applied ". . . more broadly to groups that are different in terms of age, religion, gender, sexual orientation, disabling conditions, and location (Freeman, 2000).

According to cultural theory, narrative approaches work because they challenge and support clients' cultural beliefs, values, and traditions. More specifically, narrative themes reveal clues about a group or individual's cultural conflicts, along with their cultural solutions, successes, and strengths (see Table 1.2). Seleebey (1994) suggests an analysis of those themes can instruct clients on how to survive, accept, or overcome difficult life events, while remaining culturally centered.

This process involves turning points or cultural moments that can result in the generation of lifelong cultural lessons, which further anchor the identified narrated experiences and cultural themes (Bermudez & Bermudez, 2002; Caldwell, 2005; Chadiha, Adams, Phorano, Ong, & Byers, 2002; Chan, 2003; and Lowery, 1998).

APPLYING CULTURAL THEORY TO DAVID'S NARRATED EXPERIENCE. From a cultural perspective, David experienced a difficult life event or significant lived experience involving the death of his older brother. His loss narrative reflects cultural meanings he inferred from that experience. Those inferences may have been based on his family's German American ethnicity (second generation), his previous life and cultural norms in a small rural area connected to that ethnicity (location), and on his age and gender as an eight-year-old boy. David's inferences were expressed as two cultural themes in his narrative.

One theme is cultural stoicism which is illustrated by cultural norms about German Americans, people in his rural area, and boys not crying or expressing their feelings. McGill (1992) identified correctness and natural order as similar German American narrative themes often expressed by families from that ethnic background. David's narrative works because it allows him to narrate these cultural challenges and conflicting norms in ways he might not have been able to verbalize. His narrative also reveals previously unacknowledged cultural solutions for coping with his loss related to this theme: He was coping by looking forward to a future event (his birthday party), and he wanted to incorporate Kevin into his future. Specifically, David wanted Kevin to come to his party; but his mother suggested having a picture of Kevin at the party as an alternative solution. This is an example of a cultural moment for David whereby he learned how to maintain his sibling cultural network by adopting a more realistic solution. It is not clear whether David learned any additional cultural lessons from narrating his loss experience.

A second narrative theme is cultural invisibility. That theme is reflected in David's narrated experience of loneliness and isolation from his sibling network ("I think about you at night in bed"), and in the marginalization of his loss experience as a child. Based on this theme, the cultural challenges in his narrative include the following: (1) His cultural transition from membership in a sibling network to being an only child, (2) The absence of cultural recognition and supports for his loss of a sibling as an eight year old, and (3) His upcoming birthday, which usually included a family ritual involving the sibling network. David's narrative works for him by highlighting cultural solutions such as being invited to narrate his loss experience by his mother ("Mommy said I can write you"), which reflects an increasingly empathic relationship with one adult in his life. Another solution was his mother's placement of David's narrative in her spirit bowl, a more explicit and formal acknowledgement of his loss.

Skill: Asking Timing and Context Questions

Timing and context questions are tools practitioners can use to check out their assumptions from the knowledge base discussed in the previous section. In this circular process, practitioners generate feedback from asking timing and context questions that help to test and hone their knowledge application skills, and the reverse. Table 1.3 includes some examples of timing and context questions. Practitioners can begin with the questions that seem most appropriate, whether the focus is on the narrated experience first or on the narrative itself, and whether the focus is on using timing or context questions first. Irregardless of where the questions begin, they can be directed toward clients or their significant others. The goal is to elicit more details about why a client's narrative emerges or is told at a particular time and about the narrative's context.

Applying These Questions to David's Narrative

OTHER EXPRESSIONS OF DAVID'S NARRATIVE? Questions were asked of David's mother initially about the narrative itself in order to add details and check out previous assumptions (Freeman, 2004). After reading David's letter, this author asked Ms. Wainwright if he had expressed his feelings about Kevin's death in other ways (see Table 1.3: Timing Question #3 About *the Narrative*). Had he drawn any pictures, told stories verbally, engaged in acting-out behavior (misbehaved), or sang songs about his feelings or experiences? Ms. Wainwright recalled a picture David had drawn while visiting his grandparents right after Kevin died. When David showed me this picture, it contained a well-detailed rendition of a large house centered on the page. David explained his family lived in this house in their pre-

Table 1.3
PRINCIPLE 1: THE NARRATIVE KNOWLEDGE, TIMING, AND CONTEXT
PRINCIPLE: NARRATIVE SKILLS: THE USE OF TIMING
AND CONTEXT QUESTIONS

Focus these Questions on:	*Examples of Timing Questions (Use with clients or their significant others)*	*Examples of Context Questions (Use with clients or their significant others)*
The Narrated Event or Experience:	1. When did the narrated event or experience occur (how long ago in time)? 2. When did it occur related to your life situation and circumstances (Your age, coping resources, or level of understanding). 3. Did you have a similar experience prior to that time, and if so, when did it (they) occur?	1. Where did the narrated experience occur or take place? 2. What else was going on in in your life or in your situation when the experience occurred? 3. Who else was involved in the experience?
The Narrative Itself:	1. When did you tell or share your narrative for the first time? 2. How often have you told or shared your narrative since the first time, and under what circumstances have you retold it? 3. Have you expressed or shared your narrative in other ways, and if so, when and how have you expressed it?	1. Who did you first tell your narrative to? 2. What was his/her reaction or response? 3. Where were you when you first shared the narrative? 4. What effect could that setting have had on how you told the narrative? 5. What else was going on in your life situation when you first told or shared your narrative?

vious community. One window in Kevin's bedroom had been drawn and then blacked out, while the other windows were blank. A group of three boys was drawn in the lower left corner of the picture. They were David's friends from his previous community. Another boy without feet floated above the house near a very blackened sky. The figure was David who he said flew away whenever he was sad. The sky was so dark that David was not sure Kevin was really in heaven.

This timing question about David's narrative resulted in Ms. Wainwright finding a picture narrative he had drawn about his initial experiences after Kevin's death. The question added details about what social construction theory labels as David's shattered identity (Saleebey, 1994), based not only on the loss of his sibling network but also on the loss of his old peer network. This question confirmed and then clarified more details about the nature of David's spiritual crisis. For David, it was harder to believe people like Kevin went to heaven when they died, because the darkened sky did not seem friendly or welcoming. Therefore, after seeing David's picture, it was clear that his loss narrative began from the point when he drew the picture, and that his narrative had two different but related forms (Brandell, 1988): the picture and the subsequent letter to Kevin.

WHERE AND WITH WHOM WAS THE NARRATIVE FIRST SHARED.? Responses to these questions by David and his mother indicated he had explained his drawing or told his grandparents a story about the picture (see Table 1.3: Timing and Context Questions #1 About *the Narrative*). He stayed with them from the day before Kevin died until two days after the funeral. They lived in the Wainwright's former small rural community. The grandparents responded by praising David's drawing, and then the grandmother cried in her room and the grandfather walked around the yard alone. They did not refer to his drawing again. David said he later took the picture home and placed it on the wall over Kevin's bed. His mother had seen the picture on the wall but had not commented on it.

These timing and context questions about his picture clarified the significance of one section of David's letter narrative in which he said, "I was in there {in Kevin's bedroom} one time." That was the point when David placed the picture on Kevin's bedroom wall, perhaps hoping Kevin would understand and accept it as an expression of David's loss. From a life span perspective (Thornton, (2003), those questions about the picture narrative also revealed his transition from a past community experience to a current community and family experience, involving similar losses.

Applying These Questions to David's Narrated Experience

WHEN DID THE NARRATED EXPERIENCE OCCUR? This timing question about David's narrated experience helped to revise a previous assumption about that experience (see Table 1.3: Timing Question #.1 About *the Narrated Experience*). For example, when he was asked what happened first in his picture, David said his family had moved. Moreover, the narrated experience in his picture clearly covers the period from the family's move one year earlier until right after Kevin's death. The narrated experience in David's letter began with Kevin's death and included a one-month period after his death. This indicates the experience narrated in the letter was either a subsequent event or a continuation of the narrated experience in his picture. Hence, from a life span perspective, David's transition was far more extensive and covered a longer period than was previously assumed.

WHERE DID THE EXPERIENCE OCCUR AND WHO ELSE WAS INVOLVED? Asking where the narrated experience occurred highlights the importance of David's previous community in terms of his location and peer network losses (see Table 1.3: Context Question #1 About the *Narrated Experience*). The question about who else was involved clarifies the role Kevin might have played in helping David to cope with those earlier losses (see Table 1.3: Context Question #3 About *the Narrated Experience*). More specifically, Kevin's death involved a loss of support for handling earlier losses as well as the loss of Kevin as David's sibling network. The blackened bedroom window in David's picture illustrated the pain and anger he felt about his dual loss from a cultural perspective.

Conclusions

This chapter addresses the skills of observing and applying the narrative knowledge base, and asking timing and context questions. A young boy's narrative was used to illustrate how narratives emerge informally in families' environments. The discussion also illustrates how practitioners can step outside their cultural paradigms and preassumptions, an application of the dismount metaphor from this chapter's introduction. Dismounting allows practitioners to reexamine and discard preassumptions about clients and their narratives that inhibit the narrative process. For example, this author could have assumed that David's loss narrative involved only Kevin's recent death. By asking his mother if he had expressed his loss in other ways, the narrative process was expanded rather than curtailed. Practitioners who understand this natural storytelling process can apply such lessons to their practice with clients.

Therefore the following conclusions about the author's informal work with David and his mother are relevant to narrative practice in general. Regarding Ms. Wainwright's response to David's question about Kevin's whereabouts, this author: (1) Reassured her that having David write a letter was a positive step, (2) Explored the timing and context questions described in the previous section which caused Ms. Wainwright to remember David's picture, (3) Suggested she allow me to see David's picture, (4) Agreed to meet with David to assess if he needed to be referred for services and requested that he bring his favorite toy with him, (5) Had David tell me a story about his picture narrative which led me to revise some of my theoretical assumptions about his two narratives as noted in the previous section, (6) Assessed information in his story along with my observations of his play activity with the action figures he brought to the meeting (observations revealed his figures did not cry when they were sad or had been hurt), and (7) Recommended his mother involve him in a children's group for handling his age-appropriate and natural reactions to loss. Consequently, David was involved in and benefited from an eight-week peer group at school focused on loss. It was co-facilitated by a counselor and social worker.

Finally, practitioners who work with clients like David should encourage parents to continue the process of supporting their child's expression of feelings and coping with loss. They can help parents explore and learn from other questions such as: How did they prepare their child for the impending death or other loss? What were the effects of their child's unstoried experience on his/her ability to cope prior to telling the narrative? How did they and others respond to the child's efforts to story his/her loss experience? Were adult and peer role models available who have coped effectively with loss? These questions and the timing and context questions included in Table 1.3 are essential tools for beginning narrative practice, based on the knowledge base described in this chapter.

References

Bahyham, M. (2003). Narratives in space and time: Beyond "backdrop" accounts of narrative orientation. *Narrative Inquiry, 13(2)*, 347–366.

Bermudez, J., & Bermudez, S. (2002). Altar-making with Latino families: A narrative therapy perspective. *Journal of Family Psychotherapy, 13*(3–4), 329–347.

Brandell, J. R. (1988). Narrative and historical truth in child psychotherapy. *Psychoanalytic Psychology, 5*, 241–257.

Caldwell, R. L. (2005). At the confluence of memory and meaning-life review with older adults and families: Using narrative therapy and the expressive arts to remember and re-author stories of resilience. *Family Journal of Counseling and Therapy for Couples and Families, 13*(2), 172–175.

Chadiha, L. A., Adams, P., Phorano, O., Ong, S. L., & Byers, L. (2002). Stories told and lessons learned from African American female caregivers' vignettes for empowerment practice. *Journal of Gerontological Social Work, 40*(1/2), 135–144.

Chan, D. W. (2003). Multicultural considerations in counseling Chinese clients: Introducing the narrative alternative. *Asian Journal of Counseling, 10*(2), 169–172.

Crossley, M. L. (2003). Formulating narrative psychology: The limitations of contemporary social constructionism. *Narrative Inquiry, 13(2)*, 287–300.

Dart, J., & Davies, R. (2003). A dialogical, story-based evaluation tool: The most significant change technique. *American Journal of Evaluation, 24*(2), 137–155.

Dixon, R. A. & Gould, O. N. (1996). Adults telling and retelling stories collaboratively. In P. B. Baltes & U. M. Staudinger (Eds.), *Interactive minds: Life-span perspectives on the social foundation of cognition* (pp. 221–241). New York: Cambridge University Press.

Freedman, J., & Combs, G. (1996). *Narrative therapy: The social construction of preferred realities.* New York: W.W. Norton.

Freeman, E. M. (2000). Direct practice in fields related to developmental tasks: A life-span perspective. In P. Allen-Meares & C. Garvin (Eds.), *The handbook of social work direct practice* (pp. 415–435). Thousand Oaks, CA: Sage.

Freeman, E. M. (March 4, 2004). Basic principles of effective narrative practice. Workshop presentation. Kansas City, MO: The Social Work Coalition and Social Work Leaders in Health Care.

Freeman, E. M., & Couchonnal, G. (2006). Narrative and culturally based approaches in practice with families. *Families in Society, 87*(2), 198–208.

Lowery, C. T. (1998). American Indian narratives: ". . . my spirit is starting to come back." *Reflections, 4*(3), 26–35.

Mattis, J. S. (2000). African American women's definitions of spirituality and religiosity. *Journal of Black Psychology, 26*(1), 101–123.

McGill, D. W. (1992). The cultural story in multicultural family therapy. *Families in Society, 73,* 339–349.

McLeod, J. (1997). *Narrative and psychotherapy.* London: Sage.

Potts, R. (1991). Spirits in the bottle: Spirituality and alcoholism treatment in African American communities. *Journal of Training and Practice in Professional Psychology, 5*(1), 53–64.

Saleebey, D. (1994). Culture, theory, and narrative: The intersection of meanings in practice. *Social Work, 39*(4), 351–359.

Thornton, J. E. (2003). Life-span learning: A developmental perspective. *International Journal of Aging and Human Development, 57*(1), 55–76.

Zinnbauer, B., Pargament, K., Cole, B., Rye, M., Butter, E., Belavich, T., Hipp, K., Scott, A., & Kadar, J. (1997). Religiousness and spirituality: Unfuzzing the fuzzy. *Journal for the Scientific Study of Religion, 36*(4), 549–564.

Chapter 2

LISTENING TO CLIENTS' SPONTANEOUS NARRATIVES: THE SHARED EXPERIENCE AND TRANSFORMATION PRINCIPLE

> When you live next to the cemetery
> you cannot cry for everyone.
> —Russian Proverb

Megan, a practitioner in a substance abuse treatment program, cofacilitated a women's recovery group with Dan, one of her colleagues. She noticed that when clients shared narratives about their relapses or near-relapses, he seemed to tune out their discussions with a closed facial expression. Megan wondered if group members noticed this pattern and how Dan's reactions might be affecting them. She discussed her observations with Dan during one of their facilitator planning sessions. Dan said the group members' narratives reminded him of his past relapses, some of which he had never shared as part of his own recovery. The group members' narratives made him feel more vulnerable to relapse, so he stopped listening to their narratives.

Practitioners who have significant unnarrated life experiences are often unable to listen to clients' narratives, whether the practitioner's unnarrated experiences are related to recovery, loss and grief, cultural oppression, childhood abuse, or other areas (Freeman, 2004; Gilbert & Beidler, 2001). Unnarrated experiences can prevent practitioners, clients, and others from working through and learning from the emotional issues embedded in those experiences. This chapter's epigraph is a reminder of such narrative challenges. "Living next to the cemetery" is akin to practitioners using narrative approaches with clients without the support of previous work on their own narratives. Another reason practitioners like Dan find it difficult to listen to or empathize with everyone else's narratives is they frequently misunderstand the role of listening in narrative work.

This chapter clarifies the importance of the narrative listening principle as a shared experience and transformation process, and how that principle informs narrative practice. The skill of identifying narrative forms and functions is a basic aspect of this principle. The discussion about that skill lays a foundation for another skill related to Principle 2. Listening to clients' spontaneous narratives includes hearing and observing changes in the narrator and listeners' behaviors that signal the emergence of narratives (narrative indicators). Listening also involves acknowledging those narratives and the narrator-listener transformation experience.

Overview of the Shared Experience and Transformation Principle

Main Elements of Principle Two

The process during which individuals share their narratives spontaneously was explained in Chapter 1 (Principle 1), based on life span, spiritual, and other perspectives (Table 1.1). For example, clients' narratives are often precipitated by and shared during significant life transitions or spiritual crises (timing and context factors) (Yellow Bird, 1995; Thornton, 2003). The strengths perspective and resiliency theory are also informative about this process, especially in regard to Principle 2. Both perspectives indicate that individuals' narratives allow them to shift from explaining significant experiences and beliefs to reliving and overcoming those experiences, as a way of recreating themselves, and as evidence of their strengths and resilience. Recreating the self occurs because narratives contain the necessary resources, including clients' local knowledge, for helping them to work through emotional and other issues embedded in their narratives (Freeman, 2004). In addition, clients' narratives contain information that may help practitioners to anticipate challenges to this process related to clients, practitioners, and practice settings. To summarize, this strengths and resiliency-based process (see Principle 2 in Table 1.1):

- Creates a shared emotional connection or bond between the narrator and listeners as they enter and live through or relive a client's narrative experience;

- Reveals narrative indicators that document how the narrator and listeners shift from standing outside the narrative to moving into it as a shared experience;

- Leads to a shared transformation or growth process between narrator and listeners that is integrated into future:

  - Lessons learned from being in the same emotional and narrative space, and

  - Ways of being or identity, both individually and collectively.

Significance of Principle Two to Narrative Practice

This shared process implies client-practitioner partnership roles that are consistent with the values of helping professionals and narrative practice. For example, it requires practitioners to listen from a not-knowing rather than all-knowing perspective, without directing or controlling the narrative process. It facilitates clients' roles as experts on their narratives and in the spontaneous telling or retelling of narratives. Moreover, the process strengthens the collaborative relationship with clients, which is essential for effective narrative practice. Principle 2, therefore, encourages practitioners to maintain a more equitable form of power sharing with clients (Boehm & Staples, 2004). In the practice example in this chapter's introduction, one group facilitator (Dan) disrupted the power-sharing process by not listening to clients' narratives. The other facilitator, Megan, opened up a dialogue with him about the potential effects of his behavior on their clients' empowerment process, a critical aspect of Principle Two shown in Table 1.1 (Lee, 2001).

Skill: Identifying Narrative Forms and Functions

Principle 2 assumes the skill of identifying different narrative forms and functions enhances the narrative process for clients. This basic skill can help practitioners to develop other skills such as acknowledging clients' spontaneous narratives and eliciting their narratives (Freeman, 2004). For instance, it may be easier for a practitioner to have an adolescent in mandated services analyze a song than share an individual loss narrative. Although both are elicited narratives, analyzing a song involves less risk taking for adolescents than sharing a significant individual narrative. Encouraging the client to select his or her favorite rock or rap song can make the narrative process even more age-appropriate and collaborative. This section demonstrates how practitioners can make such important clinical decisions based on the skill of identifying narrative forms and functions. A case example and a client's narrative are used to center the discussion.

Background Information on the Case Example

Thirty-five-year-old Rachael is an African American client who recently entered a substance abuse rehabilitation program for women. Two of her children were placed in foster care by Children's Protective Services (CPS) due to neglect, while her oldest child lives with Rachael's sister. Rachael is cut off from the rest of her family, including her husband who does not pay child support. Her medical records job ended three years previously after her crack cocaine addiction affected her work attendance and performance. The rehab program serves African American and Latino women primarily, but also includes white women. The services include a women's issues group cofacilitated by Megan and Dan, the social worker and psychologist identified in this chapter's introduction. The facilitators and group members provide feedback and problem-solving support to the women for their common challenges in parenting, relationships, self-esteem, gender, and addiction issues.

At the beginning of one session, Megan noticed that Rachael entered the group room quietly and slipped into a seat in the back, away from the other members. When Dan asked who wanted to start the session, one member, Beth, pointed out that Rachael was crying. Everyone turned toward Rachael who said, "I don't want to talk; it's the same old story, I screwed up my visit with my kids today. But I really did try this time, really hard." Megan asked her to tell how she tried this time, what she did differently.

Rachael's Narrative

Well, you know my youngest kids live in foster care in Pinellas County. I don't deny I've been a bad mother—when I was druggin'—I was into the street life and not takin' care of my kids at all. But since I been in rehab I've changed—I mean I've started changing. You have to cross two counties to get to Pinellas, and me without a car. It takes three hours to get there, on three different buses. I went to bed early the night before like I planned, laid out my clothes, and set my alarm clock. I was a little stressed out, but it was a good thing. It made me determined not to miss my visit again. I even called ahead, Megan, like you and Dan suggested, to let Ms. Greene, the foster mother know my plan. Like the CPS rules say—I confirmed my visit. I checked for my bus pass and a little extra money. I thought, maybe things *will* be better tomorrow when I get to see my kids.

I left a little early this morning. The first bus came on time, and so did the second one. Then the second bus got a flat tire. I'd left extra time for emergencies, but we—the riders—just had to wait. I started pacing to keep from screaming, why me, why today? Back and forth, up and down. I know the other riders thought I was losing my mind. Nobody said anything—but I could see them pretending they weren't watching me. It took over an hour before another bus picked us up. When the bus got to my stop I ran all the way to Ms. Greene's—two and a half blocks. I could hardly breathe. I was 40 minutes late.

As soon as Ms. Greene opens the door I start explainin' what happened. She's sorry she says but the CPS worker told her not to let me see my kids unless I was on time and not using drugs. I tell her, *I'm not high.* She says if it was up to her she'd let me see them, but she has to follow CPS rules. They'll land on her if she doesn't. I *plead* with her—Ms. Greene, I haven't seen my kids in three months; I need to see them and they want to see me. I can hear my kids talking and playing somewhere inside. So, I call out, Damon and Chris, Mommy's here to get you. I haven't forgotten you, like before. Ms. Greene tells me, I know you wanna' see them. Even though I'll have to report your missed visit to CPS, you should try again and not give up. By then I can hear my kids crying—calling me, Mama, Mama. Ms. Greene takes my hand off the door frame and closes the door. Even though she's trying to be nice, I don't think she's really on my side. I just stand there trying not to cry or make a bigger fool of myself. I feel like nothin', knowing my kids think I'm failing them again. And I feel like I wanna get high, real bad. So I say to myself, go to group so you don't screw up your recovery too.

Distinguishing Between Narrative Forms

CLIENTS' LIVED NARRATIVES. In response to Rachael's narrative, Dan told her the main thing he got from her story was that she had not relapsed in spite of her difficult day. Several group members consoled Rachael by saying they had similar bad experiences with CPS and foster care. One member, Felicia, went over and sat beside Rachael and gave her a hug. Felicia then shared a narrative about the day she lost custody of her children. They were later adopted by a couple in another state. Rachael said maybe losing custody is punishment for the members' drug abuse and bad parenting. It reminded her of something her grandmother used to say, "If you lay down in hell, you're bound to wake up in bed with the devil." Megan said the topic was important and that the group could continue their discussion in the next session. She indicated she would meet with Rachael individually to help address the issue of her missed visitation appointment and CPS's response.

In their postsession debriefing, Megan and Dan talked about how overwhelming the group session felt to them. Megan was deeply moved by Rachael's narrative and those of the other members. Dan wondered if the emotional intensity they all seemed to feel meant the group was out of control. He was still concerned about the issue of relapse and thought the situation might provide an opportunity to discuss relapse prevention with the group. Both facilitators said they were relieved when the session ended because each group member's "loss of custody" narrative seemed more painful than the previous one. They brainstormed some strategies they could use to respond to the members' storytelling in future sessions. They clearly did not understand how to listen to clients' narratives or how to identify different narrative forms and responses that could be helpful to clients.

Table 2.1 includes information that can help practitioners like Dan and Megan to distinguish between narrative forms in order to plan how to respond. This table indicates the two main narrative forms are lived narratives and found narratives. Each of these narrative forms consists of two subcategories: lived narratives include single event narratives and the life narrative. In contrast, found narratives involve public domain narratives and other peoples or borrowed narratives.

Rachael shared a single event lived narrative about a previously unnarrated experience. Dan and Megan observed a high level of emo-

Table 2.1
PRINCIPLE 2: THE SHARED EXPERIENCE AND
TRANSFORMATION PRINCIPLE
THE SKILLS: IDENTIFYING NARRATIVE FORMS AND FUNCTIONS

Narrative Skills Related to:	Examples of Narrative Forms and Functions
Narrative Forms: The practitioner distinguishes between:	*Clients' lived narratives, including significant unnarrated experiences:* • Single event narratives: Individual, family, community, cultural group, organizational, or projective narratives. • The life narrative: An individual's main, continuous, or all-encompassing narrative about the self and the whole life. *And Existing/Found narratives:* • Public domain forms: Proverbs, parables, metaphors, folk tales, fairy tales, poems, chants, songs, and emotional learning stories (bibliotherapy). • Other people's narratives: Borrowed from family heroes/heroines, mentors, role models, peers, other clients.
Narrative Functions: The Practitioner clarifies whether clients' narratives are:	*Regressive:* Reflect movement away from the client's goal or positive change: • Problem-saturated narratives, low currency narratives, and dead-end narratives (they limit or inhibit positive change). *Progressive:* Show movement toward the client's goal or positive change: • Inoculation narratives, turning point narratives, exception narratives, miracle narratives, getting better narratives, and preferred endings or alternative narratives (they are solution-focused or supportive of change). *Stable or Neutral:* Lack movement in a positive or negative direction: • Imposed, prescriptive, or subjugated narratives (they ignore or deny the possibility of positive change).

tional intensity among the members after Rachael shared her individual narrative. Emotional intensity is not unusual when clients share significant unnarrated experiences (Saleebey, 1994). Clients often relive their experiences when initially narrating them. Therefore, their internal emotional and psychological states, or a sense of heightened vulnerability, may become more apparent to them and to the listeners as the narrative unfolds (Freeman, 2004).

Rachael's narrative is also a cultural narrative, which added to the emotional intensity within the group. This combined individual-cultural narrative highlights universal experiences of women who have been stigmatized because of addiction, poverty, sexism, and racism (Gilbert & Beidler, 2001; Hiersteiner, 2004). The other group members, like Rachael, had not previously narrated such experiences. Listening to Rachael's narrative no doubt caused them to relive their own experiences as well as Rachael's. Moreover, dominant society often suppresses narratives about these gender-related experiences by devaluing them or by denying their occurrence. If Dan and Megan had identified the significance of Rachael's combined single event narrative, they might have understood the emotionally-charged group process that ensued. They might also have identified what the members needed from them in response during this potentially productive session.

In general, all single event lived narratives consist of experiences that are seminal to clients. Table 2.1 indicates that these narratives include family, organizational, community, and projective narratives (such as dreams), in addition to individual and cultural narratives. Cultural narratives involve experiences that are primarily centered on gender; race, ethnicity, or national origin; age or generational issues; location; social class; sexual orientation, or disabling conditions. As in Rachael's situation, clients may share combined narrative forms, such as family-community narratives, or their stories may consist of only one of the narrative forms in Table 2.1 (Freeman, 2004).

The life narrative is a second subcategory of lived narratives in Table 2.1. A person's life narrative is his or her main continuous narrative that helps to create and maintain the self. This narrative reflects values, main lessons learned, recurring life issues, heroes and heroines, and life goals, among other priorities for the individual. People reevaluate and change their life narrative in response to single event narratives when they experience conflicts between the two. The life narrative is discussed more fully in Chapter 4 regarding the meaning making principle, and in Chapters 7 and 9 which focus on adolescents and the elderly respectively.

CLIENTS' FOUND NARRATIVES. Table 2.1 also includes found narratives, the second main narrative form. The subcategories of public domain and other people's narratives require that practitioners recognize these narrative forms and become skillful in using them as part of the narrative process. For instance, a client may share or repeat one of the public domain narrative forms, such as a proverb, parable, metaphor, song, or poem (Greenbaum & Holmes, 1993). The practitioner may also share a song or proverb that seems relevant to the client's situation. In either situation, the practitioner can have the client analyze the identified found narrative form. Based on the analysis and discussion, a client can be asked to apply those analyses (or lessons) to her or his personal situation (Ucko, 1991; Freeman, 2001).

When Rachael shared her combined individual-cultural narrative in the group, she also shared an example of a public domain narrative form. She said, "Maybe losing custody is punishment for our drug abuse and bad parenting. It reminds me of something my grandmother used to say, 'If you lay down in hell, you're bound to wake up in bed with the devil'." Megan and Dan were not skillful in recognizing or acknowledging Rachael's family proverb. Therefore, they did not use this opportunity to explore the situation further. They could have explored what the proverb meant to her and her self-worth, how it explained her relationship with her grandmother, it's effect on the meaning Rachael inferred from her individual-cultural narrative, and its influence on her reactions to the missed visitation appointment.

The second subcategory of found narratives in Table 2.1 includes other people's narratives. Clients and practitioners sometimes share relevant narratives of mentors, role models, or peers, which can be analyzed and applied to clients' situations. They can "borrow" lessons learned by or about the individuals in those prototypical narratives (Carley, 1997; Chadiha, Adams, Phorano, Ong, & Byers, 2002). Several group members in the women's group facilitated by Megan and Dan shared their loss of custody narratives. The facilitators could have helped the members analyze those narratives and infer lessons that could be applied to other members' lives, including Rachael's current and future CPS encounters.

Clarifying Narrative Functions

CLIENTS' REGRESSIVE NARRATIVES. In the previous example, Rachael's individual-cultural narrative was experienced as emotionally-charged by the group members and facilitators. Such narratives weigh heavily on narrators *and* listeners, because of their function. Saleebey (1994) and Docherty and McColl (2003) characterize these as problem saturated narratives. Such narratives function as reinforcers in blaming the victim, while masking institutional or structural influences that greatly contribute to individual problems (Yeich & Levine, 1992).

Similarly, Borden (1992) identifies these as regressive narratives. Table 2.1 indicates regressive narratives tend to move clients away from their goals by limiting or inhibiting positive change. Skillful practitioners recognize such narratives have an additional function; they provide a dynamic snap shot of a client's reality rather than a static view. From the latter view, regressive narratives may emphasize the client as a powerless defeated individual, a victim, or perhaps as the problem. In contrast, a snapshot view of regressive narratives helps to explain how a client may be stuck. For example, his or her snap shot may reveal only the individual challenges in the narrated experience. Other possibilities or snap shots may be revealed when practitioners help clients to analyze their narratives, such as the existence and role of institutional barriers, as well as individual and institutional resources that are embedded in the narrative.

Megan and Dan were overwhelmed by Rachael's regressive narrative. Like many practitioners, they felt helpless and inadequate because they did not recognize the function of Rachael's narrative. The group members felt inadequate also because of common intractable custody challenges that were highlighted in Rachael's narrative. Although it is a natural reaction, being overwhelmed may have caused the group to ignore Rachael's positive actions or strengths, such as leaving home early and advocating for herself with Ms. Greene. This process led the group to ignore Dan's comment that Rachael successfully avoided relapsing in spite of her difficult day. The regressive effects of Rachael's narrative could have been limited by reinforcing these positive areas as well as by identifying common challenges (including CPS barriers) and resources among group members (relapse prevention strategies and alliances with supportive foster parents).

On the other hand, it is important to note the facilitators' strengths in conducting the group session. They provided the emotional space for Rachael to share her regressive narrative. Although overwhelmed, they also allowed time for other members to make supportive comments to Rachael and to share their previously unnarrated and narrated women's custody stories. Moreover, Dan pointed out Rachael's strength in seeking the group's help and in not relapsing, while Megan scheduled a follow-up individual session with Rachael as well as future group sessions on the topic.

CLIENTS' PROGRESSIVE AND STABILITY NARRATIVES. Progressive narratives, such as inoculation, turning point, getting better, and exception narratives, reflect movement toward a client's goal (see Table 2.1). These narratives are centered on ". . . clients' personal accounts of struggles and stories of survival that may identify multiple sources of strengths. The search for existing exception narratives about strengths and competence is difficult because often clients do not believe they have strengths or narratives about being competent" (Freeman & Couchonnal, 2006, p. 203). Essentially, progressive narratives reveal experiences in which a client's problem was managed or coped with successfully, was less noticeable, had a less troubling effect on a situation, or resulted in a lifelong lesson and growth (an inoculation for preventing/handling future challenges).

For example, Felicia was the group member who hugged and comforted Rachael in the previous vignette. When Felicia shared her loss of custody narrative, she explained the experience caused her to enter the current treatment program. The group facilitators could have asked Felicia to elaborate on the positive changes she inferred from that experience, and how the telling of her narrative reflected movement toward recovery as an outcome or goal. Possibly, losing custody of her children helped Felicia to see how severely drug addiction had affected her life. That awareness led her to enter rehab and to entitle her narrative, "An eye opening and life changing experience." This example illustrates more clearly how progressive narratives function. They exemplify movement toward positive change from a client's perspective (entering rehab to recover), although they might include other serious negative consequences that seem regressive to observers and listeners (a permanent loss of parental rights and custody) (Borden, 1992).

Stability or neutral narratives are imposed narratives that are constructed by society about particular individuals and groups. They often reflect caste and class restrictions that limit the social mobility and economic development of those groups. These narratives are retold in order to justify the power imbalances between those groups and dominant society (Saleebey, 1994), for example, women in poverty who receive public assistance for their children and addicted women (Hiersteiner, 2004). Other examples of imposed narratives are focused on gay males and lesbians, the elderly, people in poverty, the working poor, individuals with HIV/AIDS, and immigrants of color or those who are religious minorities.

Imposed narratives contain negative labels about these groups. Such labels can restrict individuals' self-identity and self-construction if they internalize those stories as their life scripts. In this manner, stability narratives help to maintain the social and political status quo at a societal level. Another function of these narratives is to ignore or deny the possibility of positive change (see Table 2.1). Borden (1992) contends they reflect a lack of movement and action by clients, either away from *or* toward positive change.

The situation of Memo, a 16-year-old Mexican American illustrates how imposed narratives function. Memo's parents immigrated to the United States when he was 10 years old. Although both parents worked, they earned less than the minimum wage standard and lived below the poverty line. Memo was a student in an alternative school. One day, his social studies teacher told his class a narrative about a former student, Mike, who happened to be a Latino. The teacher, Mr. Douglas, met with Mike two weeks after his enrollment to discuss his pattern of misbehaving in class and not completing his class work. Mike told the teacher he wanted to change—he was committed to improving his work and staying out of trouble. But when the situation did not change after a few weeks, Mr. Douglas met with Mike again. Mike admitted he was continuing to stay out late each night with the members of a neighborhood gang, and although he was not a gang member, he found it difficult to stay away from his friends.

One weekend, Mike joined the gang members in a drive-by shooting during which one rival gang member died and several others were wounded. As a result, Mike and four of his friends were sentenced to prison for 25 years. Mr. Douglas concluded that this narrative demonstrated the fate of most teenage Latino males in gangs who really do not want to succeed in life. Later, Memo discussed this narrative with his school counselor, explaining that it was a real downer for him although Mr. Douglas said he used the narrative to inspire new students to change their lives. Memo said the narrative showed Mr. Douglas really did not understand *or* respect Latino males.

The counselor recognized how such narratives function in discouraging hope for change and in denying the presence of strengths and resources in the listeners' lives. Consequently, the lack of movement and growth toward goals in these narratives is often attributed to the subjects' deficits only, while their strengths and multiple environmental factors are ignored. For instance, Mr. Douglas blamed Mike's lack of movement toward his goals for improving his school work and staying out of trouble on his gender and on his cultural lifestyle and values. Mr. Douglas did not include factors in the school, community, or public policy area in the narrative that could also be contributors.

Because the counselor realized the potentially negative effects the narrative could have on the students, he encouraged Memo to not accept Mr. Douglas's narrative as a predictor of his fate. He then helped Memo to set some goals for changes the teenager wanted in his life. They critically analyzed the conclusions Mr. Douglas had drawn from the imposed narrative, such as generalizing about all teenage Latino males. In addition, they identified some alternative competing conclusions. Examples include the importance of weighing the pros and cons of spending time with friends who engage in risky behavior, and the benefits from being involved with a cultural coach, such as a teacher or community leader, who understands and can help in handling value conflicts.

Skill: Listening for and Acknowledging Spontaneous Narratives

While the preceding skill of identifying narrative forms and functions is important, effective listening also includes hearing and acknowledging clients' narratives. Both are closely related listening skills; however, hearing and acknowledging clients' narratives is the heart of the narrative process. Practitioners typically ask, "How do I know when clients are simply discussing a concern or some aspect of their social history versus sharing an actual narrative?" Essentially, the two listening skills in this section provide the tools and competencies that practitioners need to distinguish between clients' information sharing and their fully developed narratives.

Those skills also allow practitioners to tune in and join the client by fully attending to and focusing on the narrative that is shared

(Freeman, 2004). Furthermore, effective listening requires practitioners to stop note taking or information gathering and to begin the process of experience gathering (listening to narratives). Finally, listening requires practitioners to eliminate the use of questions while clients share their narratives in order to facilitate the narrative process.

Hearing and Observing Narrative Indicators

CHANGES IN THE NARRATOR OR CLIENT'S BEHAVIOR. This skill involves hearing and observing changes in the narrator's behaviors that signal the emergence of spontaneous narratives. Such changes indicate when the shared narrative process begins between the narrator and the listeners, which ultimately transforms and stimulates growth within all participants. Table 2.2 clarifies some of these distinct behavioral changes or indicators that can be observed in the narrator and listeners during the narrative process. For instance, the narrator moves from talking objectively about facts or an experience to being lost in reliving that experience, which involves him or her completely–physically, cognitively, and emotionally (see Table 2.2, Indicator #1 related to the narrator).

Practitioners have described various indicators of these changes in clients' behaviors. For example, clients may look in the direction of the practitioner and other listeners but no longer make eye contact, talk in the present tense rather than in the past tense, make physical gestures consistent with activities occurring in the narrative, and use language that expresses the emotional intensity they are obviously reliving. Their language may reflect either the emotional and physical developmental stage they were in when the narrated experience occurred, or the stage the experience made them feel like they were in at the time (Freeman, 2000; Thornton, 2003).

In a previous section of this chapter, Rachael shared her narrative with a womens' group in a drug rehab program. When asked about their observations later in a consultation session, the group facilitators said Rachael began to pace up and down in the group room when she reached the part of her narrative where the bus had a flat tire and the riders had to wait outside. When she talked about running to the foster mother's house after she reached her bus stop, they remembered that Rachael began to breathe louder and more deeply, no doubt

Table 2.2
PRINCIPLE 2: THE SHARED EXPERIENCE AND
TRANSFORMATION PRINCIPLE
THE SKILLS: LISTENING FOR AND ACKNOWLEDGING CLIENTS'
SPONTANEOUS NARRATIVES

Narrative Skills	Examples of How to Use the Skills
Hearing and Observing Narrative Indicators:	
For the Narrator: The Practitioner Identifies:	1. A shift from discussing to reliving a narrated or unnarrated experience 2. Cultural cues related to the narrator's power and control in the experience 3. The level of emotional intensity the client attaches to the experience
For the Listener: The Practitioner Identifies:	1. A shift from observing the narrator to entering the narrative experience 2. An emotional and personal connection between the narrator and listener 3. A focus on the narrative process to guide the interaction
Acknowledging Clients' Shared Narratives:	
Regarding the Shared Experience and Transformation Process: The Practitioner:	1. Asks the client what it felt like to share the narrative 2. Explains when he or she entered the client's narrative 3. Explores the emotional intensity and cultural cues expressed by the client
Regarding the Narrative: The Practitioner:	1. Affirms the narrator's trust and risk taking in sharing the narrative 2. Suggests the narrator give the narrative a title

reflecting the emotional and physical exertion and turmoil she had experienced at the time. They also recalled that when the narrative reached the point where she came to Ms. Green's house (p. 29, the third paragraph), Rachael became so lost in her narrative that she talked about what happened in the present tense, as though it was happening there in the group room.

Moreover, Rachael said in a later group session that the experience reminded her that CPS was the parent and she *was* the child, similar to when she was a child developmentally, with very little power and self-esteem. This cultural cue related to her gender, social class, and ethnicity reveals the client's belief that Ms. Greene and the CPS system had more power than she did (see Table 2.2, Indicator #2 related to the narrator). For example, Rachael said in her narrative, "I plead with her—Ms. Greene, I need to see them (her kids) and they want to see me . . . Even though she's trying to be nice, I don't think she's really on my side."

Rachael also said this experience made her feel emotionally vulnerable, with low self-esteem like when she was 12 years old. She explained, "I just stand there trying not to cry or make a bigger fool of myself. I feel like nothin'. . . . So I say to myself, go to group so you don't screw up your recovery too." The group facilitators said Rachael was sobbing at this point in her narrative, while rocking back and forth with her arms folded tightly across her chest. They concluded these behavioral changes meant Rachael's emotional intensity peaked at that point (see Table 2.2, Indicator #3 related to the narrator). Her reaction was consistent with the guilt and pain she probably attached to the experience, as she said, "By then I can hear my kids crying—calling me, Mama, Mama. Knowing my kids think I'm failing them again . . . I feel like I want to get high—real bad."

CHANGES IN THE LISTENERS OR PRACTITIONERS' BEHAVIORS. Skillful analysis of clients' narrative indicators can help practitioners to explore their own narrative indicators as listeners. Supervision, consultation, or group facilitator planning sessions can be used for this process. In the previous example involving Dan and Megan as group facilitators in a women's rehab program, the facilitators used an external consultant for this purpose. During consultation, both facilitators remembered observing Rachael objectively as she narrated her experience, saying that it felt like they were standing outside of that experience (see Table 2.2, Indicator #1 related to listeners). They anticipated that Rachael had not kept her visitation appointment, so the detailed narration of her preparation and trials in getting to Ms. Greene's house surprised them. That part of the narrative caused them to shift from standing outside the narrative to entering it.

Listeners often enter someone else's narrative (identify with it) through the door of their own experiences (Freeman, 2004), which causes them to move into a common physical and emotional space created by a client's narrative (see Table 2.2, Indicator #1 related to listeners). Dan explained his door into Rachael's narrative involved his unnarrated experience of being late for his son's high school graduation the previous year. He recalled his efforts to keep from using drugs, including sitting for hours in front of a church that morning and going to an afternoon Narcotics Anonymous meeting. Dan felt guilty and angry with himself when he relapsed in spite of those efforts. His guilt and helplessness were exacerbated when his family realized he was late for the ceremony because he had used drugs.

Megan said her door into Rachael's narrative also involved an unnarrated experience, an illness story (Docherty & McColl, 2003). She shared confidential information with her fundamentalist minister about her recent diagnosis of diabetes. She talked about her family risk factors and about changes she had made in her diet and exercise routine. Megan thought these lifestyle changes and her prayers for good health might prevent her diabetes. In his next sermon, the minister told the congregation that certain diseases such as diabetes are caused by an individual's lack of faith. He urged church members to reexamine their spiritual values and to rededicate themselves to being more devout. Megan felt the minister's breach of trust was a misuse of his power, and that his condemnation of church members who had genetic risk factors blamed them for conditions they could not control.

The consultant said narratives such as Dan and Megan's have caused practitioners to experience an emotional and personal connection to clients (see Table 2.2, Indicator #2 related to listeners), as they listen to and enter the latter's narratives. Megan agreed by saying she now knew what it meant to be with a client in the moment, based on the process with Rachael. Dan acknowledged he had continued to listen to Rachael's narrative in spite of being overwhelmed by the emotional intensity in the room, instead of closing down as he had in previous group sessions.

Table 2.2 shows the importance of practitioners like Dan continuing to listen and stay focused on the narrative process by tuning into their emotional reactions to clients' narratives (Indicator #3 related to listeners) (Dean, 1998). Acknowledging such reactions and the experiences in which they are based, eliminates the need to mask those reactions by assuming the expert role. Conversely, not assuming this role can enhance effective listening. Skillful listening also involves acknowledging the client's narrative (that the practitioner has heard it), as well as acknowledging the shared client-helper experience.

Acknowledging Clients' Shared Narratives

THE SHARED NARRATIVE EXPERIENCE AND TRANSFORMATION. Acknowledging the shared narrative experience begins with asking clients what it was like to share their narrative (see Table 2.2, Step #1 of the shared experience) (Nevo, 1998). This question is a critical part of listening because, implicitly, it acknowledges the client's sharing of his or her narrative is a significant event. With Dan and Megan, the consultant coached them in conducting their next group session focused on acknowledging the previous narrative experience with Rachael and other members. The facilitators were asked to anticipate this step, including how to explore the situation if Rachael only responded generally. For example, if Rachael said she felt bad or relieved, the facilitators would ask her which parts of the narrative and discussion contributed to her reaction. Did she wonder what the other members thought about her and what she shared? What was her reaction when she heard Felicia and other members' narratives? How were they similar and different to her?

The facilitators decided to have group members give Rachael feedback about what her narrative meant to them. Megan and Dan would explain what Rachael's narrative meant to them as well, including how they felt connected to Rachael emotionally and personally. Sharing information with the group about when they, as facilitators, entered Rachael's narrative and asking the members to do the same was another part of their plan (see Table 2.2, Step #2 of the shared experience).

The facilitators' group session plan included pointing out some of the narrative indicators they discussed in consultation related to Rachael. In the next group session, they helped Rachael and other members to connect those indicators with the emotional reactions they had observed (see Table 2.2, Step #3 of the shared experience). As an example, they asked the members to recall whether they observed Rachael pacing up and down in the group room. Then they asked them to analyze what was going on in her narrative at that point, the emotional intensity level the pacing reflected, and the reason.

The facilitators also focused on the cultural cues the group noticed during the narrative process, an equally important aspect of listening.

Reminding the members about Rachael's crying and rocking back and forth, and eliciting how they experienced and shared her helplessness and disempowerment, allowed the facilitators to highlight the gender lessons the group learned from the narrative process. For instance, the members were able to affirm each other in terms of the strengths Rachael had demonstrated, and their common strengths as parents. They analyzed how that narrative experience mutually transformed them; helped them grow as women, parents, and practitioners; and empowered them (see Table 2.2, Step #3 of the shared experience) (Boehm & Staples, 2004).

THE NARRATIVE ITSELF. Table 2.2 indicates that affirming the client's willingness to share a particular narrative is another important aspect of listening (Step #1 regarding the narrative). This step documents that listeners have heard and understood what the narrator risked in telling his or her narrative (Hiersteiner, 2004). Dan and Megan planned to acknowledge Rachael's strengths in coming to group and in sharing her narrative about being humiliated and shamed. They then asked the group to discuss how the narrative's content was a test of Rachael's commitment to recovery, and hence a risk for her in sharing it (Nevo, 1998).

The consultant mentioned the preceding discussion could help Rachael entitle her narrative, another important aspect of listening (see Table 2.2, Step #2 regarding the narrative). This step confirms the practitioner has heard and tuned into the narrative's significance to the client. For instance, the consultant noted that although Megan and Dan called the group members' shared experiences, "loss of custody narratives" (regressive narratives), Felicia entitled her narrative, "An eye opening and life changing experience" (a progressive narrative, p. 35). The consultant suggested the facilitators repeat Felicia's title to the group in the next session and ask her and them what it meant to each member. Essentially, this revisiting process permitted the facilitators to acknowledge they tuned into the title's significance after the previous group session.

Entitling their narratives allows clients to identify the life lesson(s) they learned from those experiences (Chadiha et al., 2002). For example, the "eye opening" part of Felicia's title refers to her lesson about the loss of her children bringing her into treatment for herself, rather than to regain custody or fight severance of parental rights. Regaining custody is likely to be more successful if it is a by product of a client's treatment than the reason for it, after custody has been lost (Gilbert & Beidler, 2001). Finally, entitling narratives acknowledges that clients *and* helpers have shared an important growth experience, based on life lessons such as the one Felicia identified.

Conclusion

Practitioners often recount life lessons they learn from listening to clients' narratives. For example, they learn about clients' unique views of their life changing experiences and the personal growth they gain from narrating such experiences. Helping professionals also report being transformed themselves from listening to and observing the tremendous risks clients take in sharing their narratives. Some helpers acknowledge feeling empowered from the risk of following clients into their narrative experiences, and from getting in touch with relevant narrated and unnarrated experiences in their own lives. Other practitioners conclude that narrative practice leads to more clarity about how to listen effectively and the benefits from skillful listening, including a more authentic relationship with their clients. Most importantly, many helping professionals report that they have generalized their narrative listening skills to other approaches, because the focus is not only on improving their skills but on enhancing who they are. To summarize, those helpers believe that listening not only allows them to tune into their clients' situations and narratives, but also into themselves, both personally and professionally.

References

Boehm, A., & Staples, L. H. (2004). Empowerment: The point of view of consumers. *Families in Society, 85* (2), 270–280.

Borden, W. (1992). Narrative perspectives in psychosocial intervention following adverse life events. *Social Work, 37,* 125–141.

Carley, G. (1997). The getting better phenomena: Videotape applications of previously at-risk high school student narratives. *Social Work in Education, 19,* 115–120.

Chadiha, L. A., Adams, P., Phorano, O., Ong, S. L., & Byers, L. (2002). Stories told and lessons learned from African American female caregivers' vignettes for empowerment practice. *Journal of Gerontological Social Work, 40* (1/2), 135–144.

Dean, R. (1998). A narrative approach to groups. *Clinical Social Work Journal, 26,* 23–37.

Docherty, D., & McColl, M. A. (2003). Illness stories: Themes emerging through narratives. *Social Work in Health Care, 37* (1), 19–39.

Freeman, E. M. (March 4, 2004). Basic principles of effective narrative practice. Workshop presentation. Kansas City, MO: Sponsored by The Social Work Coalition and Social Work Leaders in Health Care.

Freeman, E. M. (2001). Restore and repair: Perinatal rehab services for women and children. *Substance abuse intervention, prevention, rehabilitation, and systems change strategies: Helping individuals, families, and groups to empower themselves* (285–307). New York: Columbia University Press.

Freeman, E. M. (2000). Direct practice in fields related to developmental tasks: A life-span perspective. In P. Allen-Meares & C. Garvin (Eds.), *The handbook of social work direct practice* (pp. 415–435). Thousand Oaks, CA: Sage.

Gilbert, M. C., & Beidler, A. E. (2001). Using the narrative approach in groups for chemically dependent mothers. *Social Work with Groups, 24* (3/4), 101–115.

Greenbaum, L., & Holmes, I. H. (1993). The use of folktales in social work practice. *Social Casework, 64*, 414–418.

Hiersteiner, C. (2004). Narratives of low income mothers in addiction recovery centers: Motherhood and treatment experience. *Journal of Social Work Practice and the Addictions, 4* (2), 51–64.

Lee, J. A. B. (2001). *The empowerment approach in social work practice* (2nd ed.). New York: Columbia University Press.

Nevo, M. (1998). What's your story? Listening to the stories of mothers from multi-problem families. *Clinical Social Work Journal, 26* (2), 177–194.

Saleebey, D. (1994). Culture, theory, and narrative: The intersection of meanings in practice. *Social Work, 39* (4), 351–359.

Thornton, J. E. (2003). Life-span learning: A developmental perspective. *International Journal of Aging and Human Development, 57*(1), 55–76.

Ucko, L. G. (1991). Who's afraid of the big bad wolf? Confronting wife abuse through folk stories. *Social Work, 36*, 414–420.

Yeich, S., & Levine, R. (1992). Participatory research's contribution to a conceptualization of empowerment. *Journal of Applied Social Psychology, 22*, 1894–1908.

Yellow Bird, M. J. (1995). Spirituality in First Nations story telling: A Sahnish-Hidatsa approach to narrative. *Reflections, 1*(4), 65–72.

Chapter 3

RESPONDING TO CLIENTS' SPONTANEOUS NARRATIVES: THE NAMING AND UNPACKING ASSESSMENT AND INTERVENTION PRINCIPLE

The student is a teacher in disguise.
—Asian Indian Proverb

Principle 3, responding to clients' spontaneous narratives, reinforces the importance of clients' unique roles in narrative practice. Those roles were discussed in Chapter 2 in terms of listening skills. In this chapter, the roles are examined in the context of skillful assessment and intervention, which involve the client as an expert partner and collaborator in narrative work (Freedman & Combs, 1996). In one example, a practitioner in a battered woman's shelter met with a client for an intake interview. The 25-year-old client, Glenda, was in a crisis because of her husband's violence and her fears that he would find the shelter and harm her again. Glenda told a story about fleeing to her husband's parents' house to get away from his violence a few months before. Her in-laws allowed him to enter the house and take her and their two children back home in spite of his violence. The practitioner, Stephanie, said she understood from Glenda's narrative the reason she was so fearful. Stephanie suggested they try to capture those family dynamics by completing a genogram.

During this assessment process, Glenda's affect became more flat and she mumbled her responses to Stephanie's enthusiastic questions about the genogram topics. While Stephanie acknowledged the importance of Glenda's narrative, she ignored the client's expert role in deciding the best venue for sharing and assessing her seminal experiences (Meichenbaum & Fitzpatrick, 1993; Norman, 2000). For instance, Stephanie did not use Glenda's spontaneous narrative to collaboratively plan the initial interventions; therefore, the effectiveness of the work and Glenda's trust were compromised. This chapter's epigraph suggests that the student, or in this discussion the client, learns and provides opportunities for the helper to understand important life lessons that are embedded in the client's narrative. Closer attention to Glenda's narrative by Stephanie could have revealed the client's themes or lessons about safety and trust. Glenda and other clients are able to assume this teaching role based on local or expert knowledge about their life situations and experiences (Kelley, 2002; Saleebey, 1994).

The next section of this chapter addresses the critical nature of clients' roles based on Principle 3. That discussion explains the principle's main elements and its significance to narrative practice, along with related solution-focused axioms. The use of solution-focused naming questions is described. This skill allows helpers to clarify narrative resources such as unacknowledged and unidentified aspects of their clients' narratives. Another skill, solution-focused unpacking questions, demonstrates how helping professionals can elicit more detailed and thicker descriptions from clients about their narratives. Both skill-based discussions include examples of clients' narratives and examples of effective responses by service providers during assessment and intervention.

Overview of Principle 3 and Solution-Focused Approaches

Main Elements of Principle Three and Solution-Focused Approaches

Principle 3 clarifies the symbolic and practical purpose of questions in narrative practice. The symbolic purpose is to acknowledge and reinforce the power of clients' expertise and local knowledge, as well as the practitioner's respect for those strengths. From a practical perspective, questions allow helping professionals to maintain a not knowing stance, an essential element for an open and ongoing assessment-intervention process (see Table 1.1) (Freeman, 2004). Questions are a common element in narrative and solution-focused approaches. They are phrased to allow maximum opportunities for clients to expand their narratives, and therefore, to generate experience and solutions. The use of questions is based on certain underlying axioms, which illustrate other elements these two approaches have in common. For example regarding (Freedman & Combs, 1996; Gingerich & Eisengart, 2000; Stalker, Levene, & Coady, 1999):

1. Perspectives About Change and Solutions:
    - Solution-focused approaches (SFA): Change is constant. Small changes in one part of a system can affect changes in another part.
    - Narrative approaches (NA): Narratives help to assess how the client's situation is already changing and what is working in the situation.
2. Preferred Assessment and Intervention Strategies:
    - SFA: The helping professional's role is to identify and amplify change. The client's role is to define her or his goals.
    - NA: The helping professional's use of the naming skill helps clients to assess relevant challenges in their narratives, such as intentions and outcomes, and reveals ways to increase and maintain changes in those areas (ways to maintain what is working).
3. Level of Optimism or Hope for Solutions and Changes:
    - SFA: The focus should be on what is possible and changeable rather than on what is impossible and intractable.
    - NA: Unpacking interventions help to elicit contextual information, such as clients' values and cultural traditions, which are manifested in their narratives. Clarifying clients' preferred endings and alternative stories reveals their preferred solutions: Past, current, and future.

Significance of Principle 3

Responding to their spontaneous narratives is a prerequisite for a collaborative assessment with clients, involving narrative resources such as naming and unpacking questions (see Table 1.1). Because these solution-focused questions are also useful for intervention, Principle 3 assumes that assessment and intervention are best accomplished in a circular, dynamic, and integrated process, rather than sequentially. This view of assessment and intervention is consistent with the perspective of social work and of other helping professions (Dimaggio, Salvatore, Azzara, Catania, Semerari, & Hermans, 2003; Docherty & McColl, 2003; Gale, Mitchell, Garand, & Wesner, 2003; Kelley, 2002).

Moreover, this principle implies that in responding to clients' stories, narrative assessment and intervention methods can be effectively combined with other methods and approaches. Other assessment methods include clinical interview inventories and guides, social histories, the DSM IV, genograms, and ecomaps. Examples of compatible intervention approaches are solution-focused brief therapy, and family systems, crisis intervention, and task-centered approaches (Freeman & Couchonnal, 2006). Principle 3 also implies that if a client shares a spontaneous narrative initially as Glenda did, the assessment and intervention process should begin with that narrative. If a narrative is shared at some other point during the helping process, it should be integrated into the ongoing assessment and intervention along with other methods (Freeman, 2001).

Skill: Using Solution-Focused Naming Questions

When helping professionals apply this skill, it allows clients to demonstrate their expertise in identifying sources of power within their narratives. Those sources of power are based on clients' opportunities to name or voice unacknowledged or unidentified aspects of their narratives (see Table 1.1). Such opportunities require a partnership between helpers and clients during narrative assessment and intervention. Because this is an integrated process, assessment and intervention can occur simultaneously or the practitioner and client can shift back and forth between these two parts of the process. Similarly, this collaborative process can simultaneously focus on using and responding to solution-focused naming and unpacking questions within a given session. The focus can also be on the use of naming questions for a session or part of a session, and then shift to unpacking questions during another session or part of a session. For clarity, however, the use of naming questions is demonstrated in this section separately from unpacking questions, which are illustrated in another section of this chapter. A case example with a client's narrative is included next to facilitate this discussion.

Background Information

Clyde Collins is a 60-year-old African American. His wife of 37 years died the previous year. He is close to his children, Bryan (33 years of age) and Katherine (36 years of age), as well as his four grandchildren who live in the next county. Mr. Collins belongs to an informal breakfast club involving several male friends. They meet at a neighborhood restaurant twice per month. He is a respected deacon in his church. His minister provided spiritual support to him when his wife died and he became depressed. When the depression continued his minister recommended that Mr. Collins meet with a mental health professional. A manager at the company where he works made the same suggestion recently, so Mr. Collins agreed to be referred to his company's employee assistance program (EAP). Mr. Collins has worked for this company as a mail clerk for 29 years. In his first session with the EAP counselor, David Thornton, a 35-year-old psychologist, Mr. Collins talked reluctantly about his depression in response to the counselor's questions. Then he shared the following narrative after David stopped asking questions and became silent for a few seconds.

Mr. Collins's Narrative:

I feel like I've been treated unfairly by my company. They recently scheduled meetings with the staff to talk about work assignments—management changes they called it. Most of us weren't surprised; we'd heard rumors for months about the company either closing or downsizing. But hearing rumors is a lot different from being sent to Human Resources (HR) for a meeting. I was a little nervous when my time came. But I'm the senior clerk in the mailroom, so I wasn't real worried about my job. So I met with the head of HR for my appointment, and that should've warned me I guess—the big guns! Well, Henry Russell was his name. He shook my hand real hard and asked me to have a seat. I got the feeling he wanted me to relax—you know how people act when they're ready to give you bad news? Anyway, he said the company *was* downsizing as I'd probably heard, and they were offering their top employees a buyout. He began explaining the buyout, giving me details and showing me forms to explain what he was saying. I felt myself just floating away from there, anything to keep from listening to him. After a while, I could see he'd stopped talking and started to watch me. I sort of came back to myself then. Are you saying I'm being laid off, I asked him. Well no, he said, but there won't be much job security for staff members who don't take the buyout. And if we don't get enough staff to take the buyout, we'll have to do a lay off to get the numbers down to 1,500 people.

I can't retire now, I say to him. I'm still paying bills from my wife's medical expenses, what the insurance company won't pay. I don't have any money saved; man I'm just getting by. Now I'm sweating a lot and shaking my head to try and think, while he keeps talking, trying to convince me about the buyout. Besides, I tell him, I've got more years yet to work, I'm still healthy and I'm strong. And management keeps telling me I'm doing a good job—they wouldn't do that if they want me to leave, would they? He tells me, just think this through later, when you're on your own. I tell *him* I don't want the buyout, but he says, "Clyde you're lucky you've been able to hold your job as long as you have and you're lucky to get the buyout benefits we're offering you." I decide to call him on that. So I ask him, "What're you saying, you think because I'm black I should be happier than other workers with what the company's offering?" But then he backs down. He said all he'd meant was I only have a high school education. I just said thanks for nothing and walked out of his office. I talked to some of the white workers later; they told me they weren't talked down to like I was.

Integrating Assessment and Intervention: Naming Questions

Table 3.1 explains the focus and purpose of naming questions. They facilitate an integrated assessment and intervention because they help to reveal, and therefore to assess, the strengths and challenges in clients' situations. Naming questions also clarify areas in the client's narrative and life situation that are already changing, and the methods and interventions they are using to initiate changes in other areas. The following section includes examples of naming questions and how practitioners can apply them effectively.

CLIENTS' FEELINGS AND THE SOURCES OF THEIR FEELINGS, Initially, helping professionals can ask about clients' current and past feelings related to their narratives (Table 3.1: Purpose: Naming clients' expressed and unexpressed feelings). Clients often do not name feelings in their narratives. Instead, they might ignore those feelings or mask them with anger. Either approach to handling feelings makes it difficult to assess and intervene as needed based on clients' narratives. Therefore the EAP counselor, David, asked Mr. Collins an initial nam-

Table 3.1
PRINCIPLE 3: THE NAMING AND UNPACKING ASSESSMENT
AND INTERVENTION PRINCIPLE
NARRATIVE SKILL: THE USE OF SOLUTION-FOCUSED NAMING QUESTIONS

The Focus of Naming Questions	The Purpose of Naming Questions for Assessment and Intervention: To Name:
1. Clients' Current and Past Feelings:	The emotions and feelings expressed by the client or others in the narrative, as well as those that were unexpressed or masked (e.g., an individual's pain is masked by anger).
2. The Sources of Those Feelings:	Experiences or events, relationships, interactions or behaviors, assumptions or attributions, and thoughts of the client or others that may have contributed to those emotions, and how they specifically affected/are affecting them.
3. Unspoken Aspects of the Narrative:	Underlying messages that could be/were inferred from the narrative but were not directly stated or observed (conclusions based on intuition or on past experiences).
4. The Outcomes or Effects of the Narrative:	The consequences or outcomes from the narrative in general. The effects of unspoken aspects of the narrative on the client or the situation, things directly stated or observed, and the emotions of the client and others (expressed and unexpressed).
5. Relative Priorities Within the Narrative:	The weight or importance given to different parts of the narrative by the client or others, what those relative weights are based on, and other factors that affected priority decisions.
6. The Themes of Meaning and the Lessons Related to Those Themes:	What the narrative means or symbolizes to the client, its purpose, or the gist of its message. Recurring symbols in a narrative that have special meaning to clients. What clients learn or are expected to learn from the narrative, and how those lessons will be used by clients currently and in the future.

ing question about his feelings, after acknowledging the client's trust in sharing his narrative and exploring his experience from doing so (see Chapter 2, "Acknowledging Clients' Shared Narratives").

David asked, "What were you feeling when the HR manager said, 'Clyde you're lucky you've been able to hold your job as long as you have and you're lucky to get the buyout benefits we're offering you'?" Mr. Collins said he was angry at the time and that in fact, just talking about what happened put him back in Henry Russell's office again, right in the middle of his anger, because the manager had implied he was ungrateful. David commented that this statement was a clear indication Mr. Collins was reliving his experience when he shared the narrative. The counselor also acknowledged the point when he entered Mr. Collins's combined individual-organizational narrative (see Chapter 2, "Hearing Narrative Indicators and Acknowledging the Shared Transformation"). He entered the narrative when the client said ". . . I got the feeling he (Henry Russell) wanted me to relax—you know how people act when they're ready to give you bad news"? David remembered several personal experiences when he too had been blind-sided by bad news.

Follow-up naming questions are essential for a continuous assessment and intervention process. Accordingly, David then said, "So you're angry even now; what specific part of the interaction or discussion that day made you so angry"? (see Table 3.1: Purpose: Naming the Sources of Clients' Feelings). Mr. Collins sat and thought for a moment and then he said, "You know—I'm 60 years old, a respected part of my community, my church, and most of all my family. Henry Russell talked to me like I was nothing. After all the loyalty and extra work I've given the company, I deserve more respect from him. And because I didn't stand up for myself, I'm a little embarrassed that I let him get away with it. Men don't talk about being hurt, but that's really what it was, now that I've had a chance to think about it here."

The counselor's initial and follow-up naming questions helped him and the client assess what was already changing in the situation. For example, the client's perspective about his feelings and what contributed to those feelings changed as he responded to David's questions. Initially, Mr. Collins identified his anger about the HR manager's assumption that he was an ungrateful employee. As the naming process continued the client admitted he felt embarrassed because he did not stand up for himself. Moreover, he had already began to reconcile two conflicting parts of his perspective by saying even though men did not admit to being hurt, he was hurt when Henry Russell did not acknowledge his loyalty and hard work or show him respect. David could have asked additional naming questions from Table 3.1 related to the client's feelings. For instance, he could have asked the client to name the assumptions he made about what happened in Henry Russell's office and to clarify how those assumptions affected his feelings (e.g., assumptions about Mr. Russell's racial attitudes) (see Table 3.1: The Sources of Clients' Feelings).

UNSPOKEN ASPECTS AND NARRATIVE CONSEQUENCES. Some aspects of clients' narratives may affect them, but because those aspects are not directly stated it is difficult for clients to identify or name them. Clients sometimes draw conclusions about such aspects based on their intuition or past experiences. Naming questions can help them to reveal and name those unspoken aspects, as well as their conclusions about what they inferred from them. Service providers can help clients use those unspoken or hidden aspects in the narrative to name and assess their strengths (what is working) and their challenges (things that are not working) (Kelley, 2002).

David asked Mr. Collins, "What did you notice about this experience that you or Henry Russell may have understood without those things being said directly?" (see Table 3.1: Purpose: Unspoken Aspects of the Narrative). The client named one aspect related to him and one related to the HR manager. Regarding himself, Mr. Collins recognized intuitively that the recent loss of his wife caused him to feel less sure of himself and less in control of his life. In comparison, he inferred that Henry Russell possessed and exercised much power in this situation. He was younger than the client; college educated and Caucasian. In addition, he had advanced very rapidly in the company in his five years there. Past organizational experience indicated the HR manager's position was used to provide initial administrative experience to employees on the fast track, who were then promoted to higher management positions.

The narrative process between David and the client continued with a follow-up naming question related to political consequences (Wood & Roche, 2005). David asked the client, "Did you notice anything that happened or did not happen because you felt less in control of your situation (the unspoken part of your experience)," and "What did you notice specifically?" (see Table 3.1: Purpose: The Consequences or Effects of Unspoken Aspects). Mr. Collins reminded David that he "sort of left the room" because the situation made him uneasy and seemed to be out of his control. Consequently, he did not hear most of what Henry Russell said about the buyout. He did not know if the buyout involved different options, or what options were available to him if he did not take the buyout. Mr. Collins also realized the HR manager did not mention that the client was at the top of his pay scale as the senior mailroom clerk. David asked if there were related advantages and disadvantages. The client pointed out his pay range might help him negotiate special advantages if he took the buyout (a strength), or his job might be a target because the company could use his salary more flexibly if he left (a challenge).

Identifying consequences from the HR manager's organizational privilege required more discussion during their second counseling session. David and Mr. Collins concluded that one consequence was the HR manager's experience and education led him to devalue older, less educated, and lower ranked employees. Another consequence was that he only presented the organization's view of the buyout without considering the employees' reactions to this process or helping them to explore their options. This discussion helped Mr. Collins assess other consequences in this situation, such as his decision to identify his strengths for the HR manager and the counselor. He said he was healthy, strong, a hard worker, and well respected in his community, family, and church.

RELATIVE PRIORITIES AND THEMES OF MEANING OR LESSONS. The second session also involved David's use of naming questions to help Mr. Collins summarize his priorities and related lessons from his narrative. Table 3.1 defines naming questions focused on these two areas (Relative Priorities within the Narrative and Themes of Meaning and Related Lessons). Mr. Collins shared the most important and valued part of his narrated experience in response to the counselor's question in this area: Clarifying what made him so angry in the meeting (the HR manager's disrespect and the client's hurt feelings). Learning the value of his pay scale position was next in importance to Mr. Collins, because that knowledge gave him potential bargaining power with the company.

David asked Mr. Collins to "Talk about what your narrative means to you" (the main themes). Mr. Collins identified two meanings or themes: His lack of power and control in the situation and his sense of not being valued by the company. Another question shifted the focus to future coping, "What did you learn from the narrative and how can you use those lessons now?" The client said he learned that information is power (a lesson he missed during the meeting with the HR manager). Consequently, he set a goal to seek out information from external sources about the buyout and his options. He also concluded that he should meet with someone else in the company who occupied a power position to request inside information on the buyout.

Integrating Narrative and Other Approaches

NARRATIVE AND SOLUTION-FOCUSED ASSESSMENTS AND INTERVENTIONS. Mr. Collins and other clients often have difficulty identifying how their situations have changed and what led to changes such as those discussed in the previous section. They may not recognize their collaborative role in responding to solution-focused naming questions and the effects on assessment and intervention, because their role in the narrative process may seem minor to them. Essentially, their responses to solution-focused questions and their identification of themes and lessons from their narratives highlight this role. The process clarifies what has changed in their situations, areas that did not change that they are still concerned about, and how they can use what they have learned to change those areas. Mr. Collins's decision to obtain buyout information from external and internal sources, based on his narrative lessons, is an example of this type of agency (Freeman, 2004).

NARRATIVE, SYSTEMS, TASK-CENTERED, AND LOSS AND GRIEF APPROACHES. Practitioners can help clients connect their goals with planned actions by using cognitive maps and other graphic assessment and intervention methods. Many of those methods are based on systems and ecological practice approaches, and therefore, they clarify resources and challenges in clients' environments. These methods can be combined effectively with narrative approaches. For example, Mr. Collins set goals for seeking information about buyouts from external sources as well as sources within his company. David and Mr. Collins used an ecomap to identify resources and challenges in the client's environment related to those goals, including his church community (see Figure 3.1).

The ecomap helped them to identify a peer, a retired attorney in Mr. Collins' breakfast club, who mediated grievances in the business field prior to his retirement. He coached Mr. Collins by providing more objective and general information about company buyouts and employee rights. His knowledge of organizational and systems dynamics helped Mr. Collins to identify another manager in the company with whom he could talk about the buyout, and formulate follow-up

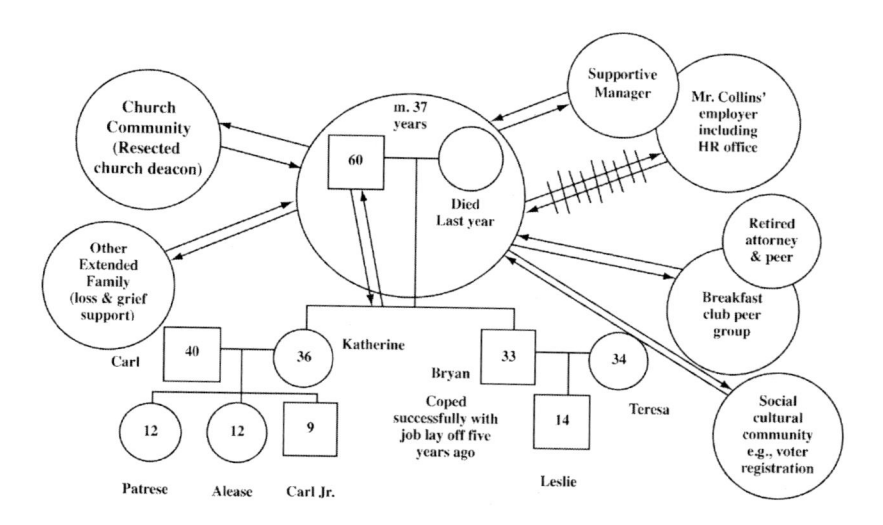

Figure 3.1. Mr. Collins's Ecomap.

questions to ask the company's HR staff, specific to the company's situation. David could have used an organizational map to enhance the systems approach and identify other organizational resources and challenges. However, the three to five sessions allowed for EAP referrals by Mr. Colllins's employer limited the amount of detailed work possible in this short-term service process.

A combination of systems and narrative approaches helped Mr. Collins to gain information and control over his situation in order to make a critical career decision. When he decided to take the company buyout, another review of the ecomap revealed his son had been laid off five years previously, and that he had successfully transitioned from being a salesman to a computer programmer. Although Mr. Collins knew a lot about his son's situation, David suggested he ask his son to be his cultural coach (Freeman, 2004), to share a narrative about what the transition had been like for the son. Another breakfast club peer encouraged Mr. Collins to apply for a part-time job as a school bus driver to supplement his retirement income after he took the buyout.

Task-centered interventions were integrated into this work involving the client's son, breakfast club peers, minister (his spiritual guide), and company manager. Planned incremental tasks and action steps included Mr. Collins consulting with his informal coaches and participating in a structured review process with his counselor about the task results during their third and fourth sessions. David used a brief loss and grief approach in those sessions focused on the loss of Mr. Collins's wife and job, which facilitated his transition into semiretirement. These two approaches were integrated with the previous narrative, solution-focused, and systems interventions that were used with the client.

Skill: Using Solution-Focused Unpacking Questions

While naming questions help clients to gain their voices or to identify sources of power in their narratives, unpacking questions can help them to expand their narratives. Expanding allows them to provide more detailed thicker descriptions of their experiences as well as contextual information. It also encourages clients to align themselves with change, rather than with the status quo, and to undertake solution-focused actions or interventions. Essentially, unpacking questions build upon or work simultaneously with naming questions, which clarify where change is already occurring and where in each narrative other initiatives for change exist. The example of Glenda, from this chapter's introduction, illustrates the use of narrative interventions near the end of long-term services, in contrast to the example in the previous section involving short-term services.

Background Information

Glenda is a 26-year-old Caucasian client who received services from a battered woman's shelter for approximately 18 months, which included a one-year aftercare or supported housing component. The client and her two children, two-year-old Adam and three-year-old Royal, had been homeless for two weeks before they entered the shelter. They slept on the streets because Glenda's in-laws allowed her to stay with them but did not protect her from her husband's violence. Glenda decided not to stay with her own family because she was afraid her husband, Michael, would become violent with them. After sharing an initial narrative about her in-laws not protecting her and the children from her husband, Glenda became more guarded in later sessions with the case manager and therapist assigned to work with her. She would talk about her husband's abuse in a matter of fact manner, including physical abuse, rape, erotic asphyxia, death threats, emotional battery, and forced bondage. During counseling and case management sessions she would not make eye contact and would seem detached and far away. In one session with the therapist, several months after she moved into the supported housing component of the program, Glenda shared a dream she had experienced the previous weekend.

Glenda's Dream Narrative

I had a dream last week that I just can't forget–it stayed with me–it's as real today as if I just had it a few minutes ago. It was emotional and so full of bright almost blinding colors it scared me. And actually, once I had that dream, I had several others, but this one was the first and the most heavy. It felt like a dream that was going to come true in my life, not like a dream from somebody else's life–like somebody rich and famous. I had a feeling that if I woke up, the dream would go away and never happen. I thought if I could keep my eyes closed and stay asleep it *would* become my life, and Royal's life, and Adam's life, too. So in this dream, I'm in my grandmother's house. It's her house, but it isn't. When the dream first starts, it's her house like it was when she was alive a few years ago. Real comfortable with big old fashioned furniture, and it feels safe because the sun is shinning in the windows like when I was a kid and thought my family would always keep me safe. Then while I'm sitting there feeling safe and enjoying myself, the house begins to change. I can feel my grandmother standing beside me, saying, "You have to make your own life, this is a safe house, but it isn't your house or your life." As the house changes, I realize that Adam and Royal are there beside me and we're walking through the house, toward one of the bedrooms. I notice the furniture is different—more like the new country style that I like now.

When we reach the bedroom Adam and Royal begin to pull away like they're afraid something bad might happen, so I tell them to come and see the bedroom with me. Then we're sitting on the bed and looking around. Suddenly Michael is there, too, as though he's been waiting for us. Only he's standing outside the bedroom window, making motions for me to unlock the back door. When I just look at him, I see him motion more angrily for me to unlock the window and let him in. He's getting upset and mean looking. I try to show Adam and Royal different things in the room, so they won't look at Michael. I can see things everywhere that Michael would be upset about if he was in the house–toys the kids like to play with, pictures of my family and friends, a journal I used to have until he burned it, a gardening basket, and tools I once used in the yard. He doesn't like me being in the yard alone and "exposing myself to other men." There's one wall with beautifully written words describing things I enjoyed doing before I married Michael—a trip to Florida with my parents, being an "A" student in school, playing with my dog, reading books to my grandmother.

When me and the kids look outside again, the sky is darker with heavy clouds. There's a terrible storm going on behind Michael. He still motions for me to let him in, but somehow I know it's me and the kids' home and not his. He's totally separate from us and I'm not afraid of him because we're inside and protected from him. The storm is outside where he is, and I suddenly know if I let him in, he'll ruin it all for us again. He'll try to get us back. But it's my house and my place like my grandmother wanted it to be. It has all the good memories from her house, but it's a home I've made for me and the kids. At the end of the dream I feel drained, because the dream is so emotional, so powerful. It's a good feeling though it's a little scary too.

Helping Clients to Unpack or Expand Their Narratives

This section addresses the context of clients' narratives, such as Glenda's previous dream narrative. The skill of contextual questions is explored also in Chapter 1 where clients' narrated experiences are analyzed, for example, "Where did this experience take place?" Such questions provide information about why a narrative emerges in a particular situation. In contrast, unpacking questions help providers to elicit thicker descriptions about the context based on more complex criteria. Specifically, these questions deconstruct the context (McQuaide, 1999) by focusing on temporal, social, individual, physical setting, and cultural criteria, as outlined in Table 3.2. They can be combined with naming questions during integrated assessment and intervention services.

TEMPORAL FACTORS OR CRITERIA. After clients share their narratives, unpacking questions can help them to add or expand details about the timing and sequence of key events. When Glenda shared her dream narrative, Stephanie listened and then asked an unpacking timing question, "When did your dream occur in terms of your life today?" (see Table 3.2, Factor #1.) Glenda said the dream included the period when her grandmother lived in the house and all was well. It was the time, ". . . when I was a kid and thought my family would always keep me safe." Stephanie asked what else was significant about that part of her past. Glenda said it was while she often visited her grandmother in the house and the latter was an important person in her life. It made her feel comfortable to dream and think about her

Table 3.2
PRINCIPLE 3: THE NAMING AND UNPACKING ASSESSMENT
AND INTERVENTION PRINCIPLE
THE SKILL: THE USE OF SOLUTION-FOCUSED UNPACKING QUESTIONS

The Focus of Unpacking Questions	The Purpose of Unpacking Questions for Assessment and Intervention: To Expand and Contextualize the Narrative Regarding:
1. Temporal Factors Related to the Narrative:	The timing of the narrative in terms of when it occurred in clients' lives. The sequence of key events and interactions within the narrative and the effects of that sequence on the situation or events.
2. Social Aspects of the Narrative:	The types and nature of relationships between individuals in the narrative, and the effects of those relationships on the actions and interactions within the narrative and the reverse. The status of and changes in the following relationship issues as noticed in the narrative: i.e., in alliances and supports, cut-offs, power differentials, and communication patterns.
3. Individual Factors Within the Narrative:	A client's life priorities, personality, coping patterns, values and beliefs, strengths, and challenges as evident in the narrative. The effects of conflicts and compatibilities between such factors within the narrative and in the client's life situation.
4. The Narrative's Physical and Emotional Setting:	The physical setting in which the narrative takes place primarily, and the effects of physical, emotional, and political factors within the setting on what happens in the narrative and on the client's life situation in general.
5. Cultural Aspects of the Narrative: Religion or spiritual, ethnicity/race and language, gender, sexual orientation, age, location, social class, and disabling conditions:	The priorities and nature of the client's culture as reflected in his or her narrative, and any similarities and differences between the client's culture and that of other individuals or systems of importance within the narrative and in the client's life situation.

grandmother because she could depend on and trust her. Stephanie asked what in Glenda's current life specifically made her think about the comfort she needed from her grandmother. Glenda pointed out she was being pressured to move out of the supported housing part of the program. The staff was insisting it was time for her to move into her own living quarters or into transitional housing. Glenda thought staff pressure about this transition made her feel unsafe and untrusting toward them; consequently, she needed her grandmother's reassurance more than ever.

Stephanie asked Glenda another timing question, whether the rest of her dream also took place during the period before her grandmother died. Stephanie looked surprised and thoughtful, and then said some of the dream seemed to be in the present. She explained the house changed while she was there; her grandmother's old fashioned furniture disappeared and was replaced by new furniture that Glenda liked. Michael was outside the window acting angry and threatening, part of his current controlling behavior. She said the children's usual reactions were in the dream; "When we reach the bedroom Adam and Royal begin to pull away like they're afraid something bad might happen." Stephanie asked what Glenda thought her grandmother meant when she said, ". . . this is a safe house, but it isn't your house or your life?" After thinking about Stephanie's unpacking question, Glenda said, "I guess she's telling me my work on the abuse and belief in myself isn't finished, and until it's finished, I won't have a life of my own."

Glenda also said she thought the last part of her dream in the bedroom might represent the future where she and the children are separate from Michael and his violence. Consequently she felt more in control and powerful in that part of the dream because, unlike in the past, she resisted Michael's efforts to enter a house that she claimed for her and the children. Some authors assume the future time dimension facilitates growth and solutions in clients such as Glenda because it highlights the possibilities for change and exceptions to their past regressive narratives (Pipher, 1994).

To help clarify or unpack the sequence of her dream, Stephanie asked Glenda what came first and the possible effects this sequence had on what happened (see Table 3.2, Factor #1). Glenda thought being in her grandmother's house at first and hearing the latter's wisdom and support made her less frightened of Michael's presence outside the bedroom window later (an exception to her past regressive narratives). Her grandmother reassured and prepared Glenda for that part of the dream, while reminding her she still had work to complete. When Stephanie asked whether her grandmother's message was consistent or inconsistent with the staff's recommendation about independent or transitional housing, Glenda concluded that the two messages were mostly consistent. Glenda also realized that having the last part of her dream focused on the future helped her to remember it more fully, and to become more hopeful about her future as an independent woman (Rasmussen, 2002).

SOCIAL AND INDIVIDUAL CRITERIA/FACTORS. The temporal unpacking questions in the previous section can often elicit related details about the social and individual context of a client's narrative. For instance, Stephanie's timing questions revealed information about Glenda's relationships with significant others and about her individual values and beliefs (see Table 3.2, Factors #2 & 3). Stephanie then used follow-up questions about these social and individual factors to help the client continue to expand her narrative. She asked Glenda, "In your dream, what type of relationship did you describe or notice between you and your grandmother?" Glenda said her grandmother's message that, ". . . you have to make your own life" shows she valued Glenda and expected she would learn to take care of herself. Glenda remembered her grandmother as her childhood ally and as a powerful female heroine in the family, whose members viewed Glenda as special because she had a "favorite" status with her grandmother.

When asked if and how that relationship changed in the dream or in her life situation (see Table 3.2, Factor #2), Glenda began to cry. Her grandmother's disappearance in the dream reinforced the real-life change that had occurred in their relationship. Her death meant she could no longer influence others on Glenda's behalf as she did while she was alive. Glenda acknowledged that her sadness came not only from her grandmother's death but also from the loss of a powerful alliance with her. Stephanie encouraged Glenda to take the time to mourn those very significant losses by sharing other stories about her grandmother like the dream narrative. Perhaps grief about those losses had been masked by anxiety and safety issues related to her husband's violence. Because Michael did not like her grandmother, he was inpatient and insecure about any outward signs of Glenda's grief or of her close relationships with others.

Based on this comment about Michael's reaction to her grief about her grandmother, Stephanie asked what the dream revealed about Glenda's relationship with her husband. Glenda concluded that the dream showed he was demanding and manipulative toward her, and that in the past, she would have given in to him. The locked windows and doors in the dream house showed a change in their relationship, that she was currently separate and protected from him. She acknowledged her "Glenda wall" in the bedroom was a reminder of her separate identity before her life with Michael. In the dream, her children seemed to accept and welcome the protection she provided to them, which represented a change in her relationship with them and in their relationship with their father. This discussion illustrates how asking unpacking questions about a particular relationship can reveal details about clients' other significant relationships.

To further expand the social context of Glenda's dream, Stephanie asked who was *not* in her dream. Glenda identified her parents, brothers, and a lifelong friend. They were cutoff from Glenda because she continued to stay with Michael in spite of his violence and their efforts to help her. Stephanie's question and the client's response demonstrate how narrative assessment and intervention occur simultaneously. Glenda was troubled by but had not assessed the cost of these cutoffs previously except to say she was protecting her family. With her agreement reconnecting and repairing those cutoffs became part of her goals and the focus of solution-focused interventions.

Glenda's dream narrative was useful for expanding information about individual as well as social factors in her life (see Table 3.2, Factor #3). For example, Stephanie asked whether any part of the dream reflected how Glenda typically coped with issues she was concerned about. Glenda said she was hoping something magical would happen when she said, "I had a feeling if I woke up, the dream would go away and never happen." She thought keeping her eyes closed was an example of something they had talked about previously in their sessions, "waiting for the next rescue party" instead of doing the difficult work herself. Their discussion highlighted a value conflict that was challenging to Glenda; waiting to be rescued (the dutiful wife or female) versus doing the work herself (self-respect/independence) (see Table 3.2, Factor #3). Glenda believed her grandmother's admonition to get her own house and life clearly supported the latter side of this value conflict. Moreover, Glenda was able to sort out her priorities based on this dream narrative, which emphasized having a safe place and control over her situation.

THE NARRATIVE'S PHYSICAL AND EMOTIONAL SETTING AND CULTURAL FACTORS. Stephanie believed narrative and solution-focused questions had helped to expand Glenda's narrative significantly, leading to her enhanced coping and self-esteem. However, certain aspects of Glenda's narrative and life situation remained unclear and challenging to their work. For example, Stephanie had been unsuccessful in helping Glenda to handle the crisis around finding transitional or independent housing. To discover how Glenda's dream narrative might be related to this crisis Stephanie asked in one session (Rasmussen, 2002), "What is the house that you dreamed about like?" Stephanie hoped this unpacking question focused on the dream's setting would open up the client's narrative even more (see Table 3.2, Factor #4). Glenda said the house was safe and comfortable. When Stephanie asked how those qualities affected her, Glenda explained they made her trusting about being able to handle the threat of Michael stalking her outside the window.

Stephanie also asked, "What is the shelter's supported housing like from your perspective?" Stephanie described the shelter and her housing as safe at one time, but said, "Now it feels threatening so it makes me feel powerless like I did when Michael hurt and bullied me. My dream about the house comforts me when I get overwhelmed." Stephanie pointed out that Glenda seemed to be talking about lacking political power or the power to decide for herself (Roche & Wood, 2005), whether it involved Michael or the shelter's staff. She asked Glenda what she needed to do to participate in the decision about her housing. Their discussion led to a plan for them to meet with the staff about this issue.

In preparation for that meeting, Stephanie asked Glenda culture-related unpacking questions about "How is the woman in the dream narrative similar to the woman in the shelter's housing unit?" "How are they different?" (see Table 3.2, Factor #5). Glenda concluded the woman in the dream was more confident, independent, and able to resist pressures from others that could lead to harm. She described the woman in her current housing (herself) in gender-stereotypical ways (Roche & Wood, 2005), such as dependent, not smart, unable to make decisions, and scared. This discussion clarified that Glenda was also being pressured by the court to allow Michael to resume his visitation with Adam and Royal. She believed moving out of supported housing could allow Michael more opportunities to abuse her and the children. Glenda had not shared her fears with staff because she thought they would assume she was using those fears to keep from moving.

When asked how Glenda believed the woman in the shelter was similar to and different from the shelter staff, Stephanie said most of the staff were a little older and better educated, while those staff members who had been abused themselves had a tough attitude about the right way to recover. Glenda's insights about these cultural differences (gender attitudes, social class, and age) helped Stephanie to understand client *and* staff challenges to resolving the crisis. She addressed some of those challenges with staff prior to the meeting with the client. In that meeting, Stephanie and Glenda proposed hiring the latter as a peer adviser in the supported housing program. A majority of the staff agreed with the proposal, leading to a decision to hire Glenda and allow the client to maintain her current housing.

Conclusion

This chapter illustrates how clients such as Glenda have an important role in the narrative assessment and intervention process, based on their expertise about their lived experiences and narratives. The discussion provides examples of the partnership clients and providers need in order to deconstruct and understand the context of clients' narratives, or what makes each narrative unique. Naming and unpacking questions are not only required narrative skills that encourage practitioners to establish such partnerships. When those skills are used effectively, they provide specific tools clients can use in the continuing process of deconstructing their narratives. Some of those tools focus clients and providers' attention on clients' feelings related to their narratives and on related lessons (naming tools), while others help these collaborators to clarify timing and cultural factors in clients' narratives (unpacking tools).

Consequently, such tools can enhance clients' growth opportunities in two critical ways. First, clients can use these tools in partnership with practitioners or alone as they gain self-confidence, which is a form of capacity building. Second, using these tools often reveals previously unidentified resources and solutions that are embedded in clients' narratives. Revelations include clients identifying changes that are already occurring in their situations as well as opportunities to revise and/or build new significant relationships. In the section on naming questions, the client, Mr. Collins, realized his perceptions and priorities about how his employer's HR office had treated him were already changing. He identified hurt feelings rather than anger as his priority concern. He also used his need for a coach in his retirement transition to establish a different adult-to-adult relationship with his son, after his narrative revealed the son had a similar work transition experience previously.

References

Dimaggio, G., Salvatore, G., Azzara, C., Gatania, D., Semerari, A., & Hermans, H. J. M. (2003). Dialogical relationships in impoverished narratives: From theory to clinical practice. *Psychology and Psychotherapy Theory, Research, and Practice, 76,* 385–409.

Docherty, D., & McColl, M. A. (2003). Illness stories: Themes emerging through narrative. *Social Work in Health Care, 37,* 19–39.

Freedman, J., & Combs, G. (1996). *Narrative therapy: The social construction of preferred realities.* New York: W.W. Norton.

Freeman, E. M. (March 4, 2004). Basic principles of effective narrative practice. Workshop presentation. Kansas City, MO. Sponsored by the Social Work Coalition and Social Work Leaders in Health Care.

Freeman, E. M. (2001). Assessment: Clients as experts on their experiences, recovery motivation, and power resources. In *Substance abuse intervention, prevention, rehabilitation, and systems change strategies: Helping individuals, families, and groups to empower themselves* (pp. 183–207). New York: Columbia University Press.

Freeman, E. M., & Couchonnal, G. (2006). Narrative and culturally based approaches in practice with families. *Families in Society, 87*(2), 198–208.

Gale, D. D., Mitchell, A. M., Garand, L., & Wesner, S. (2003). Client narratives: A theoretical perspective. *Issues in Mental Health Nursing, 24,* 81–89.

Gingerich, W. J., & Eisengart, S. (2000). Solution-focused brief therapy: A review of the outcome research. *Family Process, 39* (4), 477–498.

Kelley, P. (2002). A narrative therapy approach to brief treatment. *Journal of Brief Therapy, 1,* 91–100.

McQuaide, S. (1999). Using psychodynamic, cognitive, and solution-focused questioning to co-construct a new narrative. *Clinical Social Work Journal, 27*(4), 339–353.

Meichenbaum, D., & Fitzpatrick, D. (1993). A constructionist narrative perspective on stress and coping. In L. Goldberger & S. Breznitz (Eds.), *Handbook of stress: Theoretical and clinical aspects* (2nd ed., pp. 706–723). New York: Free Press.

Norman, J. (2000). Constructive narrative in arresting the impact of post-traumatic stress disorder. *Clinical Social Work Journal, (28)*3, 303–319.

Pietsch, U. K. (2002). Facilitating post-divorce transition using narrative therapy. *Journal of Couple and Relationship Therapy, 1*(1), 65–81.

Pipher, M. (1994). *Reviving Ophelia: Saving the selves of adolescent girls.* Ballantine Books, New York.

Rasmussen, B. M. (2002). Linking metaphor and dreams in clinical practice. *Psychoanalytic Social Work, 9*(2), 71–87.

Roche, S. E., & Wood, G. G. (2005). A narrative principle for feminist social work with survivors of male violence. *Afillia, 20*(4), 465–475.

Saleebey, D. (1994). Culture, theory, and narrative: The intersection of meanings in practice. *Social Work, 39*(4), 351–359.

Stalker, C. A., Levene, L. E., & Coady, N. F. (1999). Solution-focused brief therapy– One model fits all? *Families in Society, 80*(5), 468–477.

Chapter 4

USING NARRATIVE QUESTIONS TO CONNECT CLIENTS' SINGLE EVENT NARRATIVES AND LIFE NARRATIVES: THE MEANING-MAKING PRINCIPLE

What is the use of running when we're not on the right road?
—German Proverb

Principle 4 explains the importance of context in terms of life narratives, a central source of meaning making by individuals (Luborsky, 1993). People's life narratives affect and are affected by their single narratives over time (E. Freeman, 2004). For instance, clients' questions about their life narratives can encourage them to explore the meaning of their current and past single narratives or the reverse. Such explorations often reveal value, belief, or identity conflicts that lead clients to either revise their life narratives or to change the meaning they infer from their single narratives.

Practitioners can enhance clients' tools for constructing, reviewing, and revising their life narratives. An understanding of context in general, and of the role of clients' life narratives in particular, is required to facilitate this vital work. One hospital social worker was helping a 57-year-old Columbian man with Type II diabetes to cope with his potential kidney failure and new medical regimen. He believed the client, Carlos Riviera, should quit his job as an over-the-road truck driver in order to begin renal dialysis. The client planned to work for several months to pay the family's bills and save money for when he could no longer drive his truck. He shared a family narrative about his father's miraculous recovery from cancer based on his faith after doctors predicted he would die within a few months. The worker said the client's faith in coping with his health condition was important, but he wondered if the client might be in denial about the seriousness of his condition.

Mr. Rivera's single narrative about his father and his own decision to continue working for a while were no doubt rooted in a context that the social worker did not understand. This context involved the client's life narrative, or more specifically, his cultural and gender expectations for himself as head of his household. The client's story about his father as the family hero was also part of that context. This chapter's epigraph questions the purpose of running, even when time is of the essence, if the provider is not on the right road or helping the client to move in his or her desired direction. Clarity about the right direction emerges as the client's meanings are shared and the provider and client begin to understand that context. The process can reveal important meanings and options to clients that were not apparent initially.

This chapter illustrates how direction and meaning reside in the context of clients' life narratives and in the connections between those narratives and their single event narratives. Clients' efforts to find meaning in their narrated experiences are then explained as a search for coherence and continuity, based on the premises of Principle 4. This principle clarifies the components of life narratives and their role in the search for meaning. Providers' skillful use of narrative coherence and continuity questions demonstrates how to help clients resolve their challenges and enhance their strengths.

Overview of the Meaning-Making Principle

Defining Life Narratives and Single Event Narratives

Life narratives have been defined as powerful tools that individuals use to establish continuity and coherence in their lives over time. Thomson, Bell, Holland, Henderson, McGrellis, and Sharpe (2002) believe the life narrative consists of an accumulation of critical moments in people's lives which viewed together provide continuity over time. Therefore, the life narrative's structure is not as strong and narrative events may be less detailed and more abbreviated in comparison to single event narratives (Habermas & Paha, 2001). The life narrative fulfills its continuity function by providing a stage or context in which people can examine, understand, gain meaning from, and find coherence within their single narratives. The latter are narratives that are constructed from one significant experience or event in contrast to life narratives.

Life narratives are often elicited through "... interviews, clinical encounters, and other such interrogative venues, that entail a significant measure of reflection on either an event or experience, a significant part of life, or the whole of it" (M. Freeman, 2006, p. 132). Such narratives can also emerge spontaneously from both internal and external factors. Examples include when older adults involve themselves in the life review process, middle-age adults make major career or other life changes, and youths involved in identity development are moved from parental custody to out-of-home placements.

In these and other circumstances, the life narrative undergoes continuous revisions, rewrites, and changes as individuals integrate new lessons or meanings they have inferred from their single narratives. Such revisions are counterbalanced, however, by each person's life narrative, which provides the consistent template required for interpreting their single narratives. Consequently, this dynamic process insures that individuals have ongoing narrative opportunities to grow and change (E. Freeman, 2004; McAdams, 2001).

The Main Elements of Principle 4

The previous definition of the life narrative implies several underlying assumptions or premises, for example, many authors assume that (Luborsky, 1993; Woike & Polo, 2001; Wortham, 2000):

1. The life narrative's critical or fateful moments are selected, acknowledged as significant, and remembered by individuals because they are central to their identity, existence, world views, value priorities, beliefs, and meaning making.
2. Individuals compare values and beliefs in their life narratives with those in their single narrated experiences, which can lead to perceptions of dissonance or consonance regarding those values and beliefs.
3. While dissonance may feel uncomfortable, it can provide opportunities for people to construct new aspects of their life narratives, and to periodically review, rewrite, or maintain those narratives

over time based on the meanings they infer during the review process.
4. Hence, dissonance can lead to problem resolution, improved coping, and a sense of well-being by individuals eventually, based on values and beliefs under review in their life narratives, in a single narrated event, or in both.
5. Similarly, consonance between individuals' life and single event narratives can reinforce values and beliefs that are reflected in those narratives as well as the meanings they infer from the review process.

The Significance of Principle 4 to Narrative Practice

The definition and premises outlined in the previous sections imply that constructing and revisiting a life narrative may aid people at particular stages of development or during significant transitions. The transitions from adolescence to young adulthood (Habermas & Paha, 2000) and from adulthood to old age (Thomson et al., 2002) are critical opportunities for constructing or revising the life narrative and for conducting a life narrative review. Therefore, the life narrative may aid in youth and adult development (Luborsky, 1993) because it can be a source of coherence, self-regulation, and growth (McAdams, 2006; E. Freeman, 2004).

Narrative authors and researchers have posed questions about the relative significance of big versus small stories, or life narratives versus single event narratives. Some characterize life narratives as too distant from the present because of their focus on grand events versus small stories, which seem closer to the action and are enmeshed within "... the interactive, especially conversational, dynamics of social life" (M. Freeman, 2006, p. 132). Principle 4 acknowledges the tension implicit in these two opposing views, but suggests that the synergy between big and small stories makes them equally important and essential (Bamberg, 2006).

Components of the Life Narrative

The Dynamic Nature of These Components

Helping clients such as Mr. Rivera in this chapter's introduction to explore their life narratives often reveals the main story or running

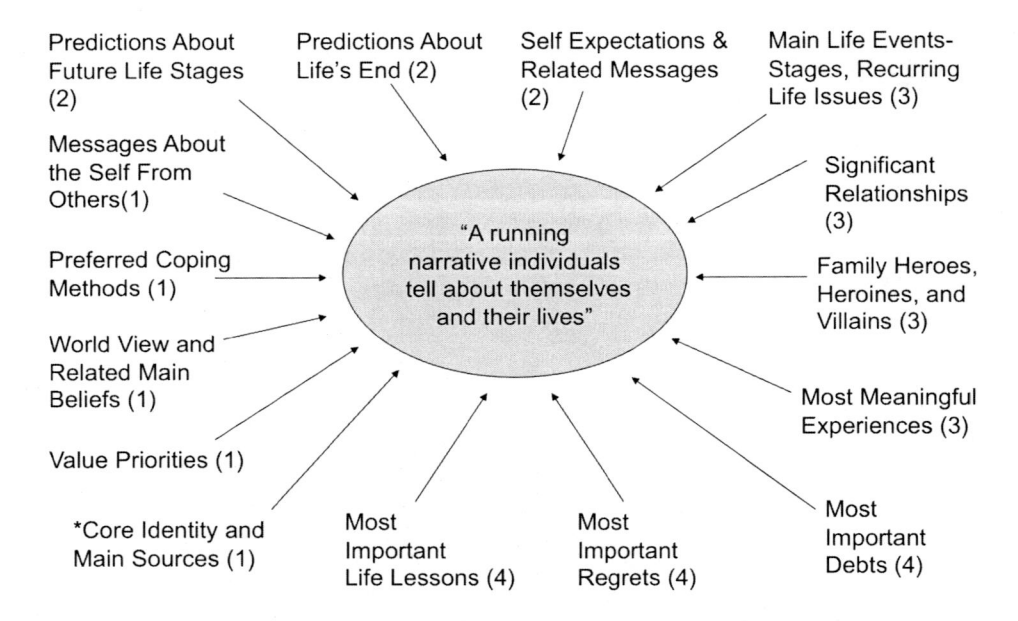

72   *Narrative Approaches in Social Work Practice*

```
Predictions About      Predictions About    Self Expectations &    Main Life Events-
Future Life Stages     Life's End (2)       Related Messages       Stages, Recurring
(2)                                         (2)                    Life Issues (3)

Messages About                                                              Significant
the Self From                                                               Relationships
Others(1)                         "A running                                (3)
                          narrative individuals
Preferred Coping          tell about themselves              Family Heroes,
Methods (1)                   and their lives"               Heroines, and
                                                             Villains (3)
World View and
Related Main                                                         Most Meaningful
Beliefs (1)                                                          Experiences (3)

Value Priorities (1)
                                                                     Most
*Core Identity and     Most              Most                        Important
Main Sources (1)       Important         Important                   Debts (4)
                       Life Lessons (4)  Regrets (4)
```

Figure 4.1. Components of the Life Narrative.

narrative they have chosen to tell about themselves and their lives. The main story may be told to themselves only, either in spoken words or as a silent voice in the individual's mind or it may be told out loud to others. To assist in this process, practitioners need to be aware of the life narrative's components and how they contribute to clients' meaning-making processes. Thomson et al. describe those components as "A combination of conditions, individual responses, timing, and chance" (2002, p. 340). Figure 4.1 includes four clusters of life narrative components which are autobiographical in nature and which interact with each other continuously. Those components are instrumental in the development and continuity of each person's life narrative (E. Freeman, 2004):

Cluster 1: The Core Narrated Self

In the lower left corner of Figure 4.1, the core identity component (*) is listed first because it is the central source of each individual's self-discovery, meaning making, and continuity (Thomson et al., 2002) in terms of this cluster and the life narrative itself. Cluster 1 also includes four other components that are each followed by the number "1" in Figure 4.1: an individual's value priorities, world view and beliefs, preferred coping methods, and messages about the self from significant others that the individual has accepted and internalized. These components address whom the individual is essentially or his or her internal and external identity, which "... is much larger, more continuous, and more stable" (Bamberg, 2006, p. 67) than single narratives typically reveal.

Cluster 2: Narrated and Unnarrated Life Predictions and Expectations

Components in this cluster can be both predictive and self-fulfilling prophecies. For example, peoples' predictions about future life stages may clarify their level of optimism or pessimism based on their parents' or other peoples' life narratives and how those individuals experienced the same stages. A person's optimism or pessimism for the future may also lead to self-fulfilling prophecies based on his or her own current life narratives. Habermas and Paha (2001) identify expectations and predictions respectively as "... causal links between event and personal change and past-present comparisons" (p. 35). Figure 4.1 indicates components followed by the number "2" include predictions about future life stages, predictions about life's end, and self-expectations and related messages to the self. Those components focus on individuals' hopes, endurance, the sources of their optimism, and for some people, on their pessimism about overcoming various life challenges at a given time or throughout their life span.

Cluster 3: Significant Narrated and Unnarrated Life Events and Actors

This cluster indicates how each life narrator developed into his or her present self. It reveals how particular people, experiences, and events contributed significantly to the narrator's life journey (components in Figure 4.1 followed by the number "3"). These components are opportunistic in nature because they often precipitate biographical changes or life transitions. For example, the death of a spouse can result in a transition from dependence to independence by the widow or widower (E. Freeman, 2004). This cluster can also involve myths about a family or cultural hero's behavior, which are both strengths and challenges. Carlos Riviera rejected the clinic's prognosis for his kidney condition, similar to his father's reaction to his cancer diagnosis. While adopting his family hero's response allowed additional time for the client to find other ways to cope (a strength), it also delayed his treatment (a challenge). Such heroic events can impact upon life narrative construction and revisions by involving ". . . a delay or postponement of insight . . . for individuals," therefore their ". . . narrative connections are made after-the-fact, when the dust has settled" (M. Freeman, 2006, p. 57).

Cluster 4: Narrated Life Opportunities for Meaning Making and Growth

The focus of Cluster 4 is on how people reflect and learn as part of their biographical changes, including the identification of life lessons, regrets, and unpaid debts (Figure 4.1, components followed by the number "4"). These components often involve a dynamic growth process, for example, when individuals address their unpaid debts that effort can help them to learn related life lessons. Moreover, the connection between individuals' regrets and debts may become more apparent as the life narrative is reviewed and revised. Cluster 4 components can also influence the other three clusters, leading to growth and lessons learned regarding an individual's identity, predictions about the future, or significant relationships (see Figure 4.1). Mark Freeman (2006) clarifies the impact of these growth components or ". . . the revelatory power of big stories–that is, their capacity to yield insight and understanding . . . by virtue of the larger constellations of meaning . . . " (p. 134) they can provide. Other authors assume these components provide individuals with an aerial view of their lives which reveals terrain and vistas that are invisible from a ground level perspective (Gusdorf, 1980).

Practice Skills: Using Life Narrative Coherence and Continuity Questions with Adolescents

Practice Overview

Age is a factor in this process of connecting big and small stories because *generally* the ability "... to coherently narrate the story of one's life seems to be acquired only during adolescence" (Habermas & Paha, 2001, p. 35). However, younger children have the ability to tell a story about a single personal experience and to learn lessons from that process. Therefore practitioners can assist them in analyzing issues of concern in their single event narratives and addressing their concerns in general. Their analyses can reveal concerns about other children and adults in their environments as well as provide tools for addressing those environmental challenges. The discussion on narrative timing and context questions in Chapter 1 and solution-focused narrative questions with children in Chapter 6 are examples of such tools and how they can facilitate this analysis process.

Similarly, practitioners can help adolescents to learn from their single event narratives as well as assist them in constructing and learning from their life narratives (Bamberg, 2006). However, some teenagers may lack the necessary knowledge about their family history and significant events in their biological and biographical contexts to construct their life narratives. In those situations practitioners can provide life narrative opportunities for adolescents to gather this history while also helping to foster the emergence of their life stories. In the following example, a practitioner helps a client construct her life narrative and then explore her knowledge gaps about the family's history and significant events. This process enhances the client's problem solving and her ongoing life narrative development.

Practice Example: Exploring Adolescents' Life Narrative/Biographical Contexts

BACKGROUND INFORMATION. Sandra is a 14-year-old African American girl. Four years previously, her father shot her mother in the head after beating her severely during an argument. Her mother almost died from the attack. She was released from the hospital after several weeks and then spent three months in a rehabilitation center where she received physical therapy. After her release from the rehab center, the mother disappeared. Since then she has recontacted the family periodically, but then she always leaves again after a few days. The children's father was sentenced to ten years in prison. Sandra and her two younger sisters were placed with their maternal grandparents, who have been very supportive and nurturing. The grandparents receive a foster care subsidy from the state which is inadequate, therefore they continue to struggle financially.

With the foster care worker's support, the grandparents encouraged the children to talk about their loss and grief from the family's disruption and also to feel safe in the grandparents' home. The worker recently referred Sandra to a family service agency for help with her low self-esteem and the effects of Post-Traumatic Stress Disorder (PTSD) due to her father's past violence. In one of her family service sessions, Sandra talked about a letter the grandparents received from her father informing them of his impending parole hearing. Sandra was fearful and ambivalent about his potential release. She liked living with her grandparents because they were stable and patient with the three children. So she worried about the possibility of having to live with their father after his release. She remembered his violence and said she could not depend on her mother to stay around and protect the children. Sandra stated it was hard to talk about her family because she did not think other people could understand her situation.

The family service worker, Diana Louis, acknowledged that other teenagers often found it difficult to discuss private information about their families. She said some of them were more comfortable discussing and learning from other people's situations. She then asked if Sandra would complete a story that she, Diana, would begin about a 13-year-old girl named Justine. Sandra was free to complete the story in her own way. Diana audiotaped the following shared storytelling process with Sandra as part of their previous agreement on how their sessions would be conducted.

THE PRACTITIONER'S SHARED STORYTELLING STRATEGY: THE STIMULUS PORTION. Justine's parents separated during the past two years. They argue a lot about which parent the children should live with. Justine likes to stay with her aunt and uncle because she feels close to them and they get along with each other. They also like having Justine and her brother around and they do not make negative comments about the family's troubles. Justine says her parents have involved her and her brother in their fights and that each of them expects the children to side with him or her. Justine is dreading a scheduled child custody court hearing, which could result in the siblings having to leave their aunt and uncle's home and live with one of their parents. One day Justine decides to go for a walk by herself. As she walks along an unfamiliar street she realizes she is lost and that she does not know where she is.

SANDRA'S SHARED STORYTELLING RESPONSE: THE COMPLETION PORTION. This girl, Justine, is walking down a real pretty street. The trees are all different colors of green. The houses are painted in bright colors—they make her feel good. The sun is shinning on her face. It's warm and soft. Maybe she's thinking to herself, this is a strange street or wondering how she got there. She knows she's lost because she hasn't seen the street before. Then someone comes out of one of the houses. It's a woman. She invites Justine inside. Justine knows this woman is inviting her inside because she's smiling and waving her hands at her. I bet she's not sure what to do—should she go in or stay outside on the street? She takes a big chance, because she doesn't know this woman, and goes inside anyway. The woman shows the girl every room in the house, just taking her time and being nice to Justine. The house is very clean, nice furniture everywhere. All of a sudden a lot of people—a few of them are kids—come into one of the rooms. They come over and say hello to the girl, one or two at a time, taking turns. They tell her their names and ask Justine to tell them her name—like they want to know who she is. She opens her mouth each time to tell them who she is, but she can't make a sound no matter how hard she tries. If I was her, I'd be scared if I didn't know my name. They start to look at her real funny. Justine probably wonders how she can get back to her street and her aunt and uncle's house if she can't remember her name. I think she's real scared because she's not sure who she can talk to and she realizes she's really lost now.

Narrative Analysis: Helping Adolescents to Construct Their Life Narratives

COHERENCE SKILLS-STAGE ONE: ANALYZING SINGLE EVENT NARRATIVES. Life narrative construction with adolescents involves a two-stage process that is often overlapping rather than consecutive. Those stages are discussed separately in the next two sections only to clarify this integrated dual process. First, practitioners can use coherence skills to help adolescents learn about and analyze aspects of their single event narratives, which ultimately, is the foundation for constructing life narratives. Second, providers' continuity skills can provide opportunities for adolescents to initiate the actual construction of those life narratives.

The coherence stage of this integrated process creates a shared language and conceptual tools for adolescents' self-reflection and growth. This stage can be initiated by listening to a client's spontaneous narrative or by eliciting a narrative from the client. A tool for eliciting narratives from reluctant clients is shared storytelling, whereby practitioners' share narratives that parallel the themes, life circumstances, and turning points in their clients' lives. The client's act of completing the relevant narrative builds an emotional bond with the practitioner because the whole process is a shared emotional experience (E. Freeman, 2004).

Accordingly, Diana created and shared a stimulus portion of a narrative in which she skillfully included a number of major themes about Justine that paralleled themes and life transitions in Sandra's situation (see Table 4.1). Diana selected those themes from background information Sandra and the foster care worker shared with her. For example Diana included themes about managing change and fears to address Sandra's concerns about her father's impending parole (see Table 4.1, Themes #4a and 5a).

A second conceptual tool for the coherence stage is the narrative analysis process, during which Diana used various narrative coherence questions shown in Table 4.2. Those questions helped Sandra to name and clarify key themes in the narrative. For instance, Diana asked Sandra to identify some of the main ideas in story about Justine that were either spoken or unspoken (Question #1a). When Sandra identified two themes, being lost and Justine's aunt and uncle being kind and trustful, Diana asked where in the story Sandra was able to "hear" those themes (see Table 4.2, Question #1b). Sandra said she thought Justine was lost because her family was separated, she was walking on an unknown street, and she had lost her name (see Table 4.1, Themes #1a, c, and e).

Sandra pointed out Justine's aunt and uncle could be trusted, because they wanted Justine and her brother to feel welcome and were not focused on themselves like their parents were (Table 4.1, Themes #3a, b, and c). She said Justine's parents reminded her of her own parents. She has had to be a grown-up for her sisters because their parents

Table 4.1
PRINCIPLE 4: THE MEANING MAKING PRINCIPLE
EXAMPLES OF THEMES FROM A STIMULUS COMPLETION NARRATIVE PROCESS

Examples of Themes: (*) Similarities between Justine and Sandra	In the Stimulus Portion of the Story: The Provider's Narrative About Justine	In the Completion Portion of the Story: Sandra's Narrative About Justine
1. Past, Current, and Future Loss	(a) Justine's parents are separated (the initial disruption) (*), (b) there is a possibility that the siblings will have to leave their aunt and uncle's home (another impending disruption) (*), and (c) Justine has become lost on an unknown street.	d) Sandra describes a warm, colorful, and welcoming street that Justine finds herself lost on, e) She says Justine realizes she is really lost now because she does not know her name, f) The nice house where Justine visits reminds Sandra she might lose her grandparents' very welcoming house.
2. Role of Guides or Mentors	(a) Justine's aunt and uncle model how to get along with each other and how to be warm and caring toward the siblings (*) (b) while not making negative comments about their family troubles.	(c) The guide in the house welcomes Justine and invites her inside, (d) Because the guide welcomed Justine in a new social situation Justine feels supported and accepted.
3. The Issue of Trust	(a) Justine's parents have attempted to get the siblings to take sides, making it difficult for the siblings to trust the parents' willingness to put the children's needs above their own needs. (b) The aunt and uncle like having the siblings around and have made them feel welcome, thus inspiring trust (*).	(c) Sandra believes Justine's aunt and uncle could be trusted because of how they care for Justine and her brother, (d) Justine must have trusted the woman in the house because even though she wasn't sure if she should go inside she decided to go in, (e) Justine cannot talk to the people in the house because she does not want to tell them who she is; she does not trust them.

Continued on next page

Table 4.1 *(continued)*
PRINCIPLE 4: THE MEANING MAKING PRINCIPLE
EXAMPLES OF THEMES FROM A STIMULUS COMPLETION NARRATIVE
PROCESS

Examples of Themes: (*) *Similarities between Justine and Sandra*	*In the Stimulus Portion of the Story: The Provider's Narrative About Justine*	*In the Completion Portion of the Story: Sandra's Narrative About Justine*
4. Managing Change	(a) The family has experienced several changes over which the siblings do not have any control. For example, Justine does not know what to expect from the impending child custody hearing, another possible transition which could make the siblings feel powerless (*). (b) Justine is in the identity development phase; the family changes may have complicated her development in this area (*).	(c) Sandra said Justine is in a new situation on a new street, she likes the pretty street and she likes the house, but she is not comfortable with so many new people and things around her, (d) Justine does not know what to do or say in the strange house.
5. Fear and Risk Taking	(a) Being pressured to take one or the other parent's side in the divorce makes Justine reluctant to make decisions because with her parents she cannot win.	(b) Justine takes a big chance by going inside the house, which is nice, but then she loses her name, b)She is not sure if the people will like her if she tells them about herself.
6. Lack of Power and Agency	(a) The parents have decided who the children should live with but Justine and her brother have not been asked to help decide.	(b)When Justine lost her name that's like losing yourself, so she cannot find her way back to her aunt and uncle's house.

have not been there for them. Sandra said now that their father might be released from prison and their mother was no longer there to protect them, their situation could become worse. Her conclusion enhanced the meaning making process because it identified how Sandra was specifically applying themes from Justine's story to her own situation. Sandra's conclusion made it unnecessary for Diana to ask the following coherence question: "What does Justine's parents' focus on themselves mean to you in your life?" (see Table 4.2, Question #1c).

Table 4.2
PRINCIPLE 4: THE MEANING MAKING PRINCIPLE
SKILL: THE USE OF NARRATIVE COHERENCE AND LINKING QUESTIONS

Tasks to Enhance Meaning of Single Event Narratives and Resolve Issues	Examples of Coherence and Linking Questions
1. Expand the Narrative: Begin the meaning making process	(a) From your perspective, what is one of the main ideas in this story, whether that idea was spoken or unspoken? (b) Where in the story specially did you notice or "hear" that idea? (c) What does that idea mean to you? (d) What do some of the other main ideas in the story mean to you?
2. Set Narrative Goals: Identify and sort priority changes	(a) If the situation in this story suddenly improved, that is a miracle occurred so you were no longer _____, what would be different about you (your behavior, feelings, or attitude)? (b) How much would you be changed in _____ on a scale from 1 (very little change) to 3 (moderate change) to 5 (major change)? (c) What about you would not change and why?
3. Access Narrative Resources: Identify or create sources of support (key actors)	(a) Who would be the first person in the story to notice you were different? (b) What would he or she say to you specifically (what would he or she notice)? (c) Who is that person similar to in your life now or in the past (if at all), and how are the two similar? (d) What is that person's role in the story (or in your life)? (e) Who else would notice you were different (in the story or outside of the story) and what would he or she say specifically?
4. Enhance Narrative Coping: Envision coping effectively and celebrate exceptions	(a) How could that person's feedback help you to cope with _____ more effectively *now*? (b) How could his or her feedback help you to prepare for coping with _____ *in the future*? (c) Have you noticed times when _____ was of less concern to you or when you managed to cope better with _____? (d) What was going on in your life during those times?
5. Seek Alternative Information and Skills: Locate family history bridges or links to life narrative construction	(a) If you could give this story a different ending what is your preferred ending? (b) Is there information you don't have currently that could help to achieve your preferred ending (knowledge about your family background or family history, developmental stages, relationships, important events, or the law). (c) Are there skills or abilities that you need in order for your preferred ending to occur (relationships, communication, problem solving, household management, education, employment, or coping skills)?

These coherence questions not only helped Sandra to expand the narrative's meaning (see Table 4.2, Task #1), but also to identify priority goals or changes and to access the narrative resources shown in Table 4.2 (see Tasks #2 and 3). For example, Diana helped the client to set a goal for identifying fears about her father's impending parole (see Table 4.2, Task #2), after discussing Sandra's themes of managing many life changes and not having power over her situation (see Table 4.1: Themes #4 and 6). Sandra said Justine did not know what to do in a new situation on a strange street, implying that like herself, Justine had difficulty managing change (see Table 4.1: Theme 4b). Sandra also pointed out Justine was not sure whether she should go inside or stay outside, consistent with "being a kid without any decision power" (see Table 4.1: Theme 6b). Discussing the role of mentors (see Table 4.1: Themes #2a and b) helped Sandra to identify narrative resources such as Justine's aunt and uncle who could help Justine to manage her struggles with change and parental pressures (see Table 4.2: Task #3).

Sandra was then able to apply the same lesson about resources to her own situation. For instance, when Diana asked about the role of the guide in Justine's narrative (the woman in the house) (see Table 4.2: Question 3d), Sandra said the guide accepted Justine like her own grandmother accepted her. When the guide welcomed Justine, Sandra believed it meant the guide could be trusted; therefore Justine allowed the woman to show her around the house (see Table 4.1: Themes #2c and d).

Several coherence questions in Table 4.2 and themes in Table 4.1 also apply to Sandra's situation and to those of other teenagers. For example, the practitioner could have asked, "How might talking with your grandmother help prepare you to cope with your father's prison release?" (see Table 4.2: Question #4b). Such questions encourage clients to envision how to cope more effectively by identifying and using their supports. Questions #4c and d in the same table, "Have you noticed times when you coped differently with fear or uncertainty?" and "What was going on in your life at those times?", can encourage teens to identify and celebrate narrative exceptions (see Table 4.2: Task #4).

CONTINUITY SKILLS–STAGE TWO: USING SINGLE NARRATIVE THEMES TO CONSTRUCT LIFE NARRATIVES. The previous analysis of themes and use of coherence questions between Diana and her client, Sandra, involved several sessions. That process created an opportunity for Sandra to begin constructing three segments of her life narrative. Hence their beginning work on single narratives led directly to the overlapping continuity stage of life narrative development. That stage includes helping adolescents to construct an "aerial view" of their lives (Gusdorf, 1980) by connecting themes from their single event narratives with their emerging whole life narratives. Practitioners such as Diana, the family service worker, can facilitate these connections through the skillful use of narrative continuity questions, shown in Table 4.3. Although examples of continuity questions are grouped according to the four life narrative clusters in Figure 4.1, in reality, many of those questions overlap across two or more clusters.

For instance, to help Sandra use their sessions for life narrative construction Diana asked, "What things are important to you based on what you included in your story about Justine?" This question is part of Cluster 1 in Table 4.3 as well as Cluster 3. The question is designed to help clients construct and simultaneously understand their life narratives by clarifying their core values or the areas that are most important to them (Cluster 1). The question also can help clients to reveal how experiences involving key actors or life events have shaped their values (Cluster 3). In response to this dual-cluster question, Sandra clarified the first segment of her emerging life narrative, along with some of the value-, event-, and key actor-related threads she was using to construct or weave the narrative:

> **Segment 1:** My grandmother calls me a blessed child. She says I have this goodness inside me and I know how to let the good things inside show on the outside. Her favorite saying is, 'It's what's inside that counts,' and I believe her because she's honest and kind. So I'm trying to be like her; she's my model. I help out with my little sisters because it makes it easier for my grandparents. Sometimes I resent helping out, but then I remember how hard it was for them when they took us in. Because they're so strong inside they've been more than good to us. That's how they let their inside-goodness show on the outside. Just like Justine's aunt and uncle are good inside. Remember the story—how she trusted them, how making her feel welcome was important to Justine? Just like my grandparents! Everybody can't be that way, but that's how I want to live *my life* and that's who *I'm* trying to be."

As a result of listening to Sandra construct and share this first segment of her life narrative, Diana concluded that her client's life narra-

Table 4.3
PRINCIPLE 4: THE MEANING MAKING PRINCIPLE
SKILL: THE USE OF NARRATIVE CONTINUITY QUESTIONS TO CONSTRUCT LIFE NARRATIVES

The Four Life Narrative Clusters	*Examples of Continuity Questions Related to Sandra's Life Narrative and Those of Other Teens*
Cluster 1: The Core Narrated Self	(1) How do you describe yourself as a person? How would you describe yourself in relation to your family? (2) What kind of person are you based on this story? What things are important to you based on this story? (3) How would/does _____ describe you as a person? What is that description based on? (4) What kind of person do you want to be in the future based on this story? Based on other factors? (5) Since _____ happened, how has that event affected the kind of person you are (or want to be)?
Cluster 2: Narrated and Unnarrated Life Predictions and Expectations	(1) Based on this story, how has your outlook on life changed or not changed? (2) How do you think _____ might affect your outlook on life in the future in terms of roles, etc? (3) What other things might affect your outlook on life in the future? In what ways might those things affect your outlook? What leads you to believe those things could affect your future outlook? (4) Based on this story, what do you think you will be doing when you are _____ years of age? What will your outlook on life be at that time? What things will be important to you then compared to now?
Cluster 3: Significant Narrated and Unnarrated Life Events and Actors	(1) Based on this story, how do you describe your family and what is your description based on? (2) How would you have described the family previously and what is that description based on? (3) Who is the most important person(s) in your life today based on this story, and for what reason? (4) Who is the most important person(s) in your life today based on other factors, and for what reason? (5) Who has been most important person to you in the past, and for what reason? (6) What past or current events, experiences, or people have affected who you are today and how?
Cluster 4: Narrated Opportunities for Meaning Making and Growth	(1) Based on the preferred title or ending you gave to your story, what things are most important to you as a person? For what reason are those things important to you now?

Continued on next page

Table 4.3 *(continued)*

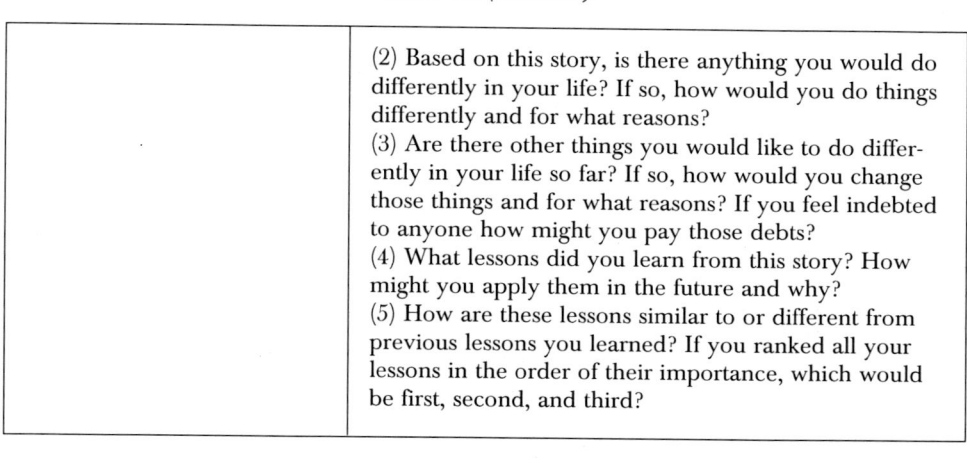

	(2) Based on this story, is there anything you would do differently in your life? If so, how would you do things differently and for what reasons? (3) Are there other things you would like to do differently in your life so far? If so, how would you change those things and for what reasons? If you feel indebted to anyone how might you pay those debts? (4) What lessons did you learn from this story? How might you apply them in the future and why? (5) How are these lessons similar to or different from previous lessons you learned? If you ranked all your lessons in the order of their importance, which would be first, second, and third?

tive was evolving overtime and that it was a work in progress. Moreover, the above segment of Sandra's life narrative revealed answers to other continuity questions from Table 4.3 that Diana had not asked yet. For example, Sandra's life narrative revealed answers to the following questions, which Diana then asked her to elaborate on:

1. What kind of person are you based on this story? (Table 4.3, Cluster 1: Question 2),
2. How does _____ (Sandra's grandmother in this situation) describe you as a person? (Cluster 1: Question 3),
3. What kind of person do you want to be in the future based on this story? (Cluster 1: Question 4),
4. Who is the most important person in your life today? What is the reason _____ is most important from your perspective? (Cluster 3: Question 3),
5. What past and current events or experiences have affected who you are today? How have those factors affected you? (Cluster 3: Question 6), and
6. What lessons did you learn from this story? (Cluster 4: Question 4).

This example indicates that some adolescents such as Sandra are able to construct parts of their life narratives spontaneously during the process of analyzing their single event narratives. However, other clients may need specific prompts to begin the construction of their narratives. In those instances, practitioners can begin the construction process by asking some of the continuity questions in Table 4.3. Regardless of whether the construction process is spontaneous or requires external prompting, practitioners should use follow-up continuity questions to help adolescents to elaborate on their life narratives (Freeman & Couchonnal, 2006). For example, regarding item #4 above (Cluster 3: Question 3), one of Diana's follow-up questions was:

> "I notice you talked about your Grandmother's influence on you. How important has she been in your life? And for what reason is she important to you?"

This example of a follow-up question helps practitioners like Diana to explore identified life narrative threads and ensures that clients have an opportunity to reflect on and understand the significance of those threads. Such questions not only facilitate clients in the construction process (M. Freeman, 2006), but they also provide opportunities for them to move their life narratives from the silent voice in their minds to words that are spoken in the presence of supportive listeners.

In subsequent sessions with Sandra, Diana used other examples of continuity questions that overlapped two or more life narrative clusters. Diana remembered from their shared story-telling session that Sandra said Justine was not comfortable in the strange house because she was in a new situation with many new people (see Table 4.1: The Managing Change Theme #4c). Consequently in a later session Diana summarized concerns and themes Sandra had identified previously and then asked a related follow-up continuity question:

> I remember how much you tuned into Justine's story, especially when you said she was in a new situation in a strange house and didn't know what to do or say. You've had several changes in *your* life too, such as when your father shot your mother, she left home, and he was sent to prison. Now that your father might be released from prison, you've said it'll be another strange situation for you and your sisters. I wonder if any of those changes have affected who you are today or how they might affect you in the future.

Diana's questions addressed the effects of past family life changes on Sandra currently (see Table 4.3: Cluster 1: Question #5), and on her future outlook on life (Cluster 2: Question #2). In response to these cross cluster questions Sandra developed a second segment of her life narrative. This segment illustrates how Sandra was continuing to construct her life narrative while, simultaneously, allowing the narrative to evolve.

> **Segment #2:** At first, I felt like I did something wrong, like I should've been able to keep our family from being pulled apart. Like me and my sisters had some kind of cloud over us that everybody could see, that told them we weren't wanted by our parents. Like none of those things you mentioned would've have happened if somebody loved us, like they were supposed to. So for a long time, everything was dark and lonely—I admit now I was scared; but couldn't admit anything back then. I think I knew it wasn't ever going to change. I'm still scared, but now I think the cloud is there because everybody knows our parents are gone; they know what our parents did. So the cloud isn't as dark now, our grandparents love us so we must not be *too* bad. If we can get through my father coming back—if the court lets us stay with our grandparents—I guess my outlook on life might get better. I won't be a lost girl anymore like Justine.

This segment of Sandra's life narrative reveals how she blamed herself for her family's disruption previously, and that she is currently working through her fears and self-esteem/self-image issues. Hence, the segment shows how Sandra and her life narrative are evolving and growing. The narrative also reveals gaps in Sandra's knowledge about her family history and important life events that could impede further development of her life narrative.

For example, Sandra wondered if her grandparents could withstand potential pressures by her father to give up custody. In terms of family history, she did not know what type of relationship existed between her father and grandparents prior to his attempt to murder her mother. She did not know how her mother functioned as a parent before she was shot or how being shot in the head affected her personality and stability. Finally, Sandra could not remember events that showed what her parents' relationship with each other was like before her father shot her mother, what their family life was like prior to the violence, and when the violence began.

Diana helped Sandra to gather information about these gaps in her family history and life events. They analyzed the effects of those gaps on various aspects of Sandra's life narrative and on how she was coping with current issues in her situation. For example, talking with her grandparents helped Sandra to identify her fears about the possibility of living with her father's violence and reassured her that they *would* fight to retain custody of Sandra and her siblings. Talking with an attorney about the possibility of her father gaining custody revealed court policies that would likely involve asking Sandra, as a 14 year old, whom she preferred to live with. In addition, her father's history of violence and his imprisonment for trying to kill their mother made it unlikely he could get custody. This knowledge-gathering process allowed Sandra to continue her life narrative construction focused on newly identified sources of power:

> **Segment #3:** If I have to I can speak up and say up front I want to live with my grandparents and that means the court will have to listen to what I want. That makes me a stronger person now, because the court will hear my voice. I think my mother was stronger before she was shot in the head—my grandmother said she was a good mother before all this happened. And the doctor you (the practitioner) and I met with told us the gun shot destroyed an important part of her brain—the part that helped her to concentrate and be responsible. Now I know it's not her fault she can't be the mother she was before. It helps to remember the good family times we had before, the times my grandmother talks about now with us. My mother loved us—I think she still loves us from what my grandmother says. So I'm—I think me and my sisters can be the ok sisters now.

This third segment of Sandra's life narrative addressed all four life narrative clusters in Figure 4.1 and Table 4.3 related to knowledge gaps in her family history and other areas. For instance, the segment addressed Sandra's past, current, and future expectations regarding her mother's role (see Table 4.3: Cluster 2: Question #2). The segment highlighted Sandra's new understanding of the effects of significant life events on her mothers' role, such as the brain injury, and on Sandra's self-image (Cluster 3: Question #6). The role of key actors was clarified, such as her grandmother and the doctor, regarding their provision of crucial family history and medical information (Cluster 3: Question #6). Moreover, Sandra's life narrative clarified that she now has a voice in court and in her ongoing life, which according to McCarthy & Weber (2005) is evidence of an individual's survival narrative. Segment #3 also illustrates the process the client experienced in establishing her core identity as a strong teen within the context of her family's history, strengths, and challenges (Cluster 1: Question #1).

Consistent with her evolving identity Sandra entitled Segment #3 of her life narrative "The OK Sisters," referring to them for the first time as a valued sibling unit. This preferred title (Cluster 4, Question #1) contrasts with the lone "Lost Girl" title she used at the end of Segment #2. Sandra used the latter title prior to identifying her lessons from engaging in legal, medical, and family history information gathering with Diana's support. This example illustrates how life narrative practice with adolescents in circumstances similar to Sandra's can be enhanced when their knowledge gaps about family history and significant life events are addressed.

Practice Skills: Using Life Narrative Continuity Questions with Older Adults

Practice Overview

The transition of Sandra and other youngsters into adolescence provides challenging opportunities for them to initiate the construction of their life narratives and to mature in significant areas. This critical process sets the stage for their future life narrative work over the life course. Old age is simply a continuation of this lifelong process in that seniors are expected to manage "growing older and being older . . . ," and to learn ". . . the meaning of important events and experiences in their lives" (Dorfman, Murty, Evans, Ingram, & Power, 2004, p. 188). Hence, this developmental phase creates a demand for seniors to revisit and rewrite their life narratives in order to accomplish those goals.

Some writers associate this revisiting process with other terms such as reminiscence, recall, life withdrawal, life review, oral history, oral biography, regressing into the past, life-story writing, and personal narrative (Dorfman et al., 2004, Shenk, 2002). While those terms represent practical methods for facilitating life narrative work, they can imply that such work is linear and time limited and that it occurs mostly during old age. Peck (2001) emphasizes, however, that looking back or life narrative work is part of an integrated process which is essential for continuous well-being and self-identify *throughout* life.

Practice Example

THE PRACTICE SETTING: A drop in medication management (MM) group was formed in a primary care health clinic in a large metropolitan area. The primary care clinic was colocated with a mental health satellite clinic, a child welfare satellite office, a homeless program, and an older adult meal and recreation site. The MM group focused on medication compliance initially based on patient needs identified by the main referral sources for the group: the primary care renal, hypertension, diabetes, and general medicine clinics, and the homeless program. The group facilitators included a social worker, his graduate school social work intern, and an internal medicine resident. As the group evolved, the focus shifted to include the members' life narrative work, which was often precipitated by their many losses and health-related identity and value issues. Concerns about past and current events as well as key actors were also part of the members' life narrative work (see Figure 4.1). Although the drop-in group was the primary venue for this work, members were encouraged to and often requested individual sessions as needed. An example of how life narrative work was initiated in this open-ended group and then evolved into several couple sessions is discussed in the next section.

THE CLIENT'S BACKGROUND INFORMATION: Carlos Riviera, in this chapter's introduction, had been diagnosed recently with kidney failure and was referred for a predialysis and family medical history assessment. He was a married truck driver with close family ties that included his four adult children who lived in the same town. He and his wife were raising one of their grandchildren. He was referred to the MM clinic because he postponed his dialysis assessment and seemed confused about taking his medication as prescribed. Mr. Riviera had applied for social security disability benefits based on the recommendation of his renal clinic doctor and the MM group facilitators.

In addition to problems with his medication, Mr. Riviera described himself as "No longer the head of household and breadwinner in my family." He stated he was ashamed and felt bad about his situation. He had regrets about his wife returning to work, their children helping with their bills, and his past addiction that led to his current health problems. Most importantly, he believed his faith was being tested because he promised his deceased son and God he would raise his grandson, and thought he might not be able to continue raising him now (see Table 4.3: Clusters 1 and 2). In a recent MM group session, in response to the facilitators' questions about whether he and other members were following their medication goals, Mr. Riviera made the following comment:

> "I can't worry about whether I'm taking my medicine now. I feel like I'm dying here and it has nothing to do with my kidneys. My wife is the only one who understands that."

USING CONTINUITY QUESTIONS AND A COLLABORATIVE ANALYSIS: After the above group session ended, the social worker and internal medicine resident asked if Mr. Riviera would meet with them in an individual session. They explained the purpose was to address some of the family concerns he brought up in group that needed individual attention, and that they wanted to include his wife because she was his primary support system. Although they did not tell Mr. Riviera at the time, they believed he might be depressed and wanted to assess whether he was also suicidal.

When the couple's session began, the facilitators thanked them for coming to the session and then reiterated that they wanted to talk about the previous group session. Specifically, the social worker summarized what happened in the group and then asked the following questions (see Table 4.3, Cluster 2: Question #1):

> "Mr. Riviera, you mentioned in the MM group last week that it's hard to focus on your health and medication because other things are getting in the way. I got the idea you're disappointed about your life. Can you talk about where you think you are today in your life, and how those thoughts are affecting your outlook on life now?"

In response, Mr. Riviera shared the following life narrative segment, which was part of his ongoing life narrative:

Life Narrative Segment #1: You're asking me what I expected out of my life and if I'm disappointed? I expected to own my truck by the time I was 50–and I'm 57 now. I figured I'd buy a second truck after that and hire another driver to work for me. I thought I'd work another 15 or 20 years after paying for my first truck. I'd be a business owner. My father started working as a helper for a stall owner at the farmers' market when he was 13. He left Columbia because their family was poor, and each year he helped other family members get to the U.S. I was the first family member who joined him in this country. By the time he was 25, my father owned a stall and had five helpers, and when he was 40 he owned five stalls. He hired family members to work for him and helped a lot of other Hispanic families in our church and community. He was the head of his house and everybody—family and neighbors—looked up to him. When he got cancer, he prayed his way out of it; his faith was strong, it saved him. Me? I'm not where I should be now. I'm not the man I was before I got kidney problems, or the man I thought I was. I had to stop driving my truck and ended up losing it. I couldn't pay the note. My wife had to get a job so we could keep our house and feed the family. Don't think I don't appreciate that you're working honey (Ms Riviera), but this isn't the way its' supposed to be. I promised my oldest son Manuel when he died three years ago I'd raise his son—I mean we'd raise him. But now my daughter and her husband want me to let them raise my grandson to help out. I know they're worried about what'll happen if I get too sick to keep my promise. I had a drinking–problem for 20 years until I sobered up about ten years ago and started going to AA. I learned to stop drinking- one day at a time. I learned I had the strength to do it with my faith and AA; and with family support. But I had to face something else; that I wasted years of my life drinking—years and years! Then the doctor told me alcohol, diabetes, and high blood pressure caused my kidney problems. If only I'd quit earlier. Honey (Ms Riviera), you keep asking me what my father would do in this situation. She's trying to help me Doc, but I don't know what my father would do. I've got to live my own life! *But* I know I'm not the man he was!

The social worker, Shane Boyd, complimented Mr. Riviera on how clearly he was able to talk about his life. As a follow-up question, he asked the couple what kind of person Mr. Riviera was based on this story about his life. Dr. Alvarez, the internal medicine resident, suggested the couple also talk about what kinds of things were important to him based on this story about his situation. Both of these questions were important as follow-up continuity questions based on the client's preceding life narrative segment (see Table 4.3, Cluster 1: Questions #2). The couple agreed he was a person who decided where he wanted to go in his life and how to get there. He was a hard worker and what was most important to him was taking care of his family and keeping his promises. Ms. Riviera added to those conclusions by saying, "In other words, he's responsible!"

Dr. Alvarez, one of the cofacilitators, asked Ms. Riviera to explain a question she raised previously: What would her husband's deceased father do in the same situation, especially about taking his medication and other requirements? Ms. Riviera said her husband was too hard on himself and he assumed his father would be hard on him too. Mr. Riviera admitted he did wonder what his father would think about his situation and that sometimes he felt down for that reason. Shane said he noticed Mr. Riviera seemed down or depressed a lot lately and wondered what made him feel that way. The client said his father was the most important influence in his life because they had struggled alone together when they first came to this country, and his father always told him he could "climb the ladder just like everybody else."

In this example, Mr. Riviera spontaneously identified the most important person in his life and the reason for his importance (see Table 4.3, Cluster 3: Question #3). He also made a connection between how his father affected his life positively in the past, and how the client's assumptions about his father's view of his current situation affected his current depression (see Table 4.3, Cluster 2: Question #2, and Cluster 3: Question #6). His life narrative segment also includes information about the client's regrets (Cluster 4: Question #3), and about some of his lessons regarding his addiction and factors that helped him to maintain his long-term recovery (Cluster 4: Question #4).

FACILITATING LIFE NARRATIVE ANALYSIS AND REWRITING: The group facilitators asked follow-up questions to help the couple elaborate on the above life narrative issues. Based on their discussion, Mr. Riviera concluded he was no longer certain about how his father would view his situation. His new doubts provided an opportunity for him to begin reauthoring his life or giving himself a second chance (Pals, 2006). The facilitators suggested the client meet with the person he said was closest to his father, a paternal uncle, to learn more about his father. The client identified questions he wanted to ask, including his father's outlook on life, what influenced his life the most, and what he thought about his son as a person.

In later sessions, Mr. Riviera rewrote his life narrative regarding his lessons, self-identity, regrets, and current and future outlook on life, based on meeting with his uncle:

Life Narrative Segment #2: I learned something from meeting with my uncle. He told me about times my father was proud of me—

some I remembered and some I didn't. When I finally stopped—I mean when I started my recovery, he told some of the neighbors I stopped drinking. I mean he was a proud man, usually he kept his business to himself, so that surprised me! Maybe I recovered when I could and should stop beating up on myself. If my father forgave me, I can forgive myself. Uncle Reuben reminded me how hard it was when my Dad got cancer. He struggled with his faith—it wasn't no miraculous recovery like I thought. It was hard on him; the only thing is he had more faith when his cancer went away. But I was still drinking then and didn't know up from down. My uncle says Pop would understand what I'm going through with the medicine and dialysis; he'd be the last one to be hard on me. What an eye-opener! He was more real than I thought; I guess I worshiped him but didn't know him. Now I'm easier on myself. And I won't be so hard on myself in the future; I promise myself I won't.

Discussion

This chapter has clarified the definition, underlying principle, components, and practice strategies related to life narratives, as well as skills for facilitating the construction, review, and revision process with adolescents and seniors. Those skills include the use of coherence and continuity questions and a collaborative analysis process. With adolescents, the importance of age-related knowledge gaps regarding family history and key life events cannot be overemphasized. Without such information, youngsters such as the teenager in one case example experience significant barriers to constructing their life narratives and allowing those narratives to evolve over time. To begin where the client is in this instance means using adolescents' single event narratives to begin the construction process. Another path is to respond to clients' spontaneous efforts to construct their life narratives without prompting.

For seniors who are managing a range of developmental and biographical changes, depression and the potential for suicide should be assessed and addressed as needed. The MM group and couple sessions with Mr. Riviera and his wife helped the facilitators to identify factors contributing to his depression and lack of medication compliance. The invitation to share his life narrative segment, the facilitators' follow-up continuity questions with the couple, and the client's meetings with a key informant uncle helped him to address his self-doubts and relieve his depression. Most importantly, the facilitators were able to initially assess his potential for suicide and to decide a psychiatric referral was not required. Instead, they encouraged the client to appropriately utilize life narrative supports within his family, and based on those meetings, to rewrite his narrative accordingly.

References

Bamberg, M. (2006). Biographic-narrative research, *quo vadis?* A critical review of "big stories" from the perspective of "small stories." In K. Milnes, C. Horrocks, & D. Robinson (Eds.), *Narrative, memory and knowledge: Representations, aesthetics and contexts* (pp. 63–79). Huddersfield, UK: University of Huddersfield Press.

Bamberg, M. (2004). Talk, small stories, and adolescent identities. *Human Development, 47*, 360–366.

Dorfman, L. T., Murty, S. A., Evans, J. J., Ingram, J. G., & Power, J. R. (2004). History and identity in the narratives of rural elders. *Journal of Aging Studies, 18*, 187–203.

Freeman, E. M. (March 4, 2004). Basic principles of effective narrative practice. Workshop PowerPoint presentation. Kansas City, MO: Sponsored by the Social Work Coalition for Social Workers in Health Care.

Freeman, E. M., & Couchonnal, G. (2006). Narrative and culturally based approaches to practice with families. *Families in Society, 87*, 198–208.

Freeman, M. (2006). Life "on holiday"? In defense of big stories. *Narrative Inquiry, 16*, 131–138.

Gusdorf, C. (1980). Conditions and limits of autobiography. In J. Olney (Ed.), *Autobiography: Essays theoretical and critical* (pp. 28–48). Princeton, NJ: Princeton University Press.

Habermas, T., & Paha, C. (2001). The development of coherence in adolescents' life narratives. *Narrative Inquiry, 11*(1), 35–54.

Luborsky, M.R. (1993). The romance with personal meaning in gerontology: Cultural aspects of life themes. *The Gerontologist, 33*(4), 445–454.

McAdams, D. P. (2006). The problem of narrative coherence. *Journal of Constructivist Psychology, 19*, 109-125.

McAdams, D. P. (2001). The psychology of life stories. *Review of General Psychology, 5*, 100–122.

McCarthy, M., & Weber, Z (2005). When bodies need voices: Sharing stories of survival. *Affilia, 20*, 368–372.

Pals, J. L. (2006). Authoring a second chance in life: Emotion and transformational processing in narrative identity. *Research into Human Development, 3*, 101–120.

Peck, M. D. (2001). Looking back at life and its influence on subjective well-being. *Journal of Gerontological Social Work, 35*, 3–17.

Shenk, D. (2002). Narratives and self-identity in later life: Two rural American older women. *Journal of Aging Studies, 16*, 401–413.

Thomson, R., Bell, R., Holland, J., Henderson, S., McGrellis, S., & Sharpe, S. (2002). Critical moments: Choice, chance, and opportunity in young people's narratives of transition. *Sociology, 36*(2), 335–354.

Woike, B., & Polo, M. (2001). Motive-related memories: Content, structure, and affect. *Journal of Personality, 69*(3), 391–415.

Wortham, S. (2000). Interactional positioning and narrative self-construction. *Narrative Inquiry, 10*(1), 157–184.

Chapter 5

HELPING MARGINALIZED CLIENTS TO SHARE AND ADVOCATE FOR THEIR NARRATED AND UNNARRATED EXPERIENCES: THE SOCIAL JUSTICE-SYSTEMS CHANGE INTERVENTION PRINCIPLE

> It is unwise to test the depth
> of a river with both feet.
> —African Proverb

This chapter discusses Principle 5, which turns the spotlight on groups that society marginalizes, in part by stigmatizing their experiences and narratives. The discussion clarifies specialized roles that key actors can assume while eliciting those narratives and helping to raise clients' awareness about some of the narratives' hidden aspects. For example, key actors can use these two micro-level interventions to assist clients in understanding their common challenges and uplifting experiences.

Key actors include practitioners, agency administrators, family and community members, and policy analysts. In addition to the previous micro-interventions, these supporters can also use mezzo- and macro-level interventions (Freeman, 2004; Kitchell, Hannan, & Kempton, 2000). Examples include educating other people about society's practice of labeling clients' marginalized narratives as low currency, and advocating against this practice. Barton (2000) states education and advocacy are effective strategies for disrupting society's pattern of ignoring or deflecting such nonsanctioned narratives, while inviting and welcoming privileged or sanctioned narratives.

Principle 5 is used to illustrate how this societal deflection versus invitational process occurs and its impact upon narrative practice with clients from marginalized *and* privileged groups. The discussion includes the main elements of Principle 5 and outlines how this principle is relevant to narrative practice at micro-, mezzo-, and macro-systems levels. Three types of narrative skills are introduced and illustrated with practice examples from the situations of clients and practitioners. Those skills consist of marginalization analysis (externalization and deconstruction), advocacy by storytelling, and systems-related power transfers. The discussion demonstrates how helpers can use these skills effectively, including using them to address underlying social justice issues.

Overview of the Social Justice-Systems Change Intervention Principle

The Main Elements of Principle 5

Figure 5.1 illustrates the roles three different discourses can play in silencing and making invisible the lives and narratives of groups that exist in the margins of dominant society. Those discourses or voices often reinforce the beliefs and values of dominant society in terms of a prescribed social, cultural, political, and economic hierarchy. They also support the asymmetrical power relationships that such hierarchies establish between the members of privileged versus marginalized groups.

Individual and family discourses include the narratives of individuals, families, and primary groups. Organizational and community discourses consist of narratives that are about and authored by organizations, neighborhoods, and larger communities. Cultural group narratives are often woven into family, organizational, and community discourses that are most relevant to a particular culture. For example, African American and Latino people often infuse their political action discourses, such as those of the National Association of Colored People and La Raza, with narratives from their respective ethnic cultures. In contrast, the discourses of dominant society consist of sanctioned narratives that portray the dominant culture, values, and life experiences as the norm against which all other narratives are evaluated and found wanting.

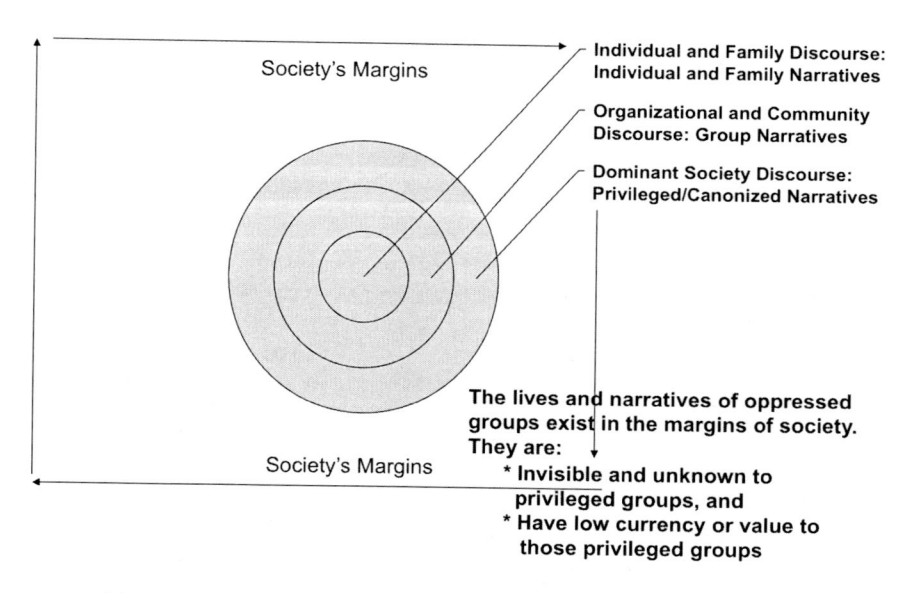

Helping Marginalized Clients Share and Advocate for Their Experiences 99

Figure 5.1. The Marginalization of People and Their Narratives.

Society's Margins

Individual and Family Discourse: Individual and Family Narratives
Organizational and Community Discourse: Group Narratives
Dominant Society Discourse: Privileged/Canonized Narratives

The lives and narratives of oppressed groups exist in the margins of society. They are:
* Invisible and unknown to privileged groups, and
* Have low currency or value to those privileged groups

In whatever ways voices from the three discourses shown in Figure 5.1 may differ, they often work together by (Boje, 2007; Freeman, 2004; Smith & Keyton, 2001):

1. Agreeing in general that the following groups should and do have a lower status and value than society's privileged groups: People of color; religious minorities; senior citizens; women; people with disabilities; poor people; and those who are sexually different (individuals who have a lesbian, gay, bi-sexual, or transgendered sexual orientation: LGBT).
2. Supporting dominant society's negative views of the groups listed in #1 above and their narratives by screening in only information from the margins that is consistent with those views, and by using discrimination and stigma to prevent changes in the overall statuses of those groups.
3. Infusing dominant society's narrative facts with emotionally and symbolically-charged meanings that capture and reflect the cultures and values of privileged individuals, families, organizations, communities, and large systems.
4. Sanctioning mainstream preferred narratives, such as bootstrap stories, that eventually become canonized or integrated without

question into the dominant society's belief systems at the highest levels.
5. Reinforcing individual acts of oppression toward the members of marginalized groups that support, but are not required, for institutionalized oppression to maintain itself or to flourish.

The Significance of Principle 5 to Narrative Practice

Clients who seek help from social agencies and other institutions are often confronted with social justice issues related to their home environments, communities, organizational or large systems' policies, and social policies. Such issues may surface whether clients are seeking help with tangible resources; or require individual, family, or group counseling; psychiatric rehabilitation; case management; medication management; family therapy; or addiction treatment. Social justice issues may be reflected in the specific reasons clients seek help or in how they respond to an agency's outreach efforts.

For instance, clients may be denied medical care by clinics and hospitals because they are poor and therefore un- or underinsured. Or they may have difficulties locating and gaining access to affordable housing because they are undocumented workers or sexually different. In addition to needing help from practitioners with the social justice barriers they encounter in other organizations and systems, clients may need help in addressing similar barriers within the practitioner's own setting, such as oppressive organizational policies in those settings (Colton, 2002; Stuart, 1999).

These examples of marginalized clients and narratives about their experiences are relevant to narrative practice for two reasons. First, marginalization decreases the quality of life for stigmatized groups and limits the types and quantity of options that are available to them. Second, marginalization serves a political control function for large systems and institutions. It allows those systems to deny the inequities that exist between marginalized and privileged groups, or to justify those inequities by spinning "boot strap" narratives to explain how privileged groups, compared to others, achieve success solely through their individual efforts (Colton, 2002).

Practitioners and other key actors can assist clients and family members by increasing their knowledge about this political control function of systems. Moreover, increasing their understanding of the low currency labels society places on their narrated and unnarrated experiences is equally important. This consciousness-raising process includes educating clients about how to use the skill of marginalization analysis, or deconstruction and externalization. These related skills help clients to clarify how some of the common roots of their narrated or unnarrated challenges are embedded in the structure and function of society's systems (Dessel, Rogge, & Garlington, 2006; Linhorst, 2002; Stuart, 1999). Freeman (2004) contends that marginalization and hidden social justice issues not only apply to clients' situations but also to those of service providers, another aspect of this narrative skill-building process.

Practice Skills: Marginalization Analysis or Externalization and Deconstruction with Helping Professionals

Practice Overview

Providers who acknowledge and address systems issues that affect their organizational lives in social agencies and other institutions are often more effective in helping clients to use similar skills in their environments. As a consequence, those providers learn how to elicit clients' previously narrated experiences related to their current and past challenges (Freeman & Couchonnal, 2006). Similarly, they understand clients often have painful unnarrated experiences that may be equally relevant to their current challenges. In such situations, clients' narrated or unnarrated experiences may be linked to punitive organizational or social policies, and macro-level systems change strategies may be required for addressing such issues.

However, the systems change process must be well planned, strategic, and incremental as noted in this chapter's epigraph. To test the depth of a river with both feet is akin to: (1) broadcasting a detailed plan to seize power within a system; (2) by deploying all human and other resources immediately; (3) without developing a counterplan "B" for when and how the system retaliates. Pilot test strategies, or testing a river's depth with one foot, are especially important in such situations. The nature of all systems is to resist and retaliate against change efforts in order to maintain themselves, without personalizing their survival-related responses (Freeman, 2008), as the following practice example illustrates.

Practice Example: Sanctioned Organizational Events and Narratives

BACKGROUND INFORMATION. A consultant was hired to complete an organizational assessment at a mental health center because the director believed the center was at a crossroad in terms of its mission and the effects of a depressed national and local economy on that mission. The assessment included interviews with the center's administrators, staff, and clients for which the consultant designed separate but similar interview guides. He reminded each individual that what they shared would be handled confidentially and recorded in a way that protected their anonymity.

A SANCTIONED AND PRIVILEGED ORGANIZATIONAL NARRATIVE. During an interview with Meera, a 42-year-old, Asian Indian social worker, the consultant asked her to provide background information about the center. He also encouraged her to include how she became employed there. His questions resulted in the following organizational narrative from Meera (Figure 5.1):

> **Meera's Sanctioned Narrative.** Well, I've worked for this mental health center for seven years. I know I was hired because of my skills in child and adolescent development and policy practice. At that time the mental health center had 11 other staff of color among its 135 employees who worked in our main office, three satellite offices, and two community-based programs. The staff of color included six African Americans, three Latinos, one Native American, and one Japanese American, I believe. Our center director is a nationally known innovator who was hired for that reason about five months before I joined the staff. He's made the center a national model for community-based programs for adults with serious mental illness and children with serious emotional disorders. And he's developed a diversified and leveraged funding base which has increased the center's survival, and put us out front of many centers that are at risk. I believe I was hired because my skills were consistent with the director's far-reaching vision at the time. His commitment to a culturally diverse staff and clients attracted me to the center, including Eastern European, African, Latino, and Muslim immigrants, along with our African American and native-born Latino clients. He's considered a giant among center directors here and nationally.

Practice Analysis

TRIAL RUN #1: CULTURAL ANALYSIS OF THE ORGANIZATION. Meera's telling of the above sanctioned narrative was her first trial run or attempt to examine her practice setting as a system in the presence of an outsider. In essence, she used this opportunity to narrate events that brought her to the center which she had not understood fully in the past, related to the organization's culture. Similarly, the consultant's goal was to elicit the type of sanctioned narrative that Meera shared to increase his understanding of the center's organizational culture. It was clear to him as he interviewed additional staff, administrators, and clients that the director had an almost mythical reputation within the organization, which contributed to a level of personal power beyond that usually afforded to most directors. Such asymmetrical power relationships within organizations support sanctioned and privileged narratives like the one shared by Meera, and similar ones as told by others in the center.

The consultant recognized Meera's sanctioned narrative also contained a hidden correlation between the director's past commitment to diversity and the presence of a critical mass of staff of color in the center. This critical mass may have kept the director's commitment in the forefront rather than in the background. Two factors may have weakened that correlation over time, a depressed economy leading to fewer staff overall and decreases in the numbers of staff of color in particular.

The consultant assumed the center's loss of staff of color was considered a low currency nonsanctioned event that was located in the margins of its organizational life (Figure 5.1). Consequently, the event might have been ignored and unnarrated by the center's power hierarchy. The consultant also assumed any attempt by insiders to narrate this and related events would be perceived as disruptive and disloyal by the system. In contrast, the rest of Meera's sanctioned narrative appeared to be situated within the mainstream of the center's organizational life, because it reinforced its world view and culture. Numerous interviews during the organizational assessment documented the story's renarration by many insiders and outsiders over the years.

Practice Example: Nonsanctioned Organizational Events and Narratives

BACKGROUND INFORMATION. The consultant's organizational assessment goals included gathering information about nonsanctioned events and experiences as well as sanctioned events. When he asked

Meera to "tell me a story that explains what its like for you to work in this mental health center today," she shared the following previously unnarrated organizational experiences related to social justice issues. Figure 5.1 shows her response was a group narrative situated in the margins of the organization's and dominant society's culture. Unlike her previous narrative, this experience and narrative were probably invisible to the organization's power hierarchy as well as unvalued.

Meera's Nonsanctioned Narrative: Let me say first that when I came here, I felt this was a rich learning environment in which I could do good social work and grow, where my work would be appreciated, respected that is. It seemed so promising. I saw staff of color as part of this multicultural climate, not as I do now, as a cultural support group. I worked closely with one African American psychologist in particular, Gloria Townsend, on the center's two community-based projects. Other staff accepted the fact that these new projects required a re-allocation of some of our resources, because of the director's vision and commitment to serving diverse families. There was a climate of cultural respect. I was primarily responsible for the youth project, while Gloria was the PI for the school-based leadership development and mentoring program. She was often outspoken in challenging some center staff about culturally insensitive statements, *and* the center itself about conflicts between its multicultural mission and practices. She did it in a patient manner, but it was easy to see that some staff resented her and responded defensively. Even so, in looking back, I can see it was a euphoric period. Then I noticed as staff of color left for various reasons, they weren't replaced. I mean the people hired for their positions were white. Staff interactions changed. No more respectful comments about the community projects and their clients, instead, more remarks about the drain they created on the center's resources. It was confusing, nothing on paper had changed, but I could sense the climate was no longer as supportive. It made me anxious and less confident in responding to some staff's innuendos about inner city families. Then Gloria left. Her leaving created a void I hadn't anticipated. What had gradually become a prickly environment suddenly became an openly hostile one to me. Now its hard to get the floor in meetings, and when I do, my comments are mostly ignored. Sometimes, after ignoring my comment, another staff member will warmly support a similar comment from a white colleague. I'd been hired as an international staff member, and I saw myself that way at first, but now I'm being treated as a minority by my colleagues. I now receive the hostile comments that were formerly reserved for Gloria, the agency scapegoat, since she's no longer a buffer for me and other staff of color. It hurts because I'd never understood fully the role she played, never even acknowledged it or validated her for that matter.

Practice Analysis

TRIAL RUN #2: MARGINALIZATION ANALYSIS: EXTERNALIZATION AND DECONSTRUCTION SKILLS. Sharing the above nonsanctioned narrative presented a second trial run or opportunity for Meera to address organizational concerns related to her practice system. The consultant asked about outcomes from the previously unnarrated events she described in the story, as part of his organizational assessment process. Meera identified her isolation as one of the outcomes she had noticed from changes within the center. As she said in her narrative, "It was hard to get the floor in meetings . . . I was now getting the hostile comments formerly reserved for Gloria. . . ."

Figure 5.2 indicates that helping individuals such as Meera to share previously unnarrated events presents opportunities for addressing underlying social justice issues. The narration process allows them to have a voice, interpret, and reauthor those events by externalizing and deconstructing the narrated situation. Externalization and deconstruction are tools for facilitating clients and providers in analyzing their marginalization experiences.

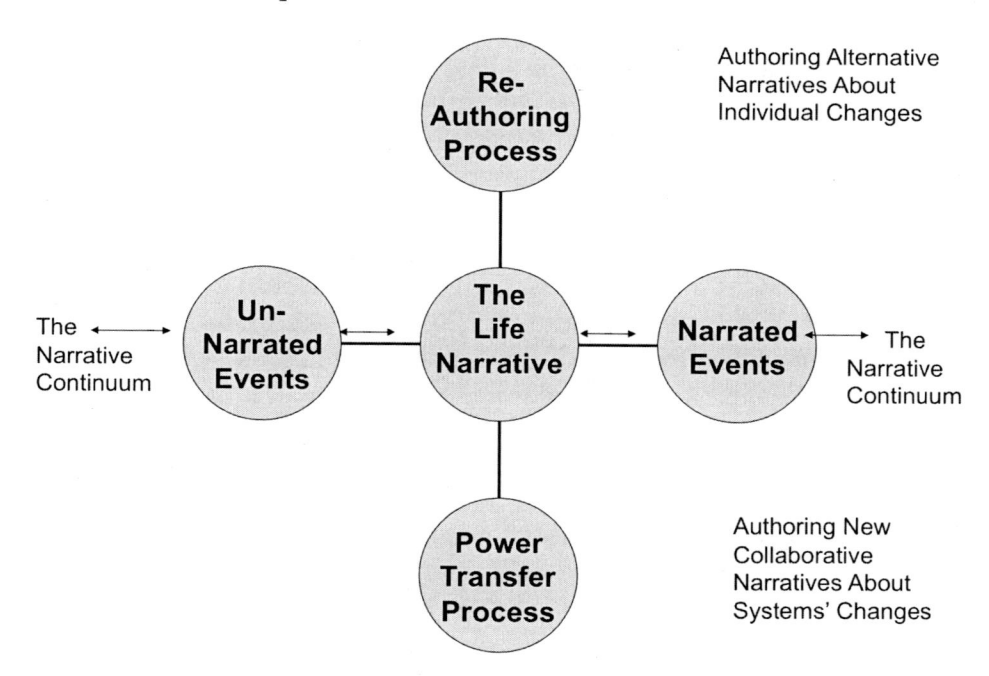

Figure 5.2. Social Justice Issues and The Narrative Continuum.

If the consultant had been in a counseling or supervisory role with Meera; he could have used externalization and deconstruction to address her loss of agency and voice, based on the related questions in Table 5.1. He actually began the externalization process by asking her to identify the consequences of being ignored or marginalized by those within the center's power hierarchy. A natural follow-up would have been to ask Meera to give her consequence, isolation, a name and to explain how that name fit her situation (see Table 5.1, Questions 1a and 1b).

While it is impossible to know exactly how Meera would have responded, in the spirit of this analysis, we can speculate that she might have named the issue, "Take Meera down a peg," or "Keep Meera in her place." If asked to visualize the issue (Questions 2a and 2b) Meera might have said, "It's a huge irregular black shape with sharp protruding edges, because I can't control it and it makes me feel helpless and crazy sometimes." From these initial externalization questions and potential responses, it is possible to see how the questions could have helped Meera to separate herself from her situation and to see it more clearly from a distance. This is the purpose of externalization.

Another useful question is whether "Keeping Meera in her place" is on the side of positive changes she desired in her organizational role or on the side of remaining stuck or marginalized (see Table 5.1, Question 3a). We can assume Meera would say the issue is keeping her stuck, which points out the organizational intent or purpose of "Keeping her in her place." This analysis could lead to the following two deconstruction questions: "Who benefits from keeping you in your place" and "What benefits do they receive in the short and long term?" (Questions 5a, 5b, and 5c). The process illustrates how the externalization and deconstruction questions in Table 5.1 can be used together in a fluid or interrelated manner rather than linearly. In response, Meera might say the director and other administrators are the primary beneficiaries, because they do not have to be as accountable in terms of the center's diversity mission. She might also include other staff who received additional resources from the reallocation of funds for community projects.

The consultant also asked whether this was the first time Meera had shared the organizational events described in her narrative. She remembered checking out her perceptions with other staff of color.

Table 5.1
PRINCIPLE 5: THE SOCIAL JUSTICE-SYSTEMS CHANGE INTERVENTION PRINCIPLE

Marginalization Analysis Skills	Examples of Narrative Questions Related to These Skills
Externalization:	
1. Name the problem/need situation:	(1a.) Based on how you described the situation in your narrative select a name for that situation. 1b. How does the name you selected fit the situation you described?
2. Visualize it:	(2a.) Select a shape and color that fit *(new name)* based on how you feel about the situation? (2b.) How do the shape and color you selected fit the situation you described?
3. Ascribe intention to it:	(3a.) Is *(new name)* on the side of changes you desire in your life or on the side of staying stuck in your life?
4. Spread it's effects/join forces:	(4a.) Who else is or might be affected by *(new name)* in similar ways to how you are affected by it? (4b.) What do you have in common with them (how are you connected)?
Deconstruction:	
5. Decode hidden sources of power and entitlement/privilege:	(5a.) Who benefitted from *(new name)* in the past and in the present? (5b.) What benefits do they receive in the short term (examples)? (5c.) In the long term? (5d.) For those who benefit from *(new name)* what spoken or unspoken messages might they receive about themselves based on those benefits? (5e.) In what other ways might they be affected by *(new name)*?
6. Decode hidden sources of disempowerment/marginalization:	(6a.) Who lost something from *(new name)* in the past and in the present? (6b.) What have you and others lost in the short term (examples)? In the long term? (6c.) For those who lose because of *(new name)* what spoken or unspoken messages might they receive about themselves? (6d.) What other more positive messages can you infer? (6e.) In what other ways might you and others be affected by *(new name)*?
7. Spread the roots of problem/need and its resolution: Join forces:	(7a.) Who benefits the most if *(new name)* stays as it is in the present or gets worse? (7b.) Who has the power to resolve (new name) or to make it better? (7c.) Who has the power to block change? (7d.) What resources and challenges might affect the resolution of *(new name)*? (7e) What do power leaders need to know from those affected by *(new name)* in order to change it?

They supported her observations, agreeing the cultural climate was much worse. Meera had not realized how much the climate had robbed her of her sense of competence and reality. Confiding in other staff of color restored some of her faith in herself. Meera's difficulty in naming her experiences and reactions with confidence was a second outcome from her organizational isolation.

Meera stated her validation experience with staff of color gave her the courage to request a meeting with the center director. She shared a less detailed narrative with the director than the one she shared with the consultant, about changes she had observed in the center's organizational policies and mission. While he listened to some of Meera's narrative before stopping her, the director's eventual angry denial was what Barton (2000) describes as ". . . a not well received reaction" (p. 345). This author described the director's type of interruption as a typical reaction, similar to leaders who reinterpret or ignore nonsanctioned narratives. Such reactions are more likely to occur in situations such as Meera's which involve asymmetrical power relationships. Finally, the director's reaction to her attempt to narrate her isolation experiences resulted in his decision to remove her from one of the center's national teams.

Practice Analysis

TRIAL RUN #3: SPREADING ISOLATION EFFECTS, ROOTS, AND RESOLUTION. Although Meera's efforts to discuss her isolation with the director backfired, the consultant was able to help her identify two reasons for that outcome. His conclusion was based on their previous analysis of the organization's culture and on the marginalization experiences shared by Meera and other staff. Table 5.1 includes two aspects of externalization and deconstruction that Meera did not utilize before her meeting with the director, which no doubt impacted upon his interruption and dismissal of her nonsanctioned narrative. It probably also led to his decision to remove her from one of the center's national teams.

First, Meera could have identified and joined forces with other center staff affected by a similar organizational isolation and marginalization (Dessel, Rogge, & Garlington, 2006). The skill of externalization includes spreading the effects of an individual's devalued role within an organization. In Meera's situation, this includes identifying "Who else in the center is affected by keeping Meera and other stakeholders in their place?" and "What are the common issues that connect you and those other stakeholders?" (see Table 5.1, Questions 4a and 4b).

The consultant's assessment interviews identified other direct practice staff, middle management, board members, and clients' family members who either had similar organizational experiences or observed other individuals in similar experiences. Meera may have assumed only staff of color were aware of or concerned about the organizational changes that had occurred. The consultant's assessment and report documented that the effects of the problem situation had already begun to spread and the situation was conducive for joining forces. Potential joiners included other staff assigned to the center's two community projects and to its three community-based satellite offices where Meera and other staff worked in collaborative teams and units. Exploring those staff members' reactions to the organizational changes and their ideas about how to address the changes could have been initial steps toward externalizing the problem (see Table 5.1, Questions 1a and 1b, 2a and 2b, 3a, and 4a and 4b).

Second, externalization could have been accompanied by deconstruction questions between Meera and other stakeholders who were affected by the organizational changes. For instance, it would be important to ask and plan how to address, "Who has the power to resolve the issue of keeping center stakeholders in their place?" and "Who has the power to keep the system from resolving these issues?" (see Table 5.1, Questions 7b and 7c). These deconstruction questions help to spread the roots of the problem and the resources for its resolution. Therefore the focus is on both organizational challenges and strengths in mental health and other practice settings (Holmes, 2003).

If this type of marginalization analysis had occurred, it could have led to a detailed planning process involving sufficient trial runs to test potential system responses to proposed organizational changes. The process also could have prevented Meera "From testing the depth of the river with both feet" in the manner that she did. How such joining should take place, who should take leading roles in the process, and when and where it should occur are important parts of planning system changes. Furthermore, the analysis and planning should not be restricted to other center staff and administrators, but in appropriate circumstances could include separate groups of clients, family members, board members, and the community.

Practice Skills: Advocacy by Storytelling and Power Transfers in Practice with Marginalized Clients

Practice Overview

This chapter's previous practice examples illustrate the importance of providers understanding their own narratives and unnarrated experiences. That understanding provides a critical foundation for their effective narrative practice with clients, especially when social justice issues are involved (Finn & Jacobson, 2003). For instance, Meera, the social worker in the first practice example was assigned to work with a client, Rachael, who requested help in handling a punitive organizational policy in her son's school. Meera tuned into Rachael's social justice concerns more effectively, because she had addressed similar concerns related to herself and other staff during the center's organizational assessment.

Rachael's two children, David and Andria, participated in the mental health center's community-based mentoring program. In addition to coordinating this program with school staff, community residents, and family members, Meera provided parenting education sessions for Rachael and other parents. This client's situation was introduced in Chapter 2 on pages 28 to 29. At that time she was receiving addiction recovery services in a rehabilitation program for women and children.

Practice Example

BACKGROUND INFORMATION. Rachael is a 35-year-old African American client with three children, two of whom were placed in foster care by Children's Protective Services (CPS) due to neglect. Her oldest daughter, Felicia, lived with Rachael's sister. After she completed her six-month rehab and aftercare program, Rachael was able to regain custody of David and Andria. She remained cut-off from the rest of her family. Her husband does not pay child support or visit their children. Rachael's medical records job ended three years previously after her crack cocaine addiction affected her work attendance and performance. The rehab program she completed serves African American and Latino women primarily, but also included white women. Many of the program participants had lost custody of their children.

In their second parenting education session, Rachael talked about a recent meeting with her son David's teacher. The teacher had decided to recommend that David be taken out of the mentoring program because his grades had dropped. Rachael tried to advocate for her son by telling his teacher about his negative experiences in foster care and her own addiction and recovery. David's teacher said his participation in the mentoring program was a privilege and that he had to earn his spot like all of the other students.

Rachael explained how the teacher's response reminded her of other people who treated her disrespectfully when she was using drugs, which made her feel ashamed. Meera asked if those interactions had been a relapse trigger for Rachael in the past, and Rachael agreed they had been. She then asked Rachael if there had ever been a similar experience when, although she felt disrespected and ashamed, she had not relapsed. In response, Rachael shared the following narrative:

Rachael's Exception Narrative. This happened about a year ago when I was in rehab. Andria and David were still in foster care two counties away. I wasn't a good mother before, but once I got in rehab, I started trying to change. CPS had strict rules about not missing parental visits. I missed my last one so I was trying hard to be on time for this one, even though I had to ride three busses. The first two buses came right on schedule, but then the third one got a flat tire right after it picked up us passengers. We waited a long time for another bus to pick us up, so I was late for my visit. The foster mother wouldn't let me see them—my kids—because CPS told her not to if I was late. I could hear them crying to see me. It made me feel good, but bad at the same time, because I let them down again; only it wasn't my fault. I told my women's group what happened later; they listened but didn't blame me. Not even when I admitted wanting to get high because I felt like less than nothing. Some of the other women had stories so much like mine it took away some of my shame, but not all of it. The more we talked the madder we got—CPS needed to know if we didn't have any say-so about our kids, we'd keep relapsing from the all the stress we had. One of our group leaders suggested we talk to CPS, so we started planning a letter about a meeting. We asked the group leaders to leave the room so we could plan on our own—this was our lives and our children! We wrote CPS saying we wanted to talk about their visitation and custody rules, and to send someone to the meeting who could make decisions. After mailing our letter, we got ready for the meeting—we made a list of questions we needed answers to and a list of changes we thought could give us some control and power. We went over a couple of our stories about our bad times with parental visits, because we'd decided to tell the stories to CPS in the first meeting. How did it all end? Well, we had four or five meetings with CPS. They changed some of the rules we asked about, and they sent a CPS worker to rehab three days a week to get things running better between them and rehab and to meet one-on-one with mothers who had individual concerns. They even improved how CPS and rehab had us do reunification plans for getting our kids back. Another thing—we asked the CPS worker to meet with the mothers' group about once a month to keep us up to date. And CPS agreed!

Practice Analysis

LESSONS FROM RACHAEL'S PERSONAL EXCEPTION NARRATIVE. Meera's request for Rachael to discuss a stressful time when she had not relapsed is an example of how providers can elicit exception narratives (see Table 5.2: Advocacy by Storytelling Skill: I-B). Equally important, Meera then helped Rachael celebrate her past successful coping experience and the lessons she learned from it by identifying how she kept from relapsing during that experience (Docherty & McColl, 2003; Gilbert & Beidler, 2001). Table 4.2 in Chapter 4 includes these two tasks related to eliciting exception narratives (Task #4). Rachael said she went to her rehab program and talked with her peers and group leaders about what happened during her attempted parental visit. Her narrative documents how she used advocacy by storytelling with her peers (see Table 5.2: Skill I-B), and how she coped better by noticing a current problem situation and handling it in a more effective way (see Table 5.2: Criteria I-B-3).

In her narrative, Rachael said, "They (her peers and group leaders) listened but didn't blame me." She explained their nonblaming response reinforced her decision to stay sober and to not relapse. In contrast, her nonrecovering peers previously pointed out reasons they and Rachael could not recover, and therefore, why they should keep using drugs. Rachael named her more effective way of coping, "Not playing the addiction- victim-blame-game," which in externalization language allowed her to separate herself from her potential relapse situation (see Table 5.1, Questions #1a and 1b). Rachael described "Not playing . . ." as having a pot of gold at the end of a colorful rainbow, all shiny and brand new like her recovery when it was working

Table 5.2
PRINCIPLE 5: THE SOCIAL JUSTICE-SYSTEMS CHANGE
INTERVENTION PRINCIPLE

Systems Change Skills	*Related Systems Change Skill Steps*
I. Types of Advocacy by Storytelling; A. A Decision-Maker's Dilemma and Resolution Narrative: Told to other decision-makers by: • the CEO in the narrative or by a third party • with power/credibility in system (a CEO, mentor, consultant, or influential organizational peer)	I-A: The Narrator shares a narrative in which a hero or heroine's systems' transformation is relevant to the listener's: (1) Power hierarchy role within a system and social justice dilemma(s) (2) Systems change opportunities, options, and resolutions (3) Narrative themes
B. A Client's Survival and Exception Narrative: Told to other clients or to decision-makers by: • the client in the narrative (a personal narrative) • a helping professional (another client's narrative)	I-B: The Narrator shares a narrative in which the usual negative outcome did not occur in the hero or heroine's problem or need situation because she/he: (1) Did not notice the situation at the time it occurred (e.g., ignored the situation or was distracted or involved elsewhere) (2) Noticed the situation but did not do anything or respond (3) Noticed the situation but handled it in a different more effective way.
II. Power Transfer/Policy Transformation Groups (Action Component) Groups develop when individuals: A: Lack sufficient personal power to change systems, and therefore B: Join forces with others to expand power and influence those who can achieve or block systems change	II-A: Based on the analysis of who has power to initiate and block system changes, the power transfer group identifies social justice barriers such as: (1) The current system policy or practice that needs to be addressed (2) The specific negative effects of the policy or practice on system participants (3) How those effects are not consistent with the system's mission, values, goals

Continued on next page

Table 5.2 *(continued)*
PRINCIPLE 5: THE SOCIAL JUSTICE-SYSTEMS CHANGE
INTERVENTION PRINCIPLE

Systems Change Skills	*Related Systems Change Skill Steps*
	II-B: The group proposes needed changes and the potential consequences (1) How the identified policy or practice can be revised, improved, or replaced (2) The benefits of proposed system changes for clients, staff, and the system

(Questions #2a and 2b). When Meera explored this issue further with Rachael, the client said "Not playing . . ." was on the side of reaching her goal of recovery rather than on the side of relapsing (Question #3a).

Their discussion about this narrative, in which her peers shared similar visitation and custody stories, helped Rachael to realize how all of them felt powerlessness related to CPS (Greene, Lee, & Hoffpauir, 2005). She said they understood that putting their concerns together made them powerful enough to get a meeting with CPS and to stick with the list of questions and changes they had agreed on (see Table 5.2, Power Transfer Groups). Essentially, their formation of an effective policy and power transfer group, as shown in Table 5.2, involved advocacy by storytelling with decision makers (Form #1). The mothers' process of spreading the effects and roots of the problem and joining each other not only helped them to achieve their planned organizational policy reforms (see Table 5.2, Criteria A1 and A2). In addition, Rachael concluded the brief process helped them to achieve unplanned outcomes (Kelley, 2002), such as a CPS staff member being permanently out-stationed in the rehab program to improve coordination and service quality to the mothers.

APPLYING THOSE LESSONS TO RACHAEL'S CURRENT SOCIAL JUSTICE CONCERNS. The previous analysis of Rachael's rehab-CPS experience and related lessons provided a path for her and Meera to address the client's current social justice concerns. Rachael realized she was feeling alone in her concerns about the teacher's decision to exclude David from the mentoring program. Without prompting from Meera, she started brainstorming about other parents with children in the program and their avenues for program input.

Based on her knowledge of the program's structure, Meera helped Rachael to identify four preliminary steps for addressing this situation: (1) review the program policies about student eligibility requirements for the program and under what circumstances exceptions are made; (2) contact the program's parent council to find out how she could raise her concerns in a future meeting; (3) informally talk with some of the other parents with children in the program who have similar concerns as well as other ones; and (4) attend the next meeting and introduce her concerns using her storytelling process to explore if other parents have been affected by program rules in a similar way. Rachael's research revealed the parent council, similar to other parent committees, was feeling challenged in their efforts to have meaningful input into the program's policies and decisions (Dessel et al., 2006). For example, they wanted more input into how mentors were selected and utilized by the program.

That issue fit with Rachael's concerns as she wanted David to be assigned to a strong African American man or college-age male, because her husband and male relatives were not currently involved in their lives. In fact, the teacher's decision to recommend that David be excluded from the program did not consider those special gender-related needs or how a mentor could help explore and resolve his academic problems. At a meeting of the parent council, Rachael and other parents stated their obvious mutual concerns, and Rachael included a brief narrative about how David became withdrawn for a few days when he heard he might not continue in the program. The council decided unanimously to request a meeting with the program's director first, and if that was not successful, to request a meeting with the Board to allow parents to air their concerns. Their meeting with the director led to policy reforms about the selection of mentors and participation criteria for the students, which allowed David to remain in the program.

Practice Skills: Advocacy by Storytelling and Power Transfers in Practice with Privileged Clients

Practice Example

BACKGROUND INFORMATION. Clients who are not marginalized often have similar concerns as those who are marginalized. Their needs may often be addressed before those of less privileged clients in some circumstances because of their higher status. In other situations, however, their needs may be ignored because their privileged status is a barrier to those who can affect systems' changes. In one Catholic Social Service Agency (CSSA), one of the staff asked the team for clients with co-occurring disorders to consider a client's request for a caregivers' support group. The team served clients with developmental disabilities (DD) who also had co-occurring serious mental illnesses (SMI), addictions, and severe hearing or vision impairments. The members discussed this request, but when they learned the family involved was one the staff considered too demanding, they decided the issue did not apply to most of their other clients.

The client whose caregivers requested a support group was 22-year-old Morton Jacobs. His caregivers are Alan and Ruth Rickman, a Jewish couple who are 69 and 66 years old respectively; this is their second marriage. Morton is Ms. Rickman's grandson. He has a co-occurring DD and SMI. He lives in a group home not far from his caregivers, where he receives some medication supervision by the staff. He also receives services from the area mental health center and from vocational rehabilitation. The couple is estranged from Mr. Rickman's two sons from his first marriage, and from Alan's mother who is divorced from Ms. Rickman's son. Mr. Rickman is a well-known former business owner in the community who is considered wealthy. Staff members view him as too aggressive in demanding services for Morton from CSSA and the area mental health center.

SYSTEMS' CHANGE PRACTICE STRATEGIES AND ANALYSIS. CSSA's psychiatric rehab nurse and administrator, Robert, decided to revisit the Rickman's request for a caregiver's support group. He believed support and education services *could* appeal to a broader range of clients' family members, so he disagreed with the team's decision. But other strategies were required to spread the effects and resolution of caregivers' burden, in terms of the client families that were affected by the issues, and the providers and administrators who could help to address it (see Table 5.1, Questions #4a and 4b, and 7a through 7e). Those strategies meant moving the Rickman couple, who were considered privileged, out of the forefront and making the need they identified for their family more universal. After talking individually with other providers and administrators to explore their concerns in this area, Robert convened two planning meetings with representatives from CSSA, Morton Jacob's group home and two others, the mental health center, the community health center, and vocational rehabilitation. They discussed different types of care giving and other issues regarding their mutual client population, and identified a range of client situations that would be appropriate for such services (Greene, Kondrat, Lee, Clement, Siebert, Mentzer, & Pinnell, 2006).

Next they scheduled a meeting involving staff from CSSA, including an administrator and the co-occurring team members, administrators and staff members from other organizations who attended the first two meetings, and two care giving families that represented different needs related to the issue who had been invited to speak during the meeting. Other families that had indicated an interest in the issue were also invited to the meeting. The goal was to establish collaborative community partnerships so the participating organizations and families could help to address care giving issues (Wertheimer, Beck, Brooks, & Wolk, 2004). This effort helped to spread the issue's resolution by developing a policy and power transfer group that included client families, and identifying barriers and supports for systems change (see Table 5.2, Power Transfer Groups, A2).

The meeting organizers presented a brief overview of some of the concerns they had noted regarding their clients with co-occurring disorders and clients' family members. They then had the two sets of family members provide stories about their care giving successes and challenges. For instance, one father said in the following:

Caregiver's Survival and Exception Narrative: A lot of people think they can't handle certain situations, like nothing they do makes a difference. I used to think like that about our daughter, Marie. That was when we first lived in Dayton. Then they encouraged us to come to the caregivers' education group, and gradually things began to change. The group leader always said, "Yes you can do it." She was honest about the hard work in being Marie's caregiver, and she cared about our family. She always asked what was going on in our lives, and she didn't just run the group. She came to our house so she could see what we were working with. There was a time when we couldn't get Marie out of bed so we were prisoners in our own home. She refused to communicate. We had to diaper and feed her like a child several times a day. I tell you it wore us out. But our coordinator and a home health care nurse came and showed us how to get her out of bed and get her going. If our coordinator said she was coming, she kept her word, and if she couldn't get there, she'd call and reschedule. It made us feel like we deserved a life of our own, and we weren't alone. That Marie could have a life too and was worth it. Now we need the same service here.

This father's story is an example of a client's survival and exception narrative, which was targeted for policy decision makers and reformers (see Table 5.2, Form #2). He brought pictures of his daughter as she looked currently and as she looked in the past, curled up in bed in the fetal position. His narrative and dramatically different pictures illustrated the value of caregiver services as clearly, but more graphically, than a case study or statistics. Mr. and Ms. Rickman also attended the meeting. He added a few appropriate comments about his family's own caregiving needs in support of the above narrative and a second caregiver who also spoke.

Robert's efforts to convene and organize the series of three planning meetings represented a cross-systems change strategy, rather than a within system change, and was therefore more unique and difficult for that reason. In his first meeting with the initial planning group, he told the participants a narrative his mentor shared with him years before called "The Reluctant Decision-Maker." Robert said whenever he found himself dragging his feet about large organizational changes as an administrator; he would retell himself and sometimes others this narrative. He recognized that narratives about decision makers' dilemmas can have the greatest impact on other decision makers. The following narrative was written by Robert's administrative mentor. It is an example of advocacy by storytelling (see Table 5.2, Form #1), because it was directed effectively toward other decision makers by Robert, their administrative peer.

> **A Decision-Makers' Dilemma and Resolution Narrative:** When I was 35, our only child died in our swimming pool. Simon, Jr. was five and a half, and my parents' only grandchild. It was devastating because I was supposed to be watching him. I turned my back for a moment, and when I looked at the pool again, I couldn't see him. I jumped in and pulled him out. He was blue and wasn't breathing. A neighbor and I took turns giving him CPR until the ambulance came. They revived him at the hospital, but then he died. Weeks later, my wife enrolled us in a loss group for parents of deceased children. I went only because I felt so guilty and wanted to support her. It was agonizing for me to hear other parents talk about the deaths of their children. At first I was closed down, locked in silence

and not hearing. But somewhere during the fourth or fifth session, something inside me shifted, that's the only way I can explain it, and I knew at that point the group was where I needed to be. It was like a thundercloud exploded over my head. It took completing the group sessions and a lot of other support to get me through my grief. Not past it; it's always there but less intense most of the time. I was an agency director then. When clients worked their way to my office with a complaint or request, they were often what I called irrational and demanding. So much so, I'd find myself digging my heels in instead of really listening to their requests. Now I had a dilemma. I'd been a client in the loss group, and although I'd been sure it wasn't for me at first, I'd had that moment when I realized the group was what I needed. So should I take my new insight and use it to listen, understand, and respond to clients' requests differently; or should I once again put on my old administrators' hat? I chose the former, because not only had I suffered an unbelievably painful loss and walked in a client's shoes, but I'd lived through it and I was a different person. Living through our own pain helps us to understand, at a visceral level, that clients do have the ability to tell us what they need. I decided our clients are really teachers in disguise, and that we should listen to them with open minds and with respect.

Conclusion

The previous Decision-Makers' Dilemma and Resolution Narrative (see Table 5.2) addresses providers and administrators' roles in respecting clients' power to name their needs and potential solutions. As this chapter illustrates, advocacy by storytelling, power transfer groups, externalization and deconstruction are powerful tools for encouraging administrators, legislators, policy analysts, providers, and consultants to consider clients' requests with open minds. The potential impact of these strategies is heightened even more when they involve decision-makers' narratives designed to influence other decision makers. However, all key actors' responses are sometimes dependent on who the client is; whether the client is marginalized, or as in the last practice example, the client has a privileged status. From a social justice framework, the responsibility for honoring clients' voices remains the same regardless of their status.

In the cross systems' planning meeting convened by Robert, the participants were reminded of that responsibility by Marie's father's narrative and the narrative of Robert's mentor. Those narratives, one oral and the other written, influenced the participants to establish caregivers' services for families of clients with co-occurring DD and SMI, as the client Alan Rickman previously requested. This community collaborative also broadened the scope of its initial planning to include a mental health peer specialist program for their mutual client population, along with several other projects.

References

Barton, E. (2000). Sanctioned and non-sanctioned narratives in institutional discourse. *Narrative Inquiry, 20*, 341–375.

Boje, D. M. (2007). *Storytelling Organization.* London: Sage.

Colton, M. (2002). Editorial. Special issue on social work and social justice. *British Journal of Social Work, 32*, 659–667.

Dessel, A., Rogge, M. E., & Garlington, S. B. (2006). Using intergroup dialogue to promote social justice and change. *Social Work, 51*, 303–315.

Docherty, D., & McColl, M. A. (2003). Illness stories: Themes emerging through narrative. *Social Work in Health Care, 37*, 19–39.

Finn, J. L., & Jacobson, M. (2003). Just practice: Steps toward a new social work paradigm. *Journal of Social Work Education, 39*, 57–78.

Freeman, E. M. (2008). Methods of practice overview. *Encyclopedia of Social Work* (20th Edition). Washington, DC: National Association of Social Workers.

Freeman, E. M. (March 4, 2004). Basic principles of effective narrative practice: Workshop PowerPoint presentation. Kansas City, MO: Sponsored by the Social Work Coalition for Social Workers in Health Care.

Freeman, E. M., & Couchonnal, G. (2006). Narrative and culturally based approaches in practice with families. *Families in Society, 87*, 198–308.

Gilbert, M. C., & Beidler, A. E. (2001). Using the narrative approach in groups of chemically dependent mothers. *Social Work With Groups, 24*, 101–115.

Greene, G. J., Kondrat, D. C., Lee, M. Y., Clement, J., Siebert, H., Mentzer, R. A., & Pinnell, S. R. (2006). A solution-focused approach to case management and recovery with consumers who have severe mental disability. *Families in Society, 87*, 339–350.

Greene, G. J., Lee, M. Y., & Hoffpanuir, S. (2005). The languages of empowerment and strengths in clinical social work: A constructivist perspective. *Families in Society, 86*, 267–277.

Holmes, J. (2003). Narrative in psychiatry and psychotherapy: The evidence? *Journal of Medical Ethics: Medical Humanities, 26*, 92–96.

Kelley, P. (2002). A narrative therapy approach to brief treatment. *Journal of Brief Therapy, 1*, 91–100.

Kitchell, A., Hannan, E., & Kempton, W. (2000). Identity through stories: Story structure and function in two environmental groups. *Human Organization, 59*, 90–105.

Linhorst, D. M. (2002). Federalism and social justice: Implications for social work. *Social Work, 47,* 201–208.

Smith, F. L., & Keyton, J. (2001). Organizational Storytelling: Metaphors for Relational Power and Identity Struggles. *Management Communication Quarterly,* November 15, 2001: 149–182.

Stuart, P. H. (1999). Linking clients and policy: Social work's distinctive contribution. *Social Work, 44,* 335–347.

Wertheimer, M. R., Beck, E. L., Brooks, F., & Wolk, J. L. (2004). Community partnerships: An innovative model of social work practice and education. *Journal of Community Practice, 12,* 123–140.

Part Two

ADVANCED NARRATIVE APPROACHES AND SKILLS WITH INDIVIDUALS, MULTIPLE CLIENT SYSTEMS, AND LARGE SYSTEMS ACROSS THE LIFE SPAN

Chapter 6

USING PLAY, INTERPRETIVE, AND IMPROVISATIONAL NARRATIVE STRATEGIES WITH CHILDREN: PREVENTION, EARLY INTERVENTION, AND TREATMENT

> Yah, my teacher said the social worker would talk to me. But I was wondering, are you a hit man? I mean my step-father said he put a contract on my mother, and . . .
>
> —Carlos

St. Amour (2003) contends that children like Carlos in the above narrative excerpt, are natural storytellers whose narratives reveal their developmental stages over time. Their narratives also reveal specific areas that are enhanced by their storytelling, such as literacy, verbal language skills, appreciation of cultural differences, and socialization or collaboration with peers (Chenfield, 2002; Fein, Ardila-Rey, & Groth, 2000; Sawyer, 2002; St. Amour, 2003). Such developmental changes often occur within the context of play, which is the universal age-appropriate work of children compared to that of adults (Freeman, 2004). Play is critical for all children's development whether they primarily participate in it individually, or as Sawyer (1997) indicates, they also collaborate in verbal or physical play with peers.

In addition to these developmental similarities, a child's narrative can illustrate developmental differences compared to other children based on: Age, gender, race or ethnicity, socioeconomic status, geographic location, religion, disabling conditions, sexual orientation, and intellectual abilities and challenges (Del Valle, McEachern, & Chambers, 2001; Hinman, 2003; Leukefeld, Godlaski, Clark, Brown,

& Hays, 2002; Toth, Cicchetti, Macfie, & Emde, 1997). Carlos' developmental differences, compared to other children, may have been affected by his Mexican-American ethnicity, and his family's involuntary relocation from a small rural southern area to a small urban northeastern area, due to poverty and family violence (Freeman, 2004; Sawyer, 2002).

When responding to developmental similarities and differences such as those involving Carlos, providers should also assess children's narratives to identify their environmental supports and challenges. Assessments should focus on family, community, school, and peer interactions. Narrative power-sharing strategies build upon such supports and on children's natural resilience. Therefore, they are more effective than verbal strategies designed primarily for adults. Coconstructed narratives and interpretive interventions, such as telling a story about a favorite toy, are examples of power-sharing.

This chapter describes how such strategies can be used with children based on practice questions typically raised by providers, for example, "How can I encourage nonverbal or untrusting children to share their narratives?" The focus is on children from six to 11 years of age in educational and community-based settings, and on how providers can adapt those strategies with children from three to five years of age. The discussion concludes with principles and strategies from Part One of the book that are relevant to this chapter.

Practice Skill: Using Power-Sharing Narrative Strategies in Education Settings

Practice Overview

Power-sharing, play, and narrative strategies help children to immerse themselves in developmentally-appropriate activities that are growth- and empowerment-oriented. These activities are also beneficial to practitioners because they provide the door through which helpers can enter, collaborate with, and understand the world of children. Table 6.1 includes examples of such strategies that are relevant to the practice example in the next section and to other children. The strategies in this table are organized to illustrate their appropriateness for children who communicate or express themselves (Csak, 2002; Freeman, 2004; Sawyer, 2002; St. Amour, 2003):

1. Primarily nonverbally (early childhood and preschool age children; abused children; those who are elective mutes, and some developmentally-disabled children),
2. Primarily verbally (some traumatized children who have Post-Traumatic Stress Disorder {PTSD}, i.e., they exhibit a blank affect or facial expression and body language),
3. Both verbally and nonverbally (school-age children with typical or normative age-and developmentally-related issues).

Practice Example

Background Information. Nine-year-old Carlos Munoz was referred by his teacher to Brent Aldrich, the school social worker in a small rural education co-op in the northeast. He and his mother and sister, Elena, moved to the area three weeks previously from Texas. The teacher was concerned because Carlos was a loner and was hesitant in sharing information about his family and past school history. The current school had requested records from his previous school, although those records had not been received yet. Consequently, the teacher was still assessing his academic abilities and achievement.

Carlos and his sister were wearing the few summer clothes they brought with them, but it was winter in their current location so they were dressed inadequately. He was a Mexican-American student who spoke clear English; however, his mother seemed more comfortable speaking Spanish and spoke very limited English. The teacher requested that Brent meet with Carlos to explore his adjustment to his new school, and then follow-up with Ms. Morales to determine areas the family might need help with. Brent assumed Carlos was coping with new social and academic demands related to his family's relocation and his developmental issues. For example, he assumed Carlos was in Erik Erickson's stage of industry versus inferiority, which is focused on developing social and educational competence (McCabe, 1997).

CONDUCTING THE INITIAL EARLY INTERVENTION CONTACT WITH THE CLIENT. When Brent met with his client, he asked what Carlos had been told about who was going to meet with him and the reason. Carlos said he had not been told anything. His teacher simply pointed Brent out in the hall and told Carlos they would meet the following day. Carlos shared a very brief narrative about his situation, which

Table 6.1
POWER SHARING SKILL: THE USE OF IMPROVISATIONAL AND SCRIPTED
NARRATIVE PLAY STRATEGIES WITH CHILDREN

Children Who Communicate at a Given Time:	Examples of Improvisational or Interpretive Play Strategies	Examples of Scripted Play Strategies
Primarily Nonverbally:	(1) Observe and interpret a child playing with with a: a. Sand tray b. Doll house and family c. Puppet family or peer group d. Play therapy with therapeutic toys	(4) Use the members' bodies and space to create a sculpting that shows: a. Family relationships based on identified issues b. Small group relationships based on the members' or an individual's issues c. Team members' relationships based on the members' or a member's issues
Primarily Verbally:	(2) Tell or read and discuss a story involving a: a. Getting better narrative b. Exception narrative c. Miracle narrative d. Alternative narrative or alternative ending e. Coconstructed poem, song, play, or narrative by a peer group or family	(5) Use a script to address identified issues by: a. Collaborating on a co-constructed narrative between a practitioner and client(s) b. Role playing a scripted issue from a client's narrative c. Engaging in Mirror work to: • Identify feelings with select emotion cards • Tell a story about the feeling(s) or the person in the mirror
Both Verbally and Nonverbally:	(3) Create a new narrative by: a. Showing and telling a story about a favorite toy, game, or possession b. Interpreting a favorite song, poem, picture, story, proverb, or parable c. Drawing and telling a story about a person, scene, or family (DAP, DAS, or DAF) d. Telling a story about a favorite event	(6) Use a script as an individual, small group members, or family members to: a. Act out a scene in a play b. Participate in scripted role plays c. Act out a proverb or parable selected by the practitioner

included the segment at the beginning of this chapter. Because Carlos asked Brent, "Are you a hit man"? Brent reassured Carlos he was not there to hurt him or his family in any way. He explained he often met with new students like Carlos to determine if they had what they needed to be successful in their new school. Before their session ended, Brent learned the family had left Texas in the middle of the night while the stepfather was sleeping, and for that reason, they left most of their clothing and other possessions. The stepfather was often violent with Carlos' mother, Ms. Munoz, and sometimes with Carlos and Elena as well.

INTRODUCING A PREINTERVENTION DRAW A SCENE NARRATIVE AND POWER-SHARING STRATEGY. Carlos stopped talking at this point in the initial contact and seemed to regret opening up to Brent about his family. He was also reluctant to talk about how he was doing in his new school other than to say "Okay." Consequently, Brent decided to have Carlos draw a picture of his last recess period on the playground, and to include every thing he remembered about the teachers, classmates, and himself, along with what happened. He explained he wanted to know from Carlos' eyes what he observed when his class was on the playground at recess.

This power-sharing strategy is included in Table 6.1, under Communicates Both Verbally and Nonverbally; and under 3c: The Draw and Tell a Story about a Scene Interpretive Strategy (DAS). The playground scene which Carlos drew is shown in Figure 6.1. Brent's previous instructions to Carlos can be adapted to situations where providers ask children to: Draw their family (DAF), at home or elsewhere; or draw a significant person in their lives (DAP) (see Table 6.1: under Communicates Both Verbally and Nonverbally, and under 3c: The Draw and Tell a Story Interpretive Strategy).

ELICITING CARLOS' STORY ABOUT HIS DAS NARRATIVE: Providers should encourage clients to complete their drawing before asking them to tell a story about it. This sequence allows practitioners to share power with children, while eliciting their ideas about the drawn narrative first, rather than interpreting it themselves. Otherwise practitioners could prevent the emergence of significant information children want to share in their own voices as experts on their situation. Follow-up questions about specific aspects of the drawing can be asked once children have shared their story about the scene (see Chapter 4: Table 4.1 for examples of useful follow-up questions). If children are unable to begin their story, a strategic question can be asked to elicit it, such as the one used by Brent, "Carlos, will you tell me who the people are in your drawing"?

CARLOS' PRE-INTERVENTION STORY ABOUT HIS DAS NARRATIVE. Well, there's Eddie by the wall playing tag with some other boys. One day he plays tag, and another time he plays kick ball or gets on the monkey bars. He gets around. Other kids like him. But they *really* like Steve; he runs the kick ball game. He lets Stephanie throw the ball, but she's not as good as he is. Nobody is! All the kids know he's the kick ball champ. He says "You're out Billy . . . Carol's in. That's my decision—my rule." I stand by the wall where I can watch the kick ball game. I can see my teacher, Ms Jones, too. So I know when recess is over. She gets mad if kids don't line up on time. Ms. Jones can't see me because of Christie and those other silly girls who play jump rope all the time, but I can see her talking to other teachers. That's Dennis and two other kids on the wall by the teachers—some kid is always standing there for hitting another kid or not playing fair. Or for throwing rocks. I'm the new kid in class, and they're all probably watching me, so I gotta' stay out of trouble.

ANALYZING THE DAS NARRATIVE AND STORY AND USING A FOLLOW-UP NARRATIVE INTERVENTION. Using the previous story Carlos told about his DAS narrative, Brent asked if there was an advantage to standing where Carlos was in his drawing (Figure 6.1). Carlos said he could watch everyone from there and figure out what they were doing and saying. Brent gave Carlos positive feedback about his "watch and learn" lesson or reframe, because it allowed him to become familiar with his new school's expectations and learn how to get along there. Carlos also said the wall kept him farther away from everyone, so they would not find out he hates being the new kid. Brent asked if Carlos had a sign on his back that showed he hated being new, what would his sign say? After thinking about it, Carlos said it might say "If you're new it's like a kick me sign on your back! Somebody might hit you—like my stepfather!" Rivett, Howarth, and Gordon (2006) indicate such PTSD-related hyper-vigilance is common in family violence situations.

Providers can encourage these children to identify the sources of their hyper-vigilance and how to objectify and manage their fears, rather than to deny them. Therefore, in their second interview, Brent suggested they make two lists: One for people Carlos trusted current-

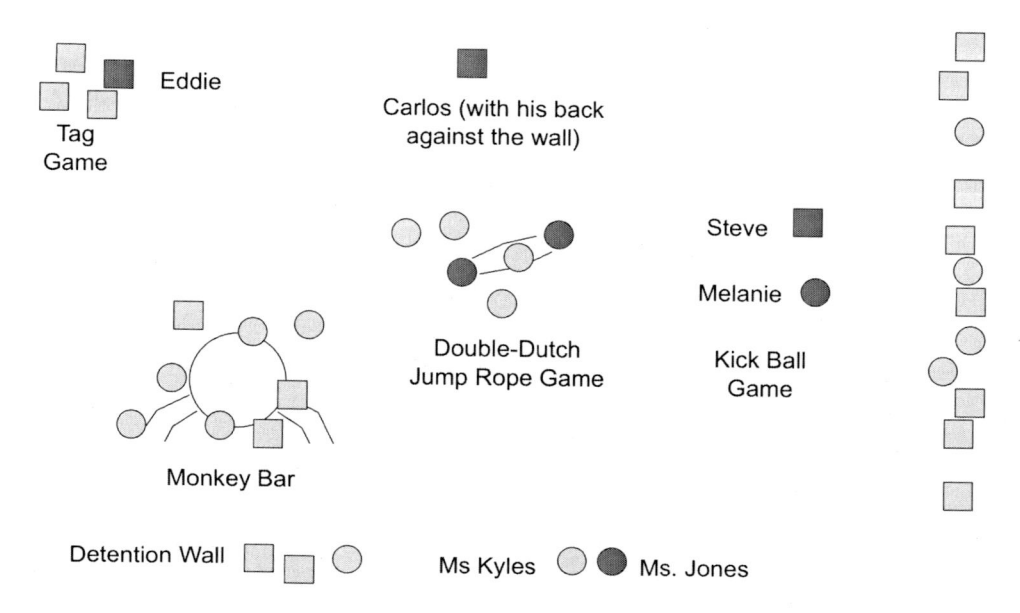

Figure 6.1. Preintervention narrative drawn by Carlos with a "Kick Me" Sign on His Back.

ly and the other for people he did not trust or was not sure about. Brent said they could start with one person on each list. Carlos put his stepfather, teacher, and classmates on his "don't trust" list. He said his teacher did not like him, and his classmates would not talk to him.

The exceptions among his peers were Eddie and Steve, whom Carlos put on his "trust" list after thinking about it. Steve was well liked and Eddie once said "Hi kid" to Carlos. Brent asked if Carlos would feel comfortable saying "hi" to Eddie and asking if he could play with him, wherever Eddie happened to be playing at the time. Carlos agreed to talk to Eddie during their next recess. Carlos said his cousin had showed him how to say "hi" and make friends in his previous school. He called it "the friendship game." This follow-up narrative intervention created peer support for Carlos in the school's social context. The result is discussed more fully in Brent's postintervention narrative analysis.

USING SYSTEMIC NARRATIVE INTERVENTIONS AND OTHER POWER-SHARING STRATEGIES. In addition to the previous narrative analysis and follow-up interventions, Brent worked with Carlos and his family in other modalities. For example, after working with Carlos in four individual sessions, Brent formed a social skills peer group with Carlos and other classmates who could benefit from the group. This gave the members an opportunity to: (1) learn and apply social skills appropriate for their developmental stage in a structured setting; and (2) engage in collaborative peer play involving power-sharing interpretive and scripted strategies (Daiute, Buteau, & Rawlins, 2001; Daiute & Buteau, 2002).

Group members were asked to take turns creating the words to a song about friendship in one session. In later sessions, they created words to a poem about preventing conflicts, using the same format. Their coconstructed poem and song, which had been typed, were distributed to members in another session, so they could decorate their copies with artwork to illustrate what their words meant to them. They shared their artwork with other members and explained their artwork choices. They also participated in scripted role plays that required them to use the social skills they were learning (see Table 6.1, under Communicates Primarily Verbally; and under #2e: Share a Story Involving a Coconstructed Interpretive Poem or Song. Also under Communicates Both Verbally and Nonverbally; and under #6b: Collaborative Play Using Scripted Role Plays).

Brent's interventions involving Ms. Munoz and Carlos' sister, Elena, consisted of individual and systems or organizational work. He began by meeting with Ms. Munoz at home to discuss the family's current needs from her perspective; and then took her to an area Clothes Closet for free winter clothing for family members; coordinated between the school and Child Protective Services to prevent the family from being hot lined for neglect; and referred her to a domestic violence women's group in the next county, which included child care and transportation to the meetings. Brent later learned Ms. Munoz attended only one meeting, because no one else in the group spoke Spanish.

His intervention might have been successful if he had helped to strengthen cultural and other environmental supports for his client (Bernal & Saez-Santiago, 2008). For instance, he could have consulted a cultural coach in Ms. Munoz's community identified by her or other knowledgeable informants. Or he could have met with the client and cultural coach to identify potential solutions regarding her needs. The coach might have supported Ms. Munoz's preference and comfort in

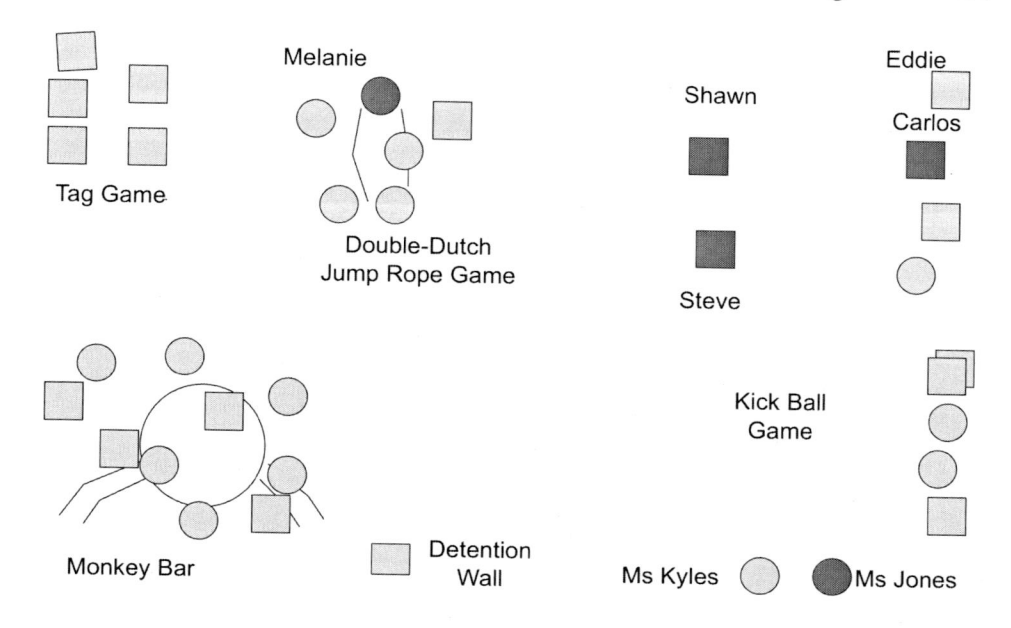

Figure 6.2. Postintervention narrative drawn by Carlos with a "Be Nice to Me" Sign on His Back.

speaking Spanish, while also encouraging her to participate in English as a Second Language (ESL) classes to facilitate her current transition. The coach might have known about a Hispanic domestic violence group or other cultural support groups. Brent also noticed that 11-year-old Elena seemed isolated from peers when he observed her in the school cafeteria and halls. After talking with her about her concerns, he successfully arranged through the school nurse for her to participate in the school's peer mentoring program with an older Hispanic female student.

CONDUCTING A POSTINTERVENTION DAS NARRATIVE ANALYSIS. Figure 6.2 shows Carlos' DAS playground drawing near the end of Brent's individual, group, family, and systems' interventions. Although some of those interventions overlapped in time, the entire intervention period covered ten weeks. Brent's work can be classified as early intervention, because Carlos' referral included early warning issues such as social isolation and the negative effects of PTSD from family violence. Figure 6.2 indicates positive changes that occurred in Carlos' situation in terms of those referral issues, which were also documented through direct observations by Brent, Ms. Munoz, and

Carlos' teacher. Ms Jones indicated he seemed less on guard, had more positive informal interactions with classmates on the playground, and was more integrated into classroom activities with peers. She said Carlos seemed less afraid of her and responded well to her efforts to draw him out in the classroom. Carlos shared the following story regarding his DAS narrative in Figure 6.2, which also documented his progress.

Carlos' Postintervention Story About His Post DAS Narrative. Eddie and me are playing kick ball. We're buddies 'cause we like some of the same games. He gets around; I mean he plays all around the playground. I used to just play on the monkey bars with Eddie, but now I like kick ball too. My sign, you remember that? It says be nice to me. Just like when me and the other kids talk about what we're doing in our skills group. There's Steve, he's in charge of the kick ball game. All the kids do what he wants. He likes Eddie, so I guess, if I'm playing with Eddie maybe that means I'm okay with Steve. Me and Melanie are in the same reading group; we talk about the stories we read sometimes. She talked to me last week during kick ball; she said, "Not bad Carlos" 'cause the bell rang, and I still wasn't out. I don't have to watch Ms. Jones much 'cause I know when it's time to go in now. I try to answer when she calls on me in class.

Practice Skill: Using Power-Sharing Narrative Strategies in Community Settings

Practice Overview

Similar to education settings, community-based programs are appropriate environments for using power-sharing narrative strategies with youngsters in the six to 11 age range. Examples include the Boys and Girls Clubs; adult-child mentoring programs such as Big Brother and Big Sister; the Young Men's Christian Association (YMCA) and Young Women's Christian Association (YWCA); faith-based Christian Sunday School programs and Jewish Saturday School programs; youth transition programs; and cultural and family service centers.

An advantage of community settings is that the stigma often associated with academic problems is not an implicit part of their services. Therefore, youngsters may perceive those settings as more neutral than schools in terms of academics. This means community settings can address academic and other school-related issues as part of the more normative group development and socialization services they typically provide (Freeman, 2004). Moreover, those normative services are often provided in primary prevention programs, while allowing community settings to also either: (1) integrate early intervention and rehabilitation with their prevention services as needed, or (2) refer their participants to more specialized child serving agencies, such as intensive substance abuse, anger management, or child abuse treatment programs.

Practice Example

BACKGROUND INFORMATION. In one Boys and Girls Club in a middle income community, the staff received a two-year grant from a private foundation to: (1) increase literacy among the organizations' young consumers, and (2) prevent the development of community problems that were of concern to the young participants and their families. The project was required to integrate graphic art and computer technology methods into the design and operation of the participants' community prevention programs. Those programs were organized into two separate groups for boys and girls in the 10 to 12 year age range, some of whom were current participants in the organization. Project staff also recruited community members in the target age range who were not current participants to increase the project's diversity.

The 40 participants in the first year's project were predominantly Caucasian but included four African Americans, six Hispanic Americans, and two Asian Americans. The lessons learned from the first year's participants would be used to improve the project's effectiveness with its second-year participants. During the project's start-up period, the boys and girls were involved in separate team-building exercises to help them learn more about and bond with their group members. The two groups also identified the youth and community issues they wanted to address as part of the project's prevention efforts.

Graduate graphic arts and computer technology students from a local university helped participants to identify creative communication methods, prevention messages, and desktop printing and marketing strategies for their prevention projects. A male recreation therapist and male social worker facilitated the boys' group, while a female community psychologist and female outreach worker facilitated the girls' group. Facilitators kept participants on target with their goals and tasks in weekly meetings, and helped to manage conflicts and decisionmaking, including the prevention issue(s) and population selected for the projects. They also coordinated the participants' collaborative tasks with community partners focused on the design and implementation of their prevention projects, and handled the foundation's grant-related paper work requirements.

THE NARRATIVE PREVENTION STRATEGIES IMPLEMENTED BY THE BOYS' GROUP. The boys' group selected prevention of prescription drug use and abuse as their community issue. They targeted youngsters in their age range who participated in two other community programs, the Boy Scouts and a YMCA summer camp. They decided to design a graphic novel in a short story format involving a 16-year-old superhero, named Pill Boy (see Table 6.1: under Primarily Verbal: and under #2e: Coconstructed narrative by a peer group). They addressed the grant's literacy requirements in three ways: By coconstructing their graphic novel as a group, involving the target population in read-ins during their community prevention sessions, and distributing their graphic novel to other youngsters who did not participate in the prevention program.

The following narrative segment illustrates how facilitators used the group process to help members coconstruct their graphic novel, plan and make group decisions, and increase their resistance to prescription drug use based on understanding and integrating their projects' prevention messages. The group facilitators were Dennis, the recreation therapist, and Michael, the social worker.

Group Process and Narrative Segment From the Graphic Short Story Designed by the Boys' Group. Michael said, "Let's pick up where we left off in our last meeting. We were trying to decide how Pill Boy would know when some kid is using prescription drugs. Shawn, you said you'd done some thinking about that part of our story—what'd you come up with?" "Well," Shawn explained, "if Pill Boy had super hearing powers, he'd hear anytime a kid opened up a pill box." Richie laughed out loud, "That's stupid Shawn; how could Pill Boy do that?" Michael reminded Richie, "You brought up a good point, but you know our rules about name calling; you can disagree with Shawn's ideas without attacking him." "Ok, I'm sorry Shawn, I shouldn't have said that." Dennis asked, "What super powers do you think Pill Boy should have Richie?" "Well, I guess he could have super hearing powers," Richie said thoughtfully, "but don't we have to explain how he got his powers?" "You're right, Richie. Shawn, do you or any of the rest of the group have ideas about how we should explain that in our story?" "Maybe Pill Boy got an electric shock when he climbed up a light pole one day. We could say the doctors saved his life, but he was different after that—like he had super hearing and sight. Yeah, and he could read minds too. That's how he'd know when a kid was getting into pills," Tyrone said excitedly. Michael said, "Should we write it just like that? Or should we say he. . . ?"

Later, Dennis asked, "Before we end our session, whose turn is it to read what we wrote today?" Scott raised his hand and said, "It's my turn." Dennis handed him the typed page they'd just finished writing, along with a drawing of Pill Boy that the graphic art student had helped them to design for their book's cover. Scott read the page Dennis gave him. "Nobody had heard of Pill Boy before 2008. When the EMTs—emergency medical technicians—took him to the hospital after the accident, he was just plain Stephen Nichols. He was a regular kid. But when he woke up in the hospital, the doctors said he'd been shocked by an electric wire on a pole he had climbed to take a picture of a long suspension bridge. The doctors didn't know he could hear and see them talking together before they got into the elevator on another floor, on their way to his room. He'd even read one doctor's mind, who was angry about a kid who died after taking his mother's prescription pills. Stephen tried to tell his best friends, Jeff and Roger, about his new super powers when they visited him in the hospital, but they laughed and looked at him real weird. He wouldn't make that mistake again. But maybe there was something he could do the next time a kid got into his mom's prescription pills. First, he'd take them to the cemetery so they could see what happened to the kid who died from taking his mom's pills. Then he'd take them to Red River Substance Abuse Treatment for teenagers so they could find out from other kids. . . ."

THE NARRATIVE PREVENTION STRATEGIES IMPLEMENTED BY THE GIRLS' GROUP. The girls' group focused on a different area of prevention. They addressed prevention of violence against girls in the nine to 12-year age range. Group members believed nine-year-old girls were also at risk for violence and decided to include them in their prevention program. The members were also concerned about low self-esteem in girls but concluded they could address that issue in conjunction with their violence prevention focus. They coconstructed a script for a play about violence prevention that they presented to students from two community middle schools (see Table 6.1: Under Both Verbal and Nonverbal; and under #6a: Use a script as small group members to act out scenes in a play).

The girls addressed the grant's literacy requirements by: coconstructing their script, memorizing the dialogue and acting out the play's scenes, designing posters to advertise the play in artwork and dialogue, designing marquee banners to market their play's violence prevention message, and providing audiences with written copies of the play's script. The facilitators used group process to help the members edit a draft of their play and begin planning their poster advertisements. Anne, a community psychologist, and Meredith, an outreach worker, facilitated the girls' group in the following segment.

Group Process and Narrative Segment From the Play Coconstructed by the Girls' Group. Anne explained they would start editing their play during the current meeting, in order to revise any dialogue, behavior, or other actions that didn't seem natural for the play's characters. She asked Tammie, a group member, to read the part of their script that began on page four. Tammie read: "Heather walked slowly toward the bed in Stephanie's room, and then plopped down on the bed, sighing loudly. She covered her face with her hands and shook her head." *Heather:* "I don't know what to do. Shawn wants to be with me every minute of every day. He says I don't need any other friends but him. Last night, he started shouting at me like he wanted to hit me. He was so loud I was scared my parents could hear him from the living room. He and I were upstairs in the den. I don't like bringing you into this, but I don't know who else to talk to!" *Stephanie* (She walks quickly over to the bed and sits next to Heather and puts her arm around her shoulder): "Were you scared? Did he really hit you or did you just think he was going to? But even if he didn't hit you, Heather, shouting at someone is a part of violence. You know—it's emotional violence." *Heather* (Standing up and walking over to the window quickly): "What makes you say that, Stephanie? That isn't really true, is it?" (Heather turns away from the window and faces Stephanie.) *Stephanie:* Well, last week I was listening to a CD by . . ."

Meredith said, "Let's stop there, Tammie. Would Stephanie really say 'emotional violence'; what do some of you think about that?" "I don't think Stephanie would say that," Leslie explained, "maybe she'd say it was verbal abuse or it was hating on Heather." Sharon said, "Definitely not emotional violence, and Heather wouldn't tell Stephanie about Shawn's behavior unless she made her agree to not tell anyone else." Holly added, "I think one of our posters should show how a boy shouting and getting in a girl's face is still violence. Some kids think it's only violence if a guy hits or kicks a girl, or chokes her. But we need a poster that shows how to tell when the hitting kind of violence happens too."

ANALYZING THE OUTCOMES OF THE TWO PREVENTION PROGRAMS. As part of the prevention project's evaluation, members of the boys' and girls' groups wrote letters to the foundation about the lessons they learned from their participation. This narrative strategy is similar to the letter narrative described in Chapter 1, and it is one of the improvisational play strategies in Table 6.1 (Under Both Verbal and Nonverbal; and under #3d: Create a new narrative about a favorite event or experience).

The boys' letter narrative highlighted the sense of power they developed from researching prescription drug abuse online, and using what they learned to educate themselves and write their graphic novel. Their letter said the novel and their main character Pill Boy helped their target audience to listen and learn about the dangers of prescription drug abuse without being preached to. The girls' letter clarified that their most valuable lesson was about the team spirit they developed from the experience, which increased their self-esteem and belief in themselves. Another valuable lesson was what the girls learned and then taught to their target audience: The different types of violence to watch for and steps girls should take to prevent violence and to protect themselves when it occurs. Finally, both boys and girls noted they had opportunities to practice their reading and writing skills, and as the girls said, "It wasn't bad at all!"

Practice Skill: Using Power-Sharing Narrative Strategies with Preschool Children

Practice Overview

Practice skills from the previous sections, for school-age children in education and community settings, should be adapted before they are used with preschool age children. Adaptations are necessary because the developmental needs of children from three to five years of age are different from those of older children. For example, preschool age children need and should be encouraged to explore their environments in order to gain control over them. This task helps them to develop a sense of initiative and purpose. However, some authors assume children who seek too much control over their environments or who receive too much adult disapproval, may develop guilt and become aggressive, as the following example illustrates (Csak, 2002).

Practice Example

BACKGROUND INFORMATION. Fatima was a five-year-old girl in a therapeutic day treatment program for abused and neglected children. Her family emigrated from the African country of Somalia five years previously. The family included Fatima's mother and stepfather, Mr. and Ms. Iman, and an older brother, Hassan, who was six years old. A local children's hospital referred the family to Children's Protective Services and to the therapeutic day program for medical neglect after they did not follow through on Hassan's treatment for hypoglycemia. The children seemed out of control during most clinic appointments, for example, jumping off chairs and throwing toys at their mother. She seemed passive and did not discipline them during clinic visits. The parents were very involved in the Muslim community where they received much of their support.

CONDUCTING INITIAL FAMILY CONTACTS. Mr. Iman refused to participate in the treatment program's intake interview for the parents after he learned an interpreter was included. He did not agree that one was needed, because he spoke English, although he preferred to speak his native language. He said he could not provide transportation for his wife to attend parent meetings once Fatima was enrolled in the program. Mr. Iman explained he drove a cab for a living and could not take time off from work. He did agree to participate in parent meetings. Ms. Iman was not employed outside the home.

Once she was enrolled, Fatima was transported to the treatment program each day by a worker from a resettlement center, who also transported Ms. Iman to the program's parent meetings. In her first session with the parents, Stephanie Baker, a child psychologist assigned to work with them, identified three challenges: (1) the parents' Somalia cultural view was that problems were nonexistent unless they interfered with everyday life; (2) their Muslim dietary practices affected their follow through on nutrition recommendations for Hassan's hypoglycemia; and (3) Ms. Imam's passivity in child rearing and during parent meetings was a gender role prescribed and supported by her culture (Grey & Hastings, 2005; Guerin, Guerin, Diriye, & Yates, 2004).

USING NARRATIVE POWER-SHARING, CULTURAL, AND OTHER INTERVENTIONS WITH FATIMA. Although the Imans did not agree that Fatima's behavior was a problem, they did agree on a goal to help her complete the treatment program as quickly as possible. To meet their goal and to be consistent with the program's treatment approach, Stephanie helped Fatima practice some of the structured classroom tasks she was learning. Those tasks enhanced Fatima's cognitive, emotional, and physical development, such as teaching her English words for the parts of her body and matching them with the same words in her African language.

In addition, Stephanie used a culturally-centered approach in individual sessions with Fatima for her behavioral issues and other psychosocial needs. For instance, she began by using one of the nonverbal, power-sharing, narrative strategies in Table 6.1, such as observing her client play with a doll family with ethnic features that resembled Fatima's family. Those observations helped identify the main repetitive elements of Fatima's play narrative with the doll family (see Table 6.1: Under Communicates Primarily Nonverbally; and under #1b: Observe Child Playing with Doll House and Family and Interpret Observations) (O'Connor, 2005; St Amour, 2003).

Fatima's Repetitive Doll Family Play Narrative as Observed by Stephanie. Fatima started each session playing with the adult male and boy dolls. Her play with them involved the adult male doll telling the adult female and girl dolls what to do, including "Fix the food," "Go over there," "Stop talking," or "Find my paper!" He also announced to them what he planned to do, such as "I'm going to work," I'm going to the mosque," or "I'm going fishing." During those times, Fatima would hold the adult male doll near the female adult and girl dolls, where she had placed them on the floor in front of her or to the side of her. Sometimes the boy doll also told the females what to do, "Stop playing with my toys" (to the girl doll), or "No, no, no, I won't" (to the adult female doll). Fatima would play with the mother and daughter dolls near the end of her sessions when Stephanie reminded her the session would soon end. In that part of her play, the female dolls were less active than the male dolls. She would hold the mother doll and tell her to, "Be good." Sometimes she'd have the daughter doll throw toys or furniture, but she seldom had her talk.

Stephanie used her observations and conclusions from Fatima's doll family play narrative to identify several other power-sharing interventions for her work with this client. One strategy involved reading Fatima a story about an African girl her age who was also in transition (Hinman, 2003). These reading segments were brief to enhance Fatima's learning. The book illustrated how the character explored and learned about her new environment by changing how she responded to her family's cultural expectations (see Table 6.1: Under Communicates Primarily Verbally; and under #2a: Share/Read and Discuss a Story Involving a Getting Better Narrative).

Stephanie then discussed the story segment with Fatima before she played with her doll family each session, asking her questions about what happened in the particular story segment. For example, she asked, "What did Yulia do when her mother said . . . ," and then gave Fatima positive feedback for her answers. The questions and answers highlighted for Fatima what the character did differently in the story and how what she learned made her smile more, and led her parents to give her more play time. By giving Fatima opportunities to apply what she learned about appropriate behavior as she played with her doll family, Stephanie helped her transition from communicating mostly nonverbally to using both verbal and nonverbal communication.

Three other power-sharing strategies were used to enhance Fatima's development. Stephanie used preselected Somalia feeling words on cards she asked Mr. Iman to write, along with the English translations, and had Fatima demonstrate those feelings in the mirror (see Table 6.1: Under Communicates Primarily Verbally; and under #5c: Identify Feelings in the Mirror with Select Emotion Cards). She also had Fatima tell a story about her favorite toy, a puzzle she received from her mother's parents in Africa. In some sessions, she and Fatima sang African and American songs together and then talked about the songs' words (Sawyer, 1997) (see Table 6.1: Under Communicates Both Verbally and Nonverbally; and under 3a: Show and Tell a Story About a Favorite Toy; and under 3b: Interpret a Favorite Song). These strategies helped Fatima to express her feelings and behave more appropriately, while providing her with developmental opportunities to explore and gain some control over her environment.

USING NARRATIVE, POWER-SHARING, AND SYSTEMS-RELATED INTERVENTIONS WITH THE PARENTS. Involving Mr. Iman in Fatima's mirror work, by having him provide feeling cards in the family's language, started the trust-building process. Then Stephanie helped the parents to enhance their support system, which was already one of their strengths. She collaborated with them in identifying and using a cultural coach, a Muslim nutrition educator who worked at the resettlement center's medical clinic. The parents trusted her to help them identify where their religious dietary practices and Hassan's recommended medical regimen for hypoglycemia were compatible. That step encouraged them to follow his medical regimen in those compatible areas, and increased their compliance.

The parent meetings encouraged parents to share their concerns and solutions about the day treatment program, and to provide peer support to each other. They also shared narratives about their sources of cultural support and stress; and they worked at staying updated on their children's progress in the program. This individual and group process helped the Imans to feel empowered and important in Fatima's progress. When she completed the program seven months later, her social behavior and development were more age-appropriate, and the Iman's expectations and support for both children were more appropriate as well. The severity of Fatima's developmental needs and the parents' challenges in meeting Hassan's medical requirements indicated a need for intensive treatment, rather than early intervention services. In the process, Stephanie, Fatima's therapist, and other staff gained valuable knowledge and skills for understanding and working more effectively with recently immigrated families, especially African families.

Conclusion

This chapter's discussion draws upon Chapter 1, which clarifies how narratives emerge at critical transition points in people's life spans, according to principle #1 and life span development theory. This chapter illustrates how the young clients' narratives emerged naturally during individual and group play. Carlos' DAS playground narrative emerged related to his development stage and his family's relocation, facilitated by the school social worker's questions. The power-sharing letter narrative strategy used as part of the Boys and Girls Club's evaluation also draws upon Chapter 1, where that strategy was introduced. It helped the participants to narrate, as a peer group, what had been a meaningful and empowering developmental experience in their young lives.

This chapter's third example and discussion about preschool children draws upon Chapter 5 and Principle 5. Fatima's example demonstrates how practitioners can elicit low currency narratives from culturally-different clients, the focus of Principle 5. In this case, however, the use of developmentally-appropriate play therapy with a mostly nonverbal child was necessary for helping her to play out her family narrative with a culturally-relevant doll family. Her developmental and social progress demonstrate how children's power and voices can be enhanced through the emergence of their narratives.

REFERENCES

Bernal, B., & Saez-Santiago, E. (2006). Culturally centered psychosocial interventions. *Journal of Community Psychology, 34,* 121–132.

Chenfield, M. B. (2002). Once upon a time. The end! *Language Arts, 79,* 332–26.

Csak, N. L. B. (2002). What's important when you're six? Valuing children's oral stories. *Language Arts, 79,* 488–497.

Del Valle, P. R., McEachern, A. G., & Chambers, H. D. (2001). Using social stories with austistic children. *Journal of Poetry, 14,* 187–197.

Daiute, C., & Buteau. E. (2002). Writing for their lives: Children's narrative supports for physical and psychological well-being. In S. J. LePore, & J. M. Smythe (Eds.), *The writing cure: How expressive writing promotes health and emotional well-being.* Washington, DC: American Psychological Association.

Daiute, C., Buteau, E., & Rawlins, C. (2001). Social-relational wisdom: Developmental diversity in children's written narratives about social conflict. *Narrative Inquiry, 11,* 277–306.

Fein, G. G., Ardila-Rey, A. E., & Groth, L. A. (2000). The narrative connection: Stories and literacy. In K. A. Roskos & J. F. Christie (Eds.), *Play and literacy in early childhood* (pp. 27–43). Mahwah, NJ: Lawrence Erlbaum Associates.

Freeman, E. M. (March 2004). Basic principles of effective narrative practice. Workshop presentation. Kansas City, MO: The Social Work Coalition and Social Work Leaders in Health Care.

Grey, I. M. & Hastings, R. P. (2005). Evidence-based practices in intellectual disability and behavior disorders. *Current Opinion in Psychiatry, 18,* 469–475.

Guerin, B., Guerin, P., Diriye, R. O., & Yates, S. (2004). Somali conceptions and expectations concerning mental health: Some guidelines for mental health professionals. *New Zealand Journal of Play Therapy, 33,* 59–67.

Hinman, C. (2003). Multicultural considerations in the delivery of play therapy services. *International Journal of Play Therapy, 12,* 107–122.

Leukefeld, C. G., Godlaski, T., Clark, J., Brown, C., & Hays, L. (2002). Structured stories: Reinforcing social skills in rural substance abusers. *Health and Social Work, 27,* 213–218.

McCabe, A. (1997). Developmental and cross-cultural aspects of children's narration. In M. Bamberg (Ed.), *Narrative development: Six approaches* (pp. 137–174). Mahwah, NJ: LEA.

O'Connor, K. (2005). Addressing diversity issues in play therapy. *Professional Psychology: Research and Practice, 36,* 566–573.

Rivett, M., Howarth, E., & Gordon, H. (2006). 'Watching the stairs': Towards an evidence-based practice in work with child witnesses of domestic violence. *Clinical Child Psychology and Psychiatry, 11,* 103–125.

Sawyer. R. K. (1997). *Pretend play as improvisation: Conversation in the preschool classroom.* Norwood, NJ: Lawrence Erlbaum Associates.

Sawyer, R. K. (2002). Improvisation and narrative. *Narrative Inquiry, 12,* 319–349.

St. Amour, M. J. (2003). Connecting children's stories to children's literature: Meeting diversity needs. *Early Childhood Education Journal, 31,* 47–51.

Toth, S. I., Cicchetti, D., Macfie, J., & Emde, R. N. (1997). Representations of self and other in the narratives of neglected, physically abused, and sexually abused preschoolers. *Development and Psychopathology, 9,* 781–786.

Chapter 7

ASSISTING YOUTHS IN EXPLORING CHOICES AND CONSEQUENCES AT CRITICAL MOMENTS THROUGH THEIR LIFE STORIES AND TRANSITION NARRATIVES

> When I returned from the inpatient psych ward, it was just like when my brother Anthony died three months ago. Nobody at school looked at me or talked to me. It was like I wasn't there, like I was a ghost . . . !
>
> —Bill T.

Bill, the teenager in the above excerpt, clearly struggled to successfully narrate his painful transition experience, similar to the struggles of other youngsters his age. Those experiences may be related to voluntary or involuntary relocations from their homes to institutions and the reverse. Their transitions can also include developmental passages from puberty to adolescence and from the teenage years to young adulthood (Coulter, 2000; Gair & Camilleri, 2003). Society views some youngsters' reactions to those experiences as attention-seeking and immature, which often increases the stigma teens may feel. However, some researchers normalize such transitions by describing them as filled with critical moments that have biographical significance to the young people who experience them (Thomson, Bell, Holland, Henderson, McGrellis, & Sharpe, 2002).

These transitions also have significance for narrative and other forms of practice with adolescents. For example, there is tremendous diversity in the transitions that youngsters experience, when they experience them, and whether or not those transitions are related to specific developmental issues such as identity, career development, peer relations, and separation from their family of origin (Freeman, 1992, 2004). Moreover, developmental and other transitional differences can affect the life choices adolescents make and the related consequences they experience, in the present and in the future (Thomson et al., 2002). Narrative strategies are useful for addressing these issues of diversity among teenagers, because those strategies focus attention on the specific world views, values, and developmental issues that are of concern to each client.

Practitioners often question how to provide effective developmental- and narrative-related services to youngsters during this period of intense changes. Chapter 7 addresses this practice question and others by defining how critical moments in teenagers' transition narratives impact upon their lives. The role of those narratives in the construction and revision of adolescents' life narratives is clarified. The chapter also illustrates the use of developmentally-sensitive narrative skills to engage and support meaningful change in partnership with adolescents, such as poetry, hip hop therapy, short novel development, and structured social skills stories. Two practice examples help to illustrate those skills with young and older teens, in short- and long-term out of home care, and involving mandated and voluntary services.

Practice Skill: Providing Developmentally-Sensitive Transition Narrative Services to Adolescents

Practice Overview

Thomson et al. (2002) contend that youth transitions are nonlinear and very diverse. Those individual factors often place adolescents on different pathways to adulthood. Some pathways make adulthood more accessible to youngsters and can lead them gradually to a more mature functional level. Other pathways can make adulthood less accessible and therefore may result in youngsters' arrested development or regressions in their functioning (Thomson et al., 2002). Adolescents' transition narratives capture the dynamic relationship between individual factors that affect their transitions, the choices that are presented to them during critical transition moments, and the consequences they experience as a result of the choices they make.

Since the transition narratives of teenagers are a type of single event narrative, as described in Chapter 4, they are directly linked to adolescents' life narratives. That chapter defined single event narratives as those "... constructed from one significant experience or event" (Freeman, 2004). Such events are often related to relocations and developmental passages, as noted in this chapter's introduction.

In contrast, life narratives were defined in Chapter 4 as, "An accumulation of critical moments in people's lives which viewed together provide continuity over time" (Thomson et al., 2002). Life narratives affect how adolescents experience and find meaning in their transition narratives. In turn, the latter help youngsters to establish, reexamine, and, sometimes, revise their life narratives. The following practice example illustrates how to use developmentally-sensitive narrative skills to help adolescents to unlock their transition narratives. A second example in a later section illustrates the intricate process of helping adolescents to connect their transition and life narratives.

Practice Example

BACKGROUND INFORMATION. Molly Nogata, a 13-year-old Japanese-Filipina adolescent and her twin brother, Mike, live on the West Coast. Their father died several months ago after serving as their mother's primary caretaker for over ten years due to her multiple sclerosis (MS). When he died, their mother's MS worsened and she and the twins went to live with her sister. Molly's father was Japanese and the mother is Filipino. Over the years, there were numerous family and cultural conflicts between their two extended families. Those conflicts were exacerbated after Mr. Nogata died and extended family members on both sides wanted custody of Mike and Molly.

However, it became clear that Ms. Nogata's health needs and Mike's behavior problems at school and in the community were more than their maternal aunt, Kara, could handle. Mike was referred to juvenile court for vandalism and for not attending school. As a result, the court then placed the twins with their paternal grandparents in a relative foster care arrangement. Mike was being assessed for a possible placement in either a group home or a residential treatment facility. Molly was receiving counseling from a local 60-day inpatient addictions program for an eating disorder and alcoholism. The program specialized in treatment for adolescents with co-occurring disorders. It also had a one-year aftercare component. This author served as a clinical consultant for that program.

Ms. Nogata's doctor told the family her condition would likely continue to get worse. She had been depressed since her husband died and was in a wheelchair by then. Her sister provided around-the-clock assistance for her activities of daily living. Therefore, the relative foster care plan for Molly and Mike was expected to be long term, pending the outcomes of the court's assessment of Mike's needs. The grandparents owned a restaurant and believed having the twins work with family members in the restaurant would help to resolve Molly and Mike's problems.

USING TRANSITION-FOCUSED POETRY WITH CLIENTS. Although Molly was involved in group sessions with peers related to her addiction problems, the program also provided her with individual sessions. Staff who facilitated client group sessions and family sessions used a combination of cognitive behavioral and family systems interventions (Chen & Davenport, 2005; Laird, 2000; Rosen & Lang, 2005). They also used solution-focused narrative naming, unpacking, and coherence questions to help clients name unacknowledged aspects of their narratives, unpack or provide more details about the narratives' context, and clarify the meaning of their narratives (see Chapters 3 and 4 for more discussion about these three types of narrative questions).

In their individual sessions, staff often used additional narrative strategies, such as song writing and poetry analysis, to work on common and unique developmental issues with clients. Therefore, the consultant suggested that the therapist assigned to work with Molly, Patty Fitzgerald, ask the client to bring in a written copy or CD of her favorite song. When Molly said she did not have a favorite song, the consultant recommended that Patty use poetry as an alternative strategy. Patty searched for poems that adolescents might identify with and, based on the consultant's encouragement, decided to include Haiku poems, one of the most important forms of traditional Japanese poetry. In a subsequent session, Patty asked Molly to select two Haiku poems from a group that she had asked the client to look over.

When Molly asked how she should select the two poems, Patty said Molly was free to determine the reasons for selecting the poems. A main goal in using narrative interventions is to provide opportunities for clients such as Molly to exercise power in their lives. Therefore, Patty was careful not to usurp Molly's power by telling her how to select the two poems. She also assured Molly there was not a right or wrong way to make her selections. Patty had preselected a group of 10 poems from the internet that were written and illustrated by boys and girls ranging in age from eight to 15 years. She included age and gender differences in how she preselected poems to ensure that they would be developmentally-sensitive to Molly's individual needs. After thinking for a while, Molly selected two separate poems written by Akihiro Yamada (age 15), and Saori Yamada (age 11) respectively (http://homepage2.nifty.com/haiku-eg/gardenE345.htm):

The Two Transition-Focused Haiku Poems Selected by Molly:

A cherry petal
falls
in front of the grave

each insect
enjoys
its own summer

HELPING MOLLY UNLOCK HER SELECTED TRANSITION HAIKU POEMS. Traditional Japanese Haiku poems are ". . . a 17-syllable verse form consisting of three metrical units of 5, 7, and 5 syllables" (Nishimoto & Shimizo, 1999). Traditional Haiku also includes a seasonal word or Kireji, to denote the present season or weather. The Kireji can be used at the end of any of the three lines to give that line a definitive ending. Each Haiku poem is expected to include a descriptive image, emotions or feelings, and "a surprise that wakes us up" (Donegan, 2003). Western and other nontraditional forms of Haiku differ from traditional poems by including from 10 to 17 syllables in the three lines (Donegan, 2003).

Patty asked Molly to choose one of the above two poems and to talk about what it meant to her. Molly picked the second poem, and explained, "Even though summer is usually when everything blooms and gets greener and more alive, I don't have the energy I used to have before my father died. As soon as we got used to our aunt's house and her rules, me and Mike had to move to our grandparents' house!" Patty asked her to talk about what those rule changes were and how they affected her and Mike. Table 7.1 indicates some of the benefits of transition narratives, such as poetry, including negotiating new social experiences and identifying and managing critical moments (The

Table 7.1
SKILL: USING DEVELOPMENTALLY-SENSITIVE TRANSITION AND LIFE NARRATIVE STRATEGIES WITH ADOLESCENTS

The Benefits of Transition Narratives	*Practice Strategies Relevant to Transition Narratives*
Opportunities for Adolescents Involve:	*Music Therapy:*
1. Negotiating New Social Experiences	1. Hip Hop Therapy
2. Identifying and Managing Critical Moments	2. Song Writing
3. Making Choices and Learning From Related Consequences	3. Dance Therapy
Outcomes for Adolescents Include:	*Bibliotherapy:*
1. Empowerment	1. Poetry Therapy
2. Skill Development	2. Structured Social Skills Stories
3. Epiphanies: Leading directly to short novel development and life narrative construction and revisions	3. Short Novel Development (related to transition narratives) a. Chapter 1: Elaborate on the old character and story b. Chapter 2: Practice a new character and story c. Chapter 3: Author/narrate new "Getting Better" story and give the novel a title (linked to life narrative construction)

Benefits of Transition Narratives: Opportunities for Adolescents: #1 and #2).

It is apparent from Molly's reaction to the second poem that she had experienced a critical moment, perhaps precipitated by the series of moves since her father's death. As Molly told Patty, "Everything changed when my father died. That's probably why I don't have much energy. I spend most of my time worrying about what's going to happen to me and Mike, can we stay together or will we be separated?" Critical moments in the lives of adolescents invariably lead to what

Thomson et al. (2002) refer to as epiphanies (see Table 7.1: The Benefits of Transition Narratives: Outcomes for Adolescents: #3).

Epiphanies are major insights teenagers experience about their lives, which can push them toward and help them manage major turning points in their lives. Molly also said, "Even though Mike and I are twins, we're different like the Haiku says, we each have to live through our own individual summer." Molly agreed she could not control whether Mike went to a group home, only her own efforts to stay in touch with him. This was an area that Patty then helped her client plan for as needed in terms of specific ways she could have ongoing contacts with Mike.

Molly also acknowledged that self-medicating with alcohol and food had not helped; it had only made things worse. She asked Patty, "Does the second Haiku mean something good, like hope, can come from bad things, like a cherry blossom falling in front of my father's grave?" Patty answered, "Yes," and wondered if this was the reason Molly chose that particular poem. Molly said her group sessions helped her to understand her individual sessions with Patty. Those group sessions included discussions about finding ways to cope with difficult times that could enhance her recovery, and believing in the possibility of change or hope. Patty reminded Molly that recovery also meant letting go of old ways of coping that could lead to relapse, such as alcohol addiction and food binging and purging.

COORDINATING ADDICTIONS COUNSELING WITH FAMILY AND SIBLING GROUP INTERVENTIONS: Near the end of Molly's 60-day inpatient recovery program, the court completed Mike's assessment and determined that he should be placed in a group home for a minimum of one year. At that point, Molly was transitioning into her program's one year aftercare component. Staff from the inpatient recovery program including Patty, and those from the aftercare component, juvenile court, and the group home Mike would be entering met to establish a coordination plan. Molly and Mike, their grandparents, and their mother's sister also participated in the planning conference. Their plans included quarterly meetings between the service providers to monitor Molly and Mike's progress, and coordinate services to them. The planned services included family systems counseling with Mike, Molly and their aunt and grandparents. The goal was to address the family's grief over Mr. Nogata's death and his wife's decreased functioning due to MS, the children's relocations and placements, and the family conflicts.

The plan also included sibling counseling for Mike and Molly to support their desire to stay connected in spite of their relocations and transitions, and to address their common and different developmental needs. Molly's recovery and aftercare services were to be coordinated with Mike's social skills and milieu services to facilitate their separate transitions back to their grandparents' home. The group home used structured social skills stories as part of their services to address many of their clients' family disruptions and relocations, and normal developmental issues (see Table 7.1: Practice Strategies: Bibliotherapy: #2 Structured Social Skills Stories). Luekefeld, Godlaski, Clark, Brown, and Hays (2002) define such stories as "narratives that target a specific skill to help clients therapeutically discuss problems and individualize possible solutions" (p. 215). These stories do not have an ending in order to leave the protagonist in situations where things can go in more than one direction, depending on the decision a group or individual make during their discussion (Freeman, (1992). Clients are then expected to apply the lessons learned from their discussions to their own narratives and situations.

In addition to this coordination planning and direct services, the service providers could have included other narrative interventions in their services to Molly, Mike, and their family members. For example, Tyson (2002) notes that hip hop therapy is both a developmentally and culturally sensitive narrative intervention for adolescents in transition. Other authors support this assumption, indicating hip hop is the most popular form of music among youth including country music (Fried, 1999); and that it transcends all race and social class differences among youth (Chappell, 2001). The goals in using this type narrative intervention with youth such as Mike and Molly are to enhance their social skills, self-concept, and peer relationships. Young clients can be asked to analyze their selected and/or favorite hip hop songs, or to analyze songs selected by the practitioner (see Table 7.1: Practice Strategies: Music Therapy, #1).

Practice Skill: Integrating Individual, Group, and Systems Strategies for Transition and Life Narrative Work with Adolescents

Practice Overview

As noted previously, the practice example in this section illustrates how practitioners can connect adolescents' transition and life narratives and help to change relevant systems. The example involves Ed Stewart, a social worker in a local mental health center. Based on a Memorandum of Understanding (MOU) between the center and an affluent suburban school district, the center agreed to out-station a social worker and psychologist in Yates High School as a pilot service. Ed and Alana Ridley, the psychologist, accept staff referrals, do social assessments and psychological evaluations on students, and provide individual and group counseling to them and their families. They also provide follow-up support services to students who are in transition between the district's regular schools and its alternative school; and inpatient psychiatric hospitals; juvenile detention; and out of home placements such as foster care, group homes, and residential treatment facilities.

The MOU was established because the center and school district were mutually concerned about those transitional students who were falling through the cracks between the education, juvenile justice, child welfare, primary health care, and mental health systems. The school district has two new Charter Schools for business and technology and for the arts. Those schools have attempted to enroll more economically and culturally diverse students from surrounding school districts, which include a rural education cooperative and an urban school district. The following practice example involves an older teen, returning to school from a short-term psychiatric hospitalization, which was voluntary; in contrast to the previous example.

Practice Example

BACKGROUND INFORMATION. Bill Tuesday is a 16-year-old Caucasian student at Yates High, the charter school for the arts. His family formerly lived in the area of the rural education cooperative from which Yates and another charter school are currently drawing students. Bill lives with his two older brothers and their parents. Another brother, Anthony, died three months ago, possibly from a suicide. Bill has recently returned to Yates after an inpatient hospitalization for depression, as noted in his narrative excerpt at the beginning of this chapter. Ed decided to observe Bill informally for a few days before approaching him to discuss his transition back to the school and his recent hospitalization. Within the first week of his return, Ed observed Bill in the following school situations:

1. Bill and two other students argued when he tried to post an announcement for a meeting involving GLBT students (gay, lesbian, bisexual, and transgendered).
2. His signed election write-in petition for a student office was thrown out by the student council.
3. He participated appropriately in a health class session on HIV/AIDS awareness and prevention that was facilitated by Ed and Alana.

After the HIV/AIDS session, Bill asked if he could come by Ed's office the next day to discuss an issue he was concerned about. During their meeting, Bill talked about feeling excluded and uninvolved in the school. He wanted to consult Ed, but emphasized he did not need counseling. He asked about how to make Yates High more open to uninvolved students, since he felt students in the more popular clubs and groups ran the school. Bill mentioned his election write-in petition for school vice-president was thrown out because a deadline the council did not announce publicly had passed.

Ed asked Bill what his interaction had been like with those students before he was hospitalized. Bill said their interaction was not good previously, but it was worse since his return to school. When he tried to post his group meeting announcement, one of the students had referred to him as a "faggot and a nut case." Ed mentioned that he and Alana had several health class sessions scheduled on handling differences and the effects of bullying on students. He reminded Bill that the health class was mandatory, so many of the students Bill was concerned about would participate in those sessions. Ed asked if there were other examples when Bill felt he did not have power or had not been allowed to participate at school. Bill said yes, and then shared the following narrative with Ed:

Bill's Transition Narrative: Well, you probably mean like when I met with Mr. H., Mr. Harwell, the principal. That was before I went to Douglas, the psych hospital. Mr. H. tells all the students he has an open door policy. "Come see me any time; there's nothing too small for my desk. The buck stops here with Mr. H.," or so he says. So I went to see him about starting a newsletter; I thought he'd at least listen. But as I was talking to him, he kept looking over my shoulder. His eyes never looked at me directly; they darted around like he was thinking about everything but me. I was telling him how important the newsletter could be to students who weren't in the regular clubs and organizations, but he didn't react or answer, just nodded his head as if to say, "Hurry up, I've got a lot to do." So I asked him what he thought about my idea. He sort of took a deep breath, and moved his shoulders back. I thought I hadn't explained my idea clearly enough, but that wasn't it. He said, "Look Tuesday, our newspaper here at Yates is for all the students." Then he said, "That's all, get back to class," still not looking at me directly. I couldn't argue, because he wasn't listening to me anyway. It was like I wasn't there, didn't matter or count at all. It probably would've been better if I'd taken a couple of other students with me, but I haven't really connected with any students at Yates. I felt totally alone, like when my older brother Anthony died this year. He was my brother Josh's twin. We were living in Rennsalier then, out in the county. We knew all the kids. Anthony started running with kids that got into trouble all the time—doing meth and other things. But he promised Josh he wasn't doing drugs. Josh found him hanging in the basement one night; we think it was an accident. My parents had the funeral and we never talked about what happened. I went back to school two days after his funeral. I didn't know what else to do. Nobody at school said anything; I guess I was invisible then too. One boy who clowns around a lot, put his hands around his neck and made his eyes get real big, like he was strangling. I didn't let on it bothered me. We moved here to Grandview after a few months, to get away from Rennsalier. That town didn't feel friendly any more.

Narrative Bibliotherapy and Other Narrative Systems Strategies

ELABORATING ON THE OLD CHARACTER AND STORY. Ed said Bill's narrative revealed several threads that made it difficult to follow his narrative. He wondered if Bill also got lost in his narrative sometimes because of those threads. Bill agreed he often lost sight of his purpose in trying to make changes in his life. As a result, when he tried to get elected to a student office and start a newsletter for uninvolved kids,

Bill said it felt like "running into another brick wall!" Ed suggested they use Bill's metaphor to clear up some of the mystery about what happened when he tried to make changes.

He said they could begin by elaborating on Bill's old brick wall story, the first step in short novel development listed in Table 7.1 (Under Bibliotherapy: #3: Short Novel Development, Chapter 1, Elaborate on the Old Character and Story). Freeman (2004) calls this first step turning up the lights in order to make parts of a story that are in the shadows more visible. Table 7.1 also indicates that Bill is missing some of the benefits of the transition narrative he shared with Ed. Bill is negotiating new social experiences at Yates High, but he is experiencing difficulties in identifying and managing critical moments in his life, and in making positive choices (Under Opportunities for Adolescents: #1-3). Therefore, he is struggling with several negative consequences, such as not becoming involved in school and increasing his risk of depression. He has also been unable to experience some of the positive outcomes from transition experiences, including developing a sense of empowerment (Under Outcomes for Adolescents: #1-3).

To continue elaborating on Bill's old story, Ed asked him to name a character from literature or the movies whose role was like Bill's in his transition narrative. Bill said he was probably playing the role of the Lone Ranger, a character in an old television show he watched when he was a little kid. Like the Lone Ranger, Bill explained, he was trying to eliminate the wrongs and injustices at Yates High. Ed asked him, "Did the Lone Ranger ride alone?" Bill remembered then that the Lone Ranger had a sidekick named Tonto. Ed also asked Bill, "Do you remember how each episode of the Lone Ranger usually ended?" Bill said who ever helped the Lone Ranger to clean up the situation in the story would wave goodbye to him as he rode off into the sunset with Tonto. Bill looked thoughtful as he said, "That means I'm *not* doing what the Lone Ranger did; he wasn't working alone at all, unlike me!"

Ed's two previous questions helped to light up the shadows in Bill's old story (Freeman, 2004), leading to a critical moment and an epiphany for Bill (see Table 7.1: Opportunities: #2, Identifying and Managing Critical Moments; and Outcomes: #3, Epiphanies {based on insights from critical moments}). Thomson et al. (2002) define critical moments as times when life course events, including transitions, come together in such a way that adolescents experience an epiphany or new understanding, leading to a fateful turning point in their lives. For instance, Bill was able to see a major inconsistency between his role and that of the Lone Ranger. He concluded that the going-it-alone role he assumed in his old story should be called the Lone Ranger without sidekicks.

In addition to the previous narrative analysis questions (see Chapter 5, Table 5.1), Ed asked Bill he helped his client develop a cognitive map to further elaborate on his old character and old story, and light up the shadows. Figure 7.1 highlights in a more visual way the power resources Bill was not aware of as his old character in his old story, the Lone Ranger without sidekicks. For example, those resources include the students who signed his petition for vice president, and the GLBT students he was trying to invite to a meeting. Those power resources may also have been unseen and ignored by Bill because he was focused on the negative rather than positive aspects in his situation. Therefore, his cognitive map highlights other power resources Bill might have taken for granted or ignored, such as Bill and Alana in the mental health unit, and other school staff such as the counselor. Bill agreed he might have also assumed that none of the straight students at Yates were sympathetic to the special needs of GLBT students.

Ed noticed from Bill's narrative he was more focused on the power challenges in his situation, perhaps because of the stresses associated with those challenges. But as Bill's cognitive map reveals (see Figure 7.1), those challenges were conflicted. For example, Bill assumed that the student council members, homophobic students and staff, and Mr H. (the principal), were all "control freaks." He believed they were conspiring to prevent him and others from gaining power. Bill's myths also included some other less obvious power challenges, for example, he believed he had to confront those he assumed were control freaks directly and often, and to maintain his old going-it-alone-role. Bill gave that role a name to help maintain his epiphany about its effects: the strong, independent, self-sufficient male (SISSM).

When Ed explored factors that might be encouraging those myths, it became clear that Bill had unmourned losses such as Anthony's death, the withdrawal of his family members in response to that death, not saying goodbye to some school peers in his old town, and a loss of familiar though painful surroundings in his old town. Moreover, Bill agreed he had not had an opportunity to share or narrate experiences and feelings related to those losses. Figure 7.1 illustrates how the

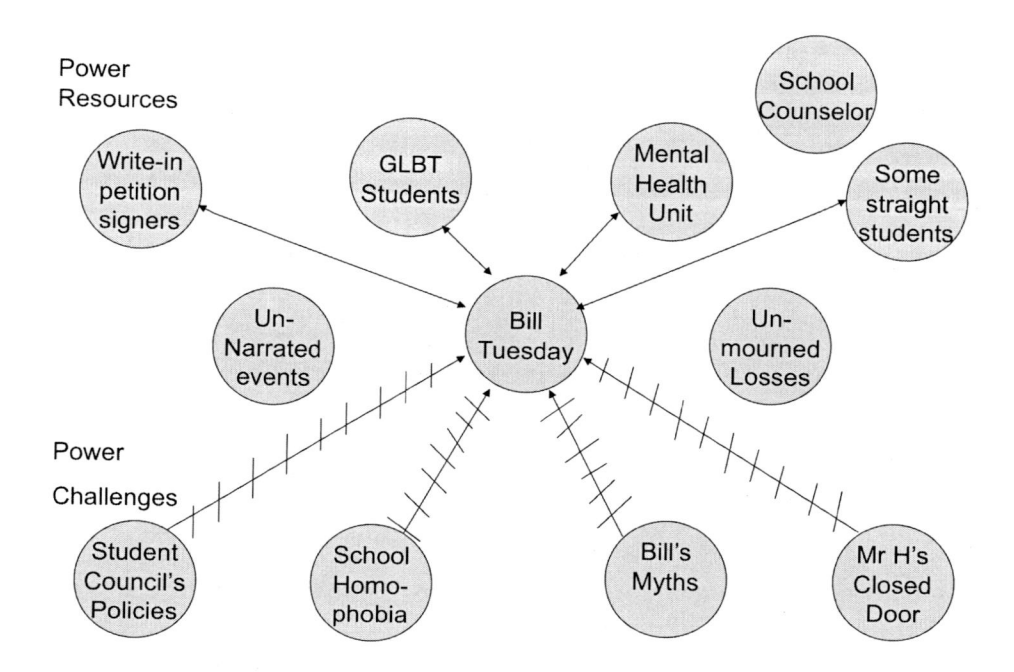

Assisting Youths in Exploring Choices and Consequences 159

Figure 7.1. Bill's Lone Ranger Cognitive Map.

unnarrated unmourned losses they discussed might make the power challenges in Bill's situation more stressful and difficult to manage, as well as prevent him from accessing his power resources. For instance, the loss of family support for narrating and mourning his losses made him less likely to trust people at Yates who represented both power challenges and potential power supports.

PRACTICE A NEW CHARACTER AND STORY. By elaborating on his old character and story, Bill learned that being a SISSM without allies encouraged him to continue hitting brick walls. In later sessions with Ed, however, Bill realized he had already established an exception to this old brick wall character and story, as revealed by his cognitive map (Figure 7.1). He had successfully built support among other students by circulating a write-in petition for a school office, based on what he learned from his unsuccessful solo effort to start a newsletter for uninvolved students. Over 100 students signed his write-in petition for vice-president. This building-allies-exception meant Bill had already started to practice a new character and story (see Table 7.1:

Under Bibliotherapy; #3: Short Novel Development; Chapter 2: Practice a New Character and Story).

Ed acknowledged that this new character and story were more consistent with the role model character and story Bill identified initially: The Lone Ranger, Tonto, and the allies they recruited in each town to work together for change. Ed asked Bill if there were other ways he could continue to practice this new character and story. Bill remembered seeing a suggestion box on the wall outside the office of Mr. Ward, the school counselor. There was a note on the box: "Zero Tolerance for Bullying." Bill wondered if that meant Mr. Ward was open to getting more students involved in the school, and whether he might be willing to sponsor a new group of GLBT and straight supporters.

Ed asked Bill how the new Lone Ranger with allies would find out the answers to those questions before hitting a brick wall. Bill decided to explore his ideas about getting more students involved in the school and finding a faculty sponsor, with a few of the students who signed his write-in petition. As a result of Bill's collaborative planning with other students, Mr. Ward agreed to sponsor the new student group and facilitate getting the principal, Mr. H's, agreement the group could become a recognized school organization. The process encouraged Bill to add Mr. Ward to his cognitive map later as a newly recognized system power resource at Yates High (see Figure 7.1).

AUTHOR/NARRATE A NEW GETTING BETTER STORY. Part of the work with Bill included adding to the transition narrative he shared with Ed in their early sessions. Additions included previously unnarrated and unmourned events surrounding Anthony's death, his brother, and the family's avoidance of acknowledging and grieving their multiple losses. The counselor and Ed facilitated an open-ended loss and grief group to meet the needs of Bill and other students with a range of losses due to parental divorce, family relocations, the deaths of significant others, and social isolation and being bullied by other students. The group leaders also focused on helping students transition from alternative schools; child welfare, mental health, and juvenile justice placements; and the reverse. Over time, the facilitators had Bill and other previous participants in the group share their getting better transition narratives with new participants, as part of a peer helper process.

LINKING SHORT NOVEL DEVELOPMENT WITH LIFE NARRATIVES. Carley (1997) assumes that such post-at-risk behavior by students, who have gotten better, represents the end of a cycle involving conflict, resolution, and stability. Similar to Freeman (2004), Carley emphasizes that in narrative language, "Characteristically, the students may then take on the roles of consultant and teacher of ways to successfully navigate high school" (p. 115). The process of video-taping students sharing their getting better transition narratives seems to clarify specific ways in which they have improved, and also allows them to predict future successful behavior based on what they have learned. Table 7.1 confirms similar outcomes for students, such as empowerment, skill development, and epiphanies or critical insights that allow them to revise and edit their life narratives. Showing the video-taped transition narratives to school staff, as well as to other students at the pre-at-risk behavior stage, is an effective way to change a large system's negative narratives about students who have gotten better (Carley, 1997; Freeman, 2004).

In addition to having Bill and other students narrate their getting better transition stories, the facilitators of the loss and grief group asked the peer helpers to give their short novels a title. This process helped the students become aware of their developmentally-relevant life narrative construction process and the content of those narratives. For example, Bill's title was, "Going It Alone: A Short Cut to a Brick Wall Collision." Bill concluded, "I've changed my mind about confronting people versus trying to figure out how to work with them, and who to invite to help plan what can be done. And there's more than one way to be a strong male!"

Conclusion

Bill, the client in this chapter's second example, was clearly working through issues of identity, gender, and perhaps sexual orientation. The practitioner helped him to address those issues as they surfaced, as well as the client's presenting problems of isolation, depression, and loss and grief. While some of the getting better narrative process between Bill and Ed took place in a loss and grief group, other practitioners can accomplish a similar process in individual sessions. Whatever combination of modalities are used, narrative interventions may be needed to help the education, mental health, primary health care, or juvenile justice systems to address the needs of students like

Bill. Hence, this chapter's focus draws upon Principle 5 and Chapter 5, which are focused on the impact of systems on an individual's ability to narrate his or her experiences and empower himself or herself within nonresponsive or oppressive systems.

REFERENCES

Carley, G. (1997). The getting better phenomenon: Videotape applications of previously at-risk high school student narratives. *Social Work in Education, 19*, 115–120.

Chappell, K. (2001). Hip hop at the crossroads: Will lyrics and perceptions change? *Ebony*, (September), 110–114.

Chen, S., & Davenport, D. S. (2005). Cognitive-behavioral therapy with Chinese American clients: Cautions and modifications. *Psychotherapy: Theory, Research, Practice, Training, 42*, 101–110.

Clendenon-Wallen, J. (1991). The use of music therapy to influence the self-confidence and self-esteem of adolescents who are sexually abused. *Music Therapy Perspectives, 9*, 73–81.

Coulter, S. J. (2000). Effect of song writing versus recreational music on Posttraumatic Stress Disorder (PTSD) symptoms and abuse attribution in abused children. *Journal of Poetry Therapy, 13*, 189–207.

Donegan, P. (2003). *Haiku: Asian arts and crafts for creative kids.* Boston: Tuttle.

Ekert, J. L. (2001). The power and vulnerability of a dream deferred: High-achieving minority adolescent girls' narratives of success. *Narrative Inquiry, 11*, 257–275.

Farmer, H. (1997). *Diversity and women's career development: From adolescence to adulthood.* Thousand Oaks, CA: Sage.

Freeman, E. M. (March 4, 2004). Basic principles of effective narrative practice. Workshop presentation. Kansas City, MO: The Social Work Coalition and Social Work Leaders in Health Care.

Freeman, E. M. (1992). The use of storytelling techniques with young African-American males: Implications for substance abuse prevention. *The Journal of Intergroup Relations, 21*, 53–71.

Fried, C. B. (1999). Who's afraid of rap: Differential reactions to music lyrics. *Journal of Applied Social Psychology, 29*, 705–721.

Gair, S., & Camilleri, P. (2003). Attempting suicide and help-seeking behaviors: Using stories from young people to inform social work practice. *Australian Social Work, 56*, 83–92.

Hakutani, Y. (1998). *Haiku: This other world: Richard Wright.* New York: Arcade.

Holman, W. D. (1996). The power of poetry: Validating ethnic identity through a bibliotherapeutic intervention with a Puerto Rican adolescent. *Child and Adolescent Social Work Journal, 13*, 371–383.

Keyes, C. L. (2000). Empowering self, making choices, creating spaces: Black female identity via rap music performance. *Journal of American Folklore, 11*, 255–269.

Kim, B. S. K., Omizo, M. M., & D'Andrea, M. J. (1998). The effects of culturally consonant group counseling on the self-esteem and internal locus of control orientation among Native American adolescents. *Journal for Specialists in Group Work, 23*, 145–163.

Laird, J. (2000). Culture and narrative as central metaphors for clinical practice with families. In D. H. Demo, K. R. Allen, & M. A. Fine (Eds.), *Handbook of family diversity* (pp. 338–358). New York: Oxford University Press.

Leukefeld, C. G., Godlaski, T., Clark, J., Brown, C., & Hays, L. (2002). Structured stories: Reinforcing social skills in rural substance abusers. *Health and Social Work, 27*, 213–218.

Mazza, N. (1999). *Poetry therapy: Interface of the arts and psychology.* Boca Raton, FL: CRC Press.

Mazza, N. (1996). Poetry therapy: A framework and synthesis of techniques for family social work. *Journal of Family Social Work, 1*, 3–18.

Nishimoto, K., & Shimizo, K. (1999). *Haiku picture book for children.* Los Angeles: Heian International.

Rosen, L.V., & Lang, C. (2005). Narrative therapy with couples: Promoting liberation from constraining influences. In M. Harvey (Ed.), *Handbook of couple's therapy* (pp. 157–178). New York: John Wiley and Sons.

Schultz, K. (1999). Identity narratives: Stories from the lives of urban adolescent females. *The Urban Review, 31*, 79–106.

Schwarz, E. D., & Perry, B. D. (1994). The post-traumatic response in children and adolescents. In D. A. Tomb (Ed.), *The psychiatric clinics of North America: Vol. 17. Post-traumatic stress disorder* (pp. 311–326). Philadelphia: W. B. Saunders.

Selman, R. L., & Adalbjamardottir, S. (2000). Developmental method to analyze the personal meaning adolescents make of risk and relationship: The case of "drinking." *Applied Developmental Science, 4*, 47–65.

Smith, M. A. (2000). The use of poetry therapy in the treatment of an adolescent borderline personality disorder: A case study. *Journal of Poetry Therapy, 14*, 3–14.

Steinman, K. J., & Zimmerman, M. A. (2004). Religious activity and risk behavior among African American adolescents: Concurrent and developmental effects. *American Journal of Community Psychology, 33*, 151–161.

Thomson, R., Bell, R., Holland, J., Henderson, S., McGrellis, S., & Sharpe, S. (2002). Critical moments: Choice, chance, and opportunity in young people's narratives of transition. *Sociology, 36*, 335–354.

Tyson, E. H. (2002). Hip hop therapy: An exploratory study of a rap music intervention with at-risk and delinquent youth. *Journal of Poetry Therapy, 15*, 131–143.

Way, N. (1998). *Everday courage: The lives and stories of urban teenagers.* New York: New York University Press.

Online Websites and Other References

Children's Poems and Interactive Poetry Lessons (Retrieved 5/13/2008). http://homepage2.nifty.com/haiku-eg/gardenE345.htm

Chapter 8

HELPING CLIENTS TO REAUTHOR CHALLENGING NARRATIVES ABOUT GENDER AND OTHER ADULT DEVELOPMENT ISSUES

> Essie, my grandmother, had a lot of guilt inside her; she called it her **woman's** pain. But she never told anyone what was hiding inside her. It was because she fell in love and married a Mormon. He never knew she was Jewish. She lived in fear that if he ever found out about her background, he'd reject her and their six children.
>
> —Margie

Some authors and researchers previously assumed that the goal of adolescence was to create fully developed adults. However, it is clear from the previous chapter and from other literature that adolescence is not just a way station toward becoming an adult. In fact, critical events occur during adolescence, including life narrative development which reflects adolescents' struggles to address identity, peer relationships, separation from the family of origin, values clarification, and educational achievement (Gair & Camilleri, 2003; Schultz, 1999; Thomson, Bell, Holland, Henderson, McGrellis, & Sharpe, 2002).

Adulthood is likewise a critical developmental stage that is more than the culmination of completing adolescence successfully. This chapter addresses young adulthood, the period from 18 to 35 years of age, and middle adulthood, the period from 36 to 54 years of age. In the above narrative segment, Margie's grandmother, Essie, refers to two of the issues young adults focus on, gender development and establishing mutually satisfying marital or romantic relationships. In addition to those issues, young adults typically work on friendship, emotional maturity, and career building; although this stage has been greatly impacted by social media, advanced electronic technology, and many sociopolitical changes (Chadiha, Veroff, & Leber, 1998; Allen, Husser, Stone, & Jordan, 2008).

Young adulthood can and does sometimes overlap with middle adulthood. However, middle adults focus on transmitting culture and values to younger generations (generativity). In addition, they address life course changes such as children leaving home, chronic health conditions, and engaging in meaningful work (Bulow & Hyden, 2003; Hall & Huenefeld, 2002; Pierret, 2001).

This chapter is focused on practice questions that service providers have raised about these two related stages of adult development: "How can you determine if clients in adult development stages simply lack information about their stage or when they need more in-depth counseling"? The chapter illustrates how practitioners can address this and other practice questions by: (1) helping clients to reauthor their life course narratives and poems, and (2) asking them solution-focused questions about those narrated or unnarrated experiences to implement adult development changes.

Practice Skills: Helping Young Adults to Reauthor Narratives and Poems

Practice Example

BACKGROUND INFORMATION. Margie Hornbeck is a 24-year-old Caucasian Midwestern student who lives in and attends college in a medium-size city of approximately 450,000 residents. She comes from a working-class family in which she is the first woman to attend college. She dropped out of college after her second year for financial reasons and because her family discouraged her from pursuing a college education. Margie decided to return to college to complete her last two years after working and saving some of the money she needed for college and obtaining loans for the rest of her college expenses.

She enrolled in a four-session seminar offered by the Women's Career Development Program at the university she is attending. This summer seminar is designed to help the enrollees to identify the resources and challenges that may affect their return to college in the fall semester. The seminar helps participants to address related gender, identity, career building, and other women's development issues. The seminar facilitator is 48-year-old June Collier, an adult education specialist, who returned to complete her college education after being a stay-at-home mother for many years.

THE SEMINAR PROCESS AND NARRATIVE METHODS. After introductions, an overview of the seminar, and an ice breaker exercise, June asked the 12 participants to write a brief family narrative. She explained their narratives could be about any family matter they believe may be affecting them currently as a young or middle adult female. Then she asked them to select a partner and to read and discuss their narratives with their partners. This part of the exercise produced high volume and enthusiastic discussions among the participants. When June asked them to reflect on what the exercise was like for them, the participants' feedback included, "Insightful, surprising, thought provoking, and somewhat disturbing."

While this feedback indicated the participants felt the exercise had an impact on them, they thought it was a stretch from doing the exercise to working out how it applied to their college success. June asked for a volunteer to share her narrative with the whole group to illustrate how the women might gain some practical value out of the experience. One of the volunteers was Margie, who shared the following more detailed version of the narrative segment included in this chapter's introduction:

> When my mother, Constance, was about 23 years old, my grandmother, Essie, told her the family was Jewish. Except for my mother's father and Essie's husband who was a Mormon. It didn't bother my mother. She said she always knew her mother kept secrets, but she never would've guessed that was it. I guess Essie swore my mother to secrecy and said she couldn't tell anyone. But eventually Essie told my grandfather about the secret. It turned out it didn't matter to him at all. Mom said Essie had a lot of guilt inside her; she called it her woman's pain. Before Essie told Grandpa, she was worried he would reject her and their children, if he found out. Mom said Essie got that guilt from her own mother, who started the secret with her husband. I mean Essie's mother married a man who didn't know she was Jewish, so she isolated herself from her family because she was afraid her husband would find out her secret. She did go to her mother's funeral in another state, but she made up stories to hide the Jewish part of the funeral and then told them to Essie so her husband wouldn't get suspicious

about her background. I guess we have two, no three, generations of secret keepers about who we are. Four generations if you count me.

ANALYSIS OF GENDER DEVELOPMENT NARRATIVES AND THE SEMINAR. After Margie shared her narrative, June asked the participants to identify any gender issues they thought were related to the narrative. Some of the issues they identified were trust, secrets between wives and husbands and mothers and daughters, guilt and shame, and identity confusion. June asked them which of those issues were gender-related. Most of the participants pointed to the secrets passed from mother to daughter and the identity confusion as examples. One participant pointed out that Margie had included herself as the fourth generation of secret keepers, which could continue the identity confusion into the next generation.

June then encouraged the group to think about how that particular gender issue might have created stress within Margie's past and current family and the possible effects of that stress on Margie as a young adult reentering college. Margie commented that her mother often gave her mixed messages about her role as a young woman (Ewing & Allen 2008; Flemke & Allen, 2008), such as, "Have a better life than I've had," but "Wouldn't it be easier to find a good job instead of wasting your time in college?" June said it was understandable that those mixed messages were probably confusing to Margie. She asked Margie and the other participants if there was a different way to interpret those messages that could reduce the stress Margie was experiencing. June's question is an example of one of the narrative reauthoring skills in Table 8.1 (Reauthoring Narratives Skill: I-A) (Golden, 2000b; McCarthy & Weber, 2005; Thomson et al., 2002).

One participant said it was possible that Margie's mother and grandmother were waiting for a family member to stop the cycle of shame and secret identity confusion, that if she could be open about her heritage, it would break the cycle of secret keepers. June pointed out that family members might have to observe Margie successfully complete college in order to fully understand what she was capable of achieving. Margie looked thoughtful and said that those ideas gave her a completely different perspective about the women in her family. She thought that perspective could free her up to stop waiting for their approval before she made decisions about her life. She also thought a different way of looking at her role as a young woman could make her

Table 8.1
REAUTHORING: ADVANCED NARRATIVE PRACTICE SKILLS
WITH YOUNG AND MIDDLE ADULTS

Practice Skill: Helping Clients to Reauthor Their Narrated Experiences (Alternative Resolutions)	
(I) Reauthoring Narratives: (A) *Alternative Meanings:* Ask the client if there is an aspect of his/her narrative that can be interpreted differently or help the client to reframe critical aspects of the narrative (B) *Alternative Endings:* Ask the client if he or she could change the narrative's ending how that ending would be different (C) *Alternative Goals:* Suggest the client aim for incremental changes or different levels of change and then revise his or her narrative to fit the revised goals (D) *Alternative Narratives:* Have the client tell a different narrative using some of the same basic facts in the original narrative	(II) Reauthoring Poems: Collective and Individual Writing (A) Client-Generated Poems: (1) Sentence stem poem (division of labor) (2) Wisdom poem (identify opposites) (3) The word list poem (free association) (B) Preexisting or Found Poems: (1) Respond to a poem (2) Modify a poem (3) Create a collective poem

feel more independent. "In my spare time this fall," Margie half seriously joked, "I could explore my Jewish heritage and see what I think about it."

The reframe suggested by one of the participants and the seminar facilitator seemed to work with Margie because it did not change the basic facts of the narrated experience, but gave those facts a different interpretation (Docherty & McColl, 2003, Freedman & Combs, 1996). That interpretation made it possible for Margie to change the meaning of her narrative, and therefore, important aspects of her family gender role. The gender secrets and shame in Margie's family dictated a kind of silence that Margie's mother, Constance, interpreted as "Keeping the pain inside of you." The rest of the first seminar included helping each participant to identify the adult gender messages in their family narratives and how they could begin to alter the meanings, goals, or endings of those narratives (see Table 8.1: Narrative Reauthoring Skills I-A, I-C, and I-B).

For example, another participant, 30-year-old Maria, shared a narrative about her younger brother who had just returned from prison to live with her parents until he could find a job and somewhere else to live. She knew that her parents wanted her to take a more active role in her brother's "rehabilitation" as the older sibling. But Maria feared more involvement in his life would hinder her success as what she called a late starter in college. Her parents were born in Puerto Rico and believed in having a close supportive family. Maria had a future vision of being responsible for her brother in their old age based on their parents' expectations.

June suggested that Maria write a second version of her narrative and share it with the other participants in the next seminar. The second version should be an alternative ending narrative, which would illustrate the desired role Maria wanted to have with her younger brother in the future (see Table 8.1: Narrative Reauthoring Skill I-B). The purpose of alternative endings narratives is to help the person visualize and work toward re-authoring their current narrative in ways that are important and empowering to him or her (Flemke & Allen, 2008).

Examples of Other Reauthoring Strategies

The Women's Career Development Seminar in the previous section involved other reauthoring strategies designed to help the participants gain their voices and experience agency (Keller-Cohen & Gordon, 2003; Kelley, 2002; McCarthy & Weber, 2005). For example, June used a reauthoring poems strategy during the third and fourth seminars with the participants. She had them to develop a list of 12 vivid, provocative, edgy, and meaningful words as a group through free association (Gillispie, 2002; Golden, 2000a). She then had each of them to write a poem using a word from the list in each line in their individual poems in the same sequence.

June asked the participants to pair off and read and discuss their poems with their partners. Golden (2002a) indicates this is a reauthoring strategy because it allows clients to recreate subjective aspects of their narrated and unnarrated experiences through the manner in which they use the word list to create their poems. Table 8.1 identifies this reauthoring strategy as The Word List Poem (Poems Reauthoring Skill: I-A-3).

After the dyad exercise, June asked for volunteers to read their poems to the larger group. In response the participants challenged each other to identify their gender, identity, career development, relationship, and other young adult themes. They also speculated on how to use what they were learning from the process to enhance their educational successes (Alschuler, 2000). June could have used other reauthoring poems skills in Table 8.1, such having the participants respond to preexisting poems that include young adult issues and themes (Poems Reauthoring Skills: I-B-1, I-B-2, and I-B-3).

Practice Skills: Helping Middle Adults Use Solution-Focused Questions to Address Important Life Course Changes

Practice Example

BACKGROUND INFORMATION. Mark Stewart is a 44-year-old Caucasian single parent. He and his wife have two children, 15-year-old Scott and 12-year-old Angel. The Stewarts have been separated for a year after Mark's wife, Grace, discovered he had an affair with a woman who works with him. The parents share custody, but Scott and Angel live with Mark primarily, with Grace having the children visit her some weekends. Grace travels a lot on work-related business trips for the bank where she is employed. At 50 years of age, Grace decided to focus on what she calls her late-start career and says its time for Mark to be the primary parent. Mark is an automobile salesman, and because of the effects of the economy on the automobile industry, he is currently earning about one-half of his usual income. Like many middle-adult-stage couples, the Stewart's dual career and marital challenges were exacerbated by the pressures from the economic depression (Hall & Huenefeld, 2002).

Mark participates in an HIV support group at Fitzsimmons' Health Center. The Center operates a specialized outreach, prevention, and treatment program for people with sexually transmitted diseases (STDs). Mark reluctantly started participating in the support group after he became severely depressed six months previously. One of the psychiatrists prescribed an antidepressant for Mark, and the social worker assigned to work with him recommended the support group. The social worker understood Mark's concerns about his coworkers and family members finding out about his medical and mental health conditions. She assured him the support group followed the AA model of confidentiality and its one-day-at-a-time philosophy.

MARK'S PROBLEM-SATURATED NARRATIVE. During Mark's second support group meeting, he explained why he has not told any of his friends or family members that he is HIV positive, although Grace is aware of his diagnosis. In the following narrative, Mark describes a revelation he experienced during a meeting with his son Scott's school principal:

> Last week Scott's principal scheduled a conference with me and Grace. She was out of town so I had to go alone. I guessed it meant Scott was in trouble. The principal, Jeff Connors, was a high school classmate of mine. That made me a little uneasy. We had Scott wait in the reception area while Jeff and I met first. Scott had been caught standing with another kid outside the school who was smoking marijuana. Scott told Jeff he wasn't involved; that he just stopped to say hello to the other student. The other kid was suspended. Jeff wanted the meeting before he decided about disciplinary actions regarding Scott. Jeff mentioned he had a no tolerance policy about drug use. He asked if I remembered his father was an alcoholic. He said it'd been hard to be the son of the neighborhood drunk. He isolated himself to keep other kids from making fun of him. Jeff said one night his father was killed when he was hit by a train. It was raining heavily and the police decided he wandered onto the train tracks by accident. Jeff didn't want Scott to use drugs and get into trouble. He talked to me about a plan for Scott to work with his school counselor to address his peer issues and bringing up his GPA to where it was the previous year. Jeff seemed a little embarrassed when we shook hands at the end of the conference. I wondered if he regretted what he'd shared about his childhood. But his openness made me see he was sincere about wanting to help Scott, and that made me feel real good.

Practice Analysis of Mark's Narrative

Although the HIV support group was run by the members, a support group coordinator participated in the group, Bert Daniels. The coordinator was a case manager for the Fitzsimmons' Center. His role included helping to obtain the resources they needed to make the group a resource for the members. Bert provided educational materials and information about the medical and social aspects of the members' STDs. He also coordinated the support group's progress with the social workers, psychiatrists, nurses, and psychologists that worked with them in other modalities. It was common for group members to experience crises at particular periods related to coping with their diseases and conditions (Asbring, 2001; Ezzy, 2000; Launer, 2002). Those periods were used by Bert and the support group as opportunities to help the members cope with their loss and grief, marital, work-related, family, stigma, and health issues.

In the session when Mark shared his narrative, Bert suggested that focusing on Mark's narrative could be helpful to all the members. This was one of the sessions when Mark was planning to share some educational materials with the group about when and how to reveal information about their health conditions. He said, "Mark's story about the school conference was really about risk taking by telling someone private information about yourself." He mentioned, "Mark said he wondered if his classmate regretted what he'd shared." Mark commented that, "When Jeff was so open with me, I had a revelation for the first time about how it must feel to be, what's the word, transparent?"

Bert said to the group, "It's clear from what Mark said, the principal seemed uncomfortable near the end of their conference, yet he was able to be transparent with Mark. How do you think he managed to be transparent in spite of being a little uncomfortable?" One of the group members, Barbara, said, "Some men think they shouldn't ever show their feelings because it makes them look weak." Edward, another group member, mentioned that, "We men are taught not to talk to each other, we do sports talking or we talk about sex; excuse me to our female members." Bert said, "Everything I read agrees with what you're saying. But the principal has apparently found a solution for getting around our male rules by not letting his discomfort keep him from being open when he needs to be."

Then Bert asked Mark, "In spite of being uncomfortable when your classmate was open about his childhood pain, and you were thinking about male rules for hiding feelings, you managed to learn something from him. How did you manage to do that, Mark?" Bert's question to Mark about what happened in his narrated experience with his classmate involves a presuppositional, solution-focused question (see Table 8.2: Question I-A). The narrative skill of using this solution-focused question works best when clients are stuck within the problem-saturated aspects of their narratives, as Mark was. The presuppositional question assumes a solution is already occurring in the problem situation, but the client remains stuck because he or she is unaware that some action is occurring (Kelley, 2002; Lee, 2003).

Mark responded to Bert's question by saying, "I think in spite of being told men aren't supposed to be open, Jeff showed me, demonstrated, how to be open while still being uncomfortable. I saw it done in living color!" Bert said, "Good, you've accomplished step 1 on how to handle revealing information about your health to whomever you choose. You've watched someone do it and you've reacted in a positive manner. Maybe you can think about how to use what you've learned for handling a similar situation in the future by being open like Jeff. Can you share with us in our next session how you might handle a future situation involving openness?"

Bert's suggestion to Mark about planning a future time when he can be open is similar to asking a unique outcomes solution-focused question about the future (see Table 8.2: Questions III-A and III-B). This type of future experience solution-focused question requires clients to identify the lesson they learned from the narrated experience. They are then expected to use their lesson to handle a similar situation in the future, as well or better than they did in the current narrated experience (Freeman, 2004; Kelley, 2002; Lee, 2003).

In Mark's situation, both male and female group participants made supportive comments to him about the difficulty men have in sharing information that makes them feel vulnerable. The consequence is that men's rules, as Bert labeled them, encourage them to hide their feelings and secrets, even to other men (Coates, 2001; Dorr, 2001; Pellegrini & Sarbin, 2002). This issue of men's rules makes them more vulnerable, rather than less vulnerable, especially when those rules hinder them from coping with and gaining support for managing the effects of long-term STDs (Pierret, 2001). Both middle adult males and females with chronic diseases may need more coping support because the rate of chronic diseases and other conditions increases with age (Asbring, 2001; Borkan, Reis, & Medalie, 2001).

Table 8.2
USING ADVANCED NARRATIVE PRACTICE SOLUTION-FOCUSED
INTERVENTIONS WITH YOUNG AND MIDDLE ADULTS

Examples of Solution-Focused Questions	Examples of Solution-Focused Questions
(I) *Presuppositional Questions:* (A) In spite of . . . (the situation you were in), how did you manage to . . . (cope with it or to respond in a preferred way)? (B) Tell me a story about that time in your life (II) *Unique Outcomes Questions: Past Experiences:* (A) Can you tell me about a time in your life when situation X was more manageable for you? (B) What was different about situation X at that time? (III) *Unique Outcomes Questions: Future Experiences:* (A) Based on the lesson you learned from . . . , how might you use that lesson in similar situations in the future? (B) What types of situations might develop in the future where retelling your narrative to yourself might be helpful? How might retelling it be helpful to you?	(IV) *Scaling Questions:* (A) From your perspective how bad is situation X, on a scale from 1 (it's tolerable) to 10 (it's unbearable)? (B) What is usually happening in situation X when it's a . . . (the number the client indicated on the scale) (C) From your perspective where would you like situation X to be in three months, on a scale from 1 (it's tolerable) to 10 (it's unbearable)? (D) What would have to happen in situation X for you to rate it a . . . (the number the client indicated on the scale above). (V) *Miracle Questions* (A) Imagine what your life would be like without situation X; what would be different and how would it be different? (B) What would have to happen in order for situation X to be different, or what would have to change? (C) If situation X changed for the better, who would be the first person to notice? What would that person do or say?

Discussion

In addition to the unique outcomes and presuppositional questions used by Bert in the previous support group, Table 8.2 includes other solution-focused questions that practitioners can use with young and middle adult clients. For example, solution-focused scaling questions encourage clients to be more precise and clear about the effects of a problem situation on them and what is influencing the situation (see Table 8.2: Scaling Questions IV-A and IV-B). Therefore, scaling questions may be effective when middle adult couples are trying to cope with parenting conflicts; or when young adults are addressing identity conflicts with parents, spouses, or friends. The reauthoring strategies that were used with young adults in a prior section of this chapter can be used with middle adults, even though the development issues the two groups are addressing are different.

Many of hose narrative skills and strategies can also be used with clients in other age groups. The discussion of those skills and strategies in this chapter draws upon Principle 1 in Chapter 1. It clarifies the role adult development plays as part of the context in which the narratives of young and middle adults emerge. The chapter also illustrates how gender roles and gender development issues are part of that developmental context, and in what ways some of those issues are different for males and females.

References

Allen, K. R., Husser, E. K., Stone, D. J., & Jordan, C. E. (2008). Agency and error in young adults: Stories of sexual decision making. *Family Relations, 57*, 517–529.

Alschuler, M. (2000). Healing from addictions through poetry therapy. *Journal of Poetry Therapy, 13*, 165–173.

Asbring, P. (2001). Chronic illness: A disruption in life: Identity transformation among women with chronic fatigue syndrome and fibromyalgia. *Journal of Advanced Nursing, 34*, 312–319.

Borkan, J., Reis, S., & Medalie, J. (2001). Narratives in family medicine: Tales of Transformation: Points in breakthrough for family physicians. *Families, Systems, & Health, 19*, 121–134.

Bulow, P. H., & Hyden, L. (2003). In dialogue with time: Identity and illness in narratives about chronic fatigue. *Narrative Inquiry, 13*, 71–97.

Chadiha, L. A., Veroff, J., & Leber, D. (1998). Newlywed's narrative themes: Meaning in the first year of marriage for African American and White couples. *Journal of Comparative Family Studies, 29*, 115–133.

Coates, J. (2001). "My mind is with you": Story sequences in the talk of male friends. *Narrative Inquiry, 11*, 81–101.

Docherty, D., & McColl, M. A. (2003). Illness stories: Themes emerging through Narrative. *Social Work in Health Care, 37*, 19–39.

Dorr, C. (2001). Listening to men's stories: Overcoming obstacles to intimacy from childhood. *Families in Society, 82*, 509–515.

Ewing, J., & Allen, K. R. (2008). Women's narratives about God and gender: Agency, tension, and change. *Journal of Systemic Therapies, 27*, 90–107.

Ezzy, D. (2000). Illness narratives: Time, hope, and HIV. *Social Science and Medicine, 50*, 605–617.

Flemke, K., & Allen, K. R. (2008). Women's experiences of rage: A critical feminist Analysis. *Journal of Marital and Family Therapy, 34*, 92–110.

Freeman, E. M. (March 5, 2004). The intersection of culture and gender with narrative interventions. Workshop presentation. Kansas City, MO. The Social Work Coalition and Social Work Leaders in Health Care.

Freedman, J., & Combs, G. (1996). *Narrative therapy: The social construction of preferred realities.* New York: W. W. Norton.

Gair, S., & Camilleri, P.(2003). Attempting suicide and help-seeking behaviors: Using stories from young people to inform social work practice. *Australian Social Work, 56*, 83–92.

Gillispie, C. (2002). Recovery poetry 101: The use of collaborative poetry in a dual-diagnosis drug and alcohol treatment program. *Journal of Poetry Therapy, 15*, 83–92.

Golden, K. (2000a). Exploring the therapeutic fairy tale motifs of silence, betrayal, and the search for a voice in the film "The Piano." *Journal of Poetry Therapy, 23*, 209–217.

Golden, K. M. (2000b). The use of collaborative writing to enhance cohesion in poetry therapy groups. *Journal of Poetry Therapy, 13*, 125–137.

Hall, M. E., & Huenefeld, N. E. (2002). The storied approach: A constructivist perspective on counseling dual-career couples. In D. S. Sandhu (Ed.), *Counseling employees: A multifaceted approach* (pp. 221–238). Alexandria, VA: American Counseling Association.

Keller-Cohen, D., & Gordon, C. (2003). "On trial": Metaphor in telling the life Story. *Narrative Inquiry, 17*, 1–40.

Kelley, P. (2002). A narrative therapy approach to brief treatment. *Journal of Brief Therapy, 1*, 91–100.

Launer, J. (2002). *Narrative-based primary care: A practical guide.* London: Radcliffe Medical Press.

Lee, M. Y. (2003). A solution-focused approach to cross-cultural social work practice. *Families in Society, 84*, 285–395.

McCarthy, M., & Weber, Z. (2005). When bodies need voices: Sharing stories of Survival. *Affilia, 20*, 368–372.

Pellegrini, R. J., & Sarbin, T. R. (Eds.) (2002). *Between fathers and sons: Critical incident narratives in the development of men's lives.* New York: Haworth Press.

Pierret, K. (2001). Interviews and biographical time: The case of long-term HIV nonprogressors. *Sociology of Health & Illness, 23*, 159–179.

Schultz, K. (1999). Identity narratives: Stories from the lives of urban adolescent females. *The Urban Review, 31*, 79–106.

Thomson, R., Bell, R., Holland, J., Henderson, S., McGrellis, S., & Sharpe, S. (2002). Critical moments: Choice, chance, and opportunity in young people's narratives of transition. *Sociology, 36*, 335–354.

Chapter 9

FACILITATING OLDER ADULTS' USE OF LIFE NARRATIVES FOR PERSONAL WELL-BEING, PEER SUPPORT, AND MENTORING

> I tell my children and other young people I see in my church and in the neighborhood-you have to help yourself first and then try to help someone else. That's the number one lesson I've learned in life. When you get on a plane they tell you; if you're sitting next to some one who needs help, 'Put your oxygen mask on first.'! Then give a hand to the one who needs help with his or her mask.
>
> —Myra Littlejohn

Just as Myra Littlejohn demonstrates in the above life narrative segment, older adults can identify sources and examples of their wisdom when they have opportunities to review and revise their narratives. "It is through the process of telling one's own life story that individuals are able to make meaning of their lives, construct and better understand the self, and maintain a sense of personal identity" (Dorfman, Murty, Evans, Ingram, & Power, 2004, p.1). The life narrative process not only enhances the personal identity of older adults, but it also increases their well-being from a developmental perspective. For example, this process can lead to a sense of integrity during the older adult stage rather than regret and despair (Erikson, 1994; Webster, 1999).

The focus of this chapter is on the role of older adult development and other transitions in precipitating and supporting an individual's life narrative review and revision process. Such transitions can also lead to opportunities for individuals to support peers and mentor younger generations of family members and other individuals. The chapter summarizes resources for reviewing, revising, and sharing life narratives by older adults from 55 years of age to death. Three life narrative practice skills allow practitioners to help older adults access those resources: facilitating the life review process, facilitating the life story-writing process, and coaching clients in the use of life narratives for intergenerational mentoring.

Those skills are useful in traditional practice settings such as nursing homes and hospitals, and in nontraditional settings which include senior meal sites and religious institutions. Narrative work in the latter settings provides opportunities for service providers to use a normative rather than problem-focused approach with clients. A normative approach can limit the age-related stigma that some older adults experience in their lives.

Resources for Reviewing, Revising, and Sharing Life Narratives

As noted in this chapter's introduction, the life narrative review process helps older adults come to terms with their previous and current lives and with the aging process itself (Jarvinen, 2004; Pals, 2006; Peck, 2002; Shenk, 2002). The review is a normal development-related opportunity that often contributes to their sense of well-being and integrity. Examples of resources for facilitating the life narrative process include an individual's family tree and family health history development. The U.S. Surgeon General's Family History Initiative recommends that people learn more about their family health histories as a prevention and educational resource (U.S. Surgeon General, 2010).

These and other resources included below have been affected by four main trends. For instance, family tree and family health history development have been affected by the trends of family genealogy, technology advances, and higher education (Andereck & Pence, 1991; Anderson, 2010; Caldwell, 2005; Clark, 2001; Brown, 1995; Burroughs, 2001; Howells, 2004; Osher Lifelong Learning Institutes, 2010).

1. **The Family Genealogy Movement:** There has been a rapid increase in the number of individuals who are involved in family biographical and genealogical research, family health history development, and family reunions. This trend has led to the development of family research

forms, reunion planning packages, and interview techniques for gathering family stories and other genealogical data. The result is a greater appreciation of culture as a source of pride and identity within all racial, ethnic, religious, and national origin groups. This trend received a major support from Alex Haley's *Roots: The saga of an American Family*, and the television adaptation of that book (Haley, 1976).

2. **Technology:** Major advances in computer hardware and software resources are an international phenomenon. Those resources include social networking websites, free genealogical search engines and websites, genealogy collections in public libraries, state and federal genealogy archives, and fee-based genealogy document collection services such as Ancestry.com and Footnote.

3. **Higher Education:** Courses in the helping professions now address family tree development and analysis, and family history development. There are increased resources for courses and workshops in family genealogy. National private funding supported the development of 123 Osher Life Long Learning Institutes (OLLIs) in colleges and universities in 49 states. OLLIs are funded by the private Osher Foundation in Maine. They are run by older adults and they offer life story writing courses as the hub of a variety of other course offerings of interest to this age group.

4. **Government and Private Funding Trends:** Although funding trends have no doubt been affected by the current national economic recession, some funding has been continued for intergenerational mentoring and storytelling projects between older adults and youth. Examples of such projects are gang prevention and intervention (neighborhood gardening and beautification), African American and Latino mentoring circles (pro-social cultural rituals and mentoring), and social skills development (in rural communities).

Practice Skill: Facilitating the Life Narrative Review Process

Practice Example

BACKGROUND INFORMATION. Related to the above resources for life narrative review services, a drop in center for older adults was cosponsored by a mental health center and a county Department of Aging. Included in the drop in center was a meal site for the elderly, a small library and reading room, the services of a nurse practitioner, and scheduled recreation activities. This center also provided a life review information session and peer discussion group. The two-hour information session was open to participants of any age; it introduced the topic and provided them with some basic facts. The follow-up peer discussion group for older adults helped them to apply some of the ideas and issues presented during the informational session and learn new related facts.

Some of the mental health center's administrators, staff, clients, and the latter's relatives were introduced in Chapter 5, including 69-year-old Alan Rickman. That chapter focused on narrative approaches for addressing social justice and organizational change issues in partnership with marginalized staff and clients. Alan was a volunteer at the current meal site, helping to deliver meals to older adult shut-ins in the area. He also participated in some of the drop in center's recreational and social activities. His current wife was the primary caregiver for her adult grandson who had co-occurring developmental disabilities and a serious mental illness. The grandson lived in a small group home near the Rickman couple. Alan, who is Jewish, lost a number of family members during the Holocaust. He emigrated from Germany to the United States after World War II at the age of 14. He has been estranged from his two sons from a previous marriage for many years.

The specific goals of the drop in center's discussion group were for the members to: (1) apply certain life review methods from the information session to their lives, (2) assess their sources of well-being and stress, and (3) resolve or cope effectively with stress in order to come to terms with their lives and the aging process. The group facilitator, Ruth Evans, a social worker, assumed the achievement of these group goals would automatically address any age-related stigma the members might be experiencing.

When Ruth invited the five members to react to those goals or to add others during their first session, they decided they did not want the group to be problem focused. Seventy-five year old Mason summed up the group's consensus, "Let's talk about what we can change and then just live with the rest!" In addition to Mason and Alan, the other members included 73-year-old Myra whose narrative segment was introduced at the beginning of this chapter, 80-year-old Edna, and 71-year-old Gladys.

In their second session, Ruth reminded the group that one of the life review methods introduced during the information session was telling stories. She asked the members to tell a story about using one of the sites' services and to include some aspect of their current or previous lives. Alan shared the following narrative segment:

Alan's Life Narrative Review Segment: I've been coming to this meal site for over a year. I usually stay around after my deliveries. I like to shoot pool and I play dominoes. You can stay by yourself or do things. The domino game started when my friend, Milt, told me about this great domino player, a black guy, who couldn't be beat. He was only over here now and then; that's why I hadn't seen him before. So one day we were here at the same time and Milt challenged this guy Hinton to a game–only he wanted me to play too. Well, I beat Hinton that day, but just barely. I never admitted to him how close that game was. Since then, we managed to play each other once a week or so. I started looking forward to our games. All the guys would crowd around and watch. Some days he'd win and some days I'd win. I guess we were pretty evenly matched. We'd joke sometimes or kid each other. We got along, OK. One day after one of our games, as the other guys were starting to leave, I said to him, joking a little, "Well here we are, enjoying beating each other, when we didn't know anything about each other at first." Hinton said we'd gotten to know each other all right, but I reminded him of someone, and he'd finally figured out who. It was his uncle I reminded him of–he was more like Hinton's brother because they were close in age. They played dominoes and cards a lot in the small Georgia town where they lived. I wondered if his uncle was still living, but he said no, his uncle died when he was just 18. He'd gone to the next town to visit a friend. The family began to worry when he didn't return home that evening. He'd never done that before. He was found dead the next week–they never found out what happened to him. I said that was a long time ago, and Hinton said, "I know it was. But the way I see it, he's as much my brother today as the day he died. And I'll be 74 next month." I was a little surprised when he said that. I didn't know what to say. We sat there for a while, not saying anything, and then stood up at the same time. I shook his hand and we looked each other in the eyes. He said, "Well I'll see you next time," and walked off. I didn't tell him about losing my family in the war, it didn't seem necessary. We understood each other. You know, before then, I didn't think about my family. But to tell you the truth, after that, I started to remember things I'd never talked about before, things I forgot about many years ago.

Practice Analysis

THE USE OF BASIC LIFE NARRATIVE REVIEW SKILLS. This analysis builds on the basic life narrative practice skill of continuity questions included in Table 4.3. Those questions were discussed in Chapter 4 regarding the construction and revision of life narratives. Because the questions are organized according to the four life narrative clusters they are focused on, they are useful for tracking the primary focus of a client's life narrative segment (see Figure 4.1). For example, the last part of Alan's life narrative segment shifts the focus of the narrative, beginning with, "It was his uncle I reminded him of. . . ." That part of the narrative refers to a previously narrated painful event and a relative who was and is important to Hinton. That part of the narrative also refers to mostly unnarrated life events and actors that seem significant to Alan (see Table 4.3: Life Narrative Cluster #3).

Ruth asked questions that were similar to those listed in Cluster #3, and encouraged other group members to participate in the questions and discussion. For example, she asked about, "Who and what events or experiences Alan forgot years ago," and then, "Who were the most important people in his life then and why were they important to him?" (see Table 4.3: Life Narrative Cluster #3, Questions #5 and 6). The discussion revealed that all of his family members who lived in Germany had died in the Holocaust, including his parents, siblings, grandparents, aunts and uncles, and cousins. The pain Alan felt from that experience was evident in the following comment, as was his relief in being able to acknowledge the pain he was still experiencing, "Everyone I knew died in Germany, including our Jewish neighbors in the town where I grew up!"

The last part of Alan's life narrative segment is also related to Cluster #1, in terms of his preferred coping methods and value priorities (see Table 4.3: Life Narrative Cluster #1). From the group discussion it became clear that Alan's preferred coping method in the past and present had been to deny and suppress painful information about his family and his losses. In contrast, he realized from Hinton's narrative, that his domino partner's pattern was to grieve openly, to try to heal, and to remember his losses. Hence, the group discussions helped Alan and other members to not only review their life narratives, but also to assess and revise those narratives based on their current perspectives.

For example, Alan's coping pattern was no doubt based on the incredible amount of trauma and PTSD he experienced during and after the war. Those experiences ranged from being forcibly removed from their hometown with his family, to witnessing the killing of his extended family and other concentration camp residents. Alan was only ten when he and his family arrived at the concentration camp.

Ruth asked him to describe what type of child he had been at that point (see Table 4.3: Cluster #1, Question #1). His response and the follow-up group discussion led to another affirming life narrative continuity question by Myra, "How on earth were you able to survive, Alan, under such terrible conditions?" Myra is the group member whose life narrative segment at the beginning of this chapter clarified one of her life lessons, "Put your oxygen mask on first, before helping others" (see Table 4.3: Cluster #4, Question #4). Discussion about Ruth's lesson helped Alan to understand that nothing he could have done at ten years of age would have saved his family; and that his survival was a gift to his family in circumstances which he could not otherwise control.

THE USE OF ADVANCED LIFE NARRATIVE REVIEW SKILLS. In addition to using the basic life narrative skill of continuity questions, practitioners can use advanced life narrative skills that are particularly relevant developmentally to older adults. Table 9.1 indicates facilitating the life narrative review process allows providers to help clients address their individual well-being and integrity, as well as provide and receive peer support, such as Myra's support to Alan in the previous section. This process can occur in individual and peer group counseling or in psychoeducation sessions. Table 9.1 includes some of the advanced skill questions providers like Ruth can use with clients in those sessions. As noted previously, in one of her peer group counseling sessions, Ruth began their life narrative review by asking members to tell a story about using the meal site's services that included aspects of their current and previous lives (see Table 9.1: Skill #I-A).

In other sessions, Ruth had the members select particular advanced life narrative review questions to focus their discussion, such as "Where are you today in coming to terms with your life?" and, "How have you changed over the years in terms of what is important to you?" (i.e., in terms of your values) (see Table 9.1: Skill #I-B-3 and Skill #I-B-1). The discussions during those sessions helped the members clarify regrets that were creating stress in their lives and identify resources that could facilitate coming to terms with their lives (Shenk, 2002; Bruner, 1999).

For instance, Gladys was able to share a narrative segment about a close friend she previously vacationed with once per year before the

Table 9.1
ADVANCED LIFE NARRATIVE PRACTICE SKILLS WITH OLDER ADULTS

Skill: Facilitating the life narrative review and life story writing process with older adults:	*Skill: Coaching older adults in intergenerational life narratives and mentoring:*

I. *Life Narrative Review Process:* The provider says/ suggests:
  A. Please tell me a story about . . . and include aspects of your current or previous life.
  B. Let's select one of the following questions for our discussion in today's session:
    1. How have you changed over the years (values, identity, goals, lessons, relationships, regrets, etc.)
    2. What events, experiences, or individuals influenced those changes and how did they influence them?
    3. Where are you today in coming to terms with your life?
    4. What challenges have hindered you? What resources have helped you?
    5. Where are you in coming to terms with the aging process? What things have helped or hindered you?
 	
II. *Life Story Writing (LSW) Process:* The provider:
  A. Explores the availability of LSW courses.
  B. Facilitates the marketing of the courses to older adults.
  C. Consults with older adults by:
    1. Answering questions and providing information about LSW courses.
    2. Listening to life stories and helping to explore who to share them with.
    3. Supporting older adults' decisions to publish stories.
	III. *Intergenerational Life Narrative Process and Mentoring (Family and community historian development):*
	
	  A. *Informal Opportunities:* Mentoring younger individual family members in other generations in historian role.
	
	  B. *Formal Programs:* Mentoring other young people in intergenerational storytelling programs in the historian community stewardship role.
	
	IV. *Service Provider Roles in Informal and Formal Arrangements Involving Older Adults:* The provider asks:
	
	  A. Who in the client's previous generation told family stories, explained family history, and researched the family's genealogy?
	  B. Who in the client's generation fulfilled those roles?
	  C. What role is the client interested in related to the intergenerational legacy role?
	    1. Related to his/her identity and coming to terms with life and the aging process?
	    2. Related to mentoring other generations?
	    3. Related to the concerns that brought the client in for services/program participation?

friend assumed custody of her step-granddaughter. Raising her granddaughter meant the friend could no longer afford to travel with Gladys. The latter regretted and resented the loss of her travel companion, and not talking about it previously had been stressful for her. The stress made her feel life was passing her by at an age when she wondered how much longer she would be physically able to travel long distances. Older women in particular may experience this type of conflict when they have assumed caregiving roles with their spouses, adult children, and/or parents (Allen & Walker, 2009). Other group members shared similar regrets and provided support to each other, such as helping Gladys identify alternative travel companions and other activities that the aging process would not hinder her from doing in the present.

Practice Skill: Facilitating the Life Story Writing Process

Life Story Writing Courses

OLLI COURSE STRUCTURE AND CURRICULUM. Life story writing (LSW) courses usually include from eight to 12 weekly sessions that last from two to three hours per session. They are typically taught by older adults who have taken the courses previously and are involved in writing their own life stories in addition to teaching and mentoring peers. The courses are designed and organized as study groups and the instructors are identified as study group leaders (OLLI, 2010). Like in most courses offered to older adults, the participants' stories are not graded. Instead, the leader and the participants offer class members constructive verbal and written feedback on their stories.

LSW courses are offered by OLLIs. A range of related courses are also offered in history, computer science, literature, business, art, dance, exercise, genealogy, and other areas; however, the LSW courses are the core of each OLLI's curriculum (OLLI, 2010). Some participants take genealogy courses simultaneously with LSW courses or they take those courses in sequence, because family stories can provide information for successful genealogy research; and the latter can document or clarify information learned from family stories. The classes meet in university campus classrooms and continuing education centers, religious institutions, community centers, shopping malls, local history centers, assisted living or other senior-specific facilities, and fitness and exercise centers.

THE COURSE PROCESS. Study group leaders provide course outlines about the types of stories participants are expected to write. Examples include childhood stories and love stories in beginning LSW courses, and stories about a parent's last days and turning point stories in advanced courses. Although participants are expected to write a story on the identified topic for each session, they have flexibility in the selection of topics for their stories. Participants provide other class members with copies of their stories so the members can read along as individuals take turns reading their stories out loud (OLLI, 2010).

Study group leaders model how to provide constructive feedback by pointing out what they like about a participant's story, what additional information they would like to know, and how the story can be improved (OLLI, 2010). They encourage class members to provide feedback in these and related areas for each participant's story. Study group leaders also provide resource materials on effective writing techniques, examples of effective and ineffective life stories and fiction, and publishing options and resources. Class discussions about resource materials help participants to clarify how such materials can be used specifically to improve the members' writing skills. These courses could be adapted for older adults with literacy challenges by having them audio tape their stories and then play the recordings during class sessions. LSW courses typically cost from $30 to $50 per course, so for some low-income participants subsidies would need to be provided.

The Practitioner's Role Regarding LSW Courses for Older Adults

EXPLORING AVAILABILILTY AND MARKETING IN NONTRADITIONAL PRACTICE SETTINGS. Service providers can be helpful to older adults who might benefit from LSW courses or who have taken such courses and are interested in continuing their LSW practices. They can explore the availability of such courses in the communities where they practice and facilitate the marketing of those courses to older adults (see Table 9.1: #II-A and B). For instance, they can find out where LSW and other OLLI courses are being offered, the schedules, and the costs; and then provide written announcements about that information. They can also facilitate marketing these courses by inviting OLLI Board members and study group leaders to talk about the courses to older adults in senior meal sites, assisted living facilities, public housing, university continuing education centers, and religious institutions (Freeman, 2004).

EXPLORING AVAILABILITY AND MARKETING IN TRADITIONAL PRACTICE SETTINGS. In addition to these nontraditional settings, practitioners and administrators can help market and advertise the availability of such courses in more traditional organizations that serve older adults. Such organizations are skilled care nursing homes, hospitals and medical clinics, rehabilitation centers, 55-plus subsidized housing, and mental health centers, particularly those with specialized geriatric services. Freeman (2004) notes that marketing LSW courses includes having providers explain how LSW courses can help older adults as a prevention strategy. For instance these courses can help them to: (1) manage the aging process, (2) develop and maintain a positive identity, and (3) understand themselves and their past and current lives.

PROVIDING ONGOING SUPPORT FOR OLDER ADULTS' LIFE STORING WRITING EFFORTS. In the process of exploring and helping to market LSW courses, providers can answer questions from older adults who are considering or have already enrolled in those courses (see Table 9.1: II-C-1). With prior knowledge about the courses, practitioners can consult with clients about their course participation or listen to their written stories when requested to (see Table 9.1: #II-C-2). Providers can support story writers in their decision to self-publish their stories, based on resource materials and information they received from LSW courses, or in their decision to seek other publishing options (see Table 9.1: #II-C-3).

Service providers can help older adults identify individuals with whom they can share their written stories and poetry, such as spouses, siblings, adult children, grandchildren, or peers (see Table 9.1: #II-C-2) (Diaz de Chumaceiro, 2000; Freeman, 2004; Taylor, 1985). Seventy-seven-year-old Michael asked a psychologist who facilitated a poetry group in his senior housing complex if he should share his LSW course stories with family members. He showed the psychologist Bob Logan the following story about how his young adult World War II experiences were affecting him as an older adult.

Michael's Written Life Story Segment: I had four years of combat during WWII, the war to end all wars; some of it was in Hawaii right after Pearl Harbor. It was a tough place to be at the time. A lot of soldiers died out there. At least twice I thought it was my turn, but I kept living through situations where I knew I might not make it. I had a wife and little boy I promised to return home to. It was the only thing that kept me going. I saw things I never told a living soul—it was the only thing I could do, especially when I knew at last the war was over and I was going home to my little family. I grew up in the South so not much about it could surprise me. But when I was on the way back to my hometown on the train, they moved me and other black soldiers to another car so German Generals and other officers from Rommel's North African campaign could have our seats. They were being taken to a POW camp not far from my hometown. I later found out the POW officers didn't have to work according to the Geneva Convention; they had everything they needed for free from our government, and I couldn't even find work. The German enlisted men had to work, so they worked the farms and factories that wouldn't hire me. It meant I had to move my family up north in order to find a job so I could feed them. The move changed our lives because we left a place we knew for one we didn't know. We made a good life here no matter what. Writing about what happened made me realize I resent it still today as a 77-year-old man with some wisdom. I thought I came to grips with what happened years ago. But maybe I wasn't finished with it after all.

In their discussion after Bob read Michael's life story segment, Michael explained that his grandson had fought in the Gulf War and later suffered PTSD and other mental health problems from that experience. When Bob pointed out the possible similarities in Michael's and his grandson's war and postwar experiences, Michael decided he would share his story with his grandson. Later he told Bob that sharing his story encouraged his grandson to begin talking about his experiences and how he continued to struggle and cope with the effects on his daily life. Michael was grateful that both he and his grandson benefited from the life story he'd shared and that they understood each other more.

In another example, after tearfully reading a story about her mother's death in one LSW class session, 56-year-old Pam, a new retiree, sent the following note to the study group leader the next week:

Pam's Written Life Story Segment. I took this course because I thought I'd get to write about the fun times—the best times in my life. I felt awful last week when I read my mother's story to the class. It brought up all the pain I thought I'd worked through two years ago. She was such a wonderful mother and person. She didn't deserve to die when she did or how she died. And I did everything I could for her, so I don't have any regrets about her last days or her death. I don't need a course like this to make me feel sad. So I'm dropping. I'm planning on taking a computer course or a salsa dancing course. I'm still young and I intend to enjoy what time I have left without crying and feeling bad about me and my life!

Pam's life story segment in the form of a written letter indicates the importance of timing and of participants being at a place in their lives where they are able to examine who they are and come to peace with their lives. The study group leader wrote to Pam in response to her letter to assure her that, ". . . people are often in different places in their lives in terms of wanting to write their life stories and deciding what parts of their lives they want to write about. Some of them want to write their life stories now, some will write them later, and some will decide they don't want to write their life stories at all. It's possible that two years after your mother's death is too soon for you to try writing about her. If you decide to take the course again in the future, you'll be welcome to write about any aspects of your life story you choose to write about." Hopefully, if Pam shared the above letter with a helping professional, the latter would react in a supportive manner similar to the study group leader's response.

Practice Skill: Coaching Intergenerational Narrative Mentoring

The Mentoring Process

Most families have members who assume the family historian role, which involves listening to and sharing family and life stories over the years. Often historians are self-selected or they may be designated by other family members within their or other generations. Storytelling occurs continuously over the years, but the most frequent venues are family funerals, holidays, reunions, weddings, birthday celebrations, and the historian's own life review process. Historians share their stories informally with all family members, but often during their life narrative review process or at other times; they typically increase their storytelling with a member or members of the next generation. This process supports the development of future historians and allows time for older historians to mentor interested family members. When this legacy or hand-off process does not occur, family stories and life narratives can be lost because they are not passed down to potential historians.

How the Process Differs Among Families

New historians may be groomed because they are interested in the role, or an older historian may identify their storytelling potential. The interaction between older and younger historians may involve discussions about their roles and the mentoring process in some families, but in other families the process may be more implicit and unstated. The first example below illustrates an explicit mentoring process, while the second example clarifies an implicit unstated mentoring process:

> **Example of an Explicit Life Narrative Historian and Mentoring Role: 80-Year-Old Everett Smalls:** I used to visit my four sisters over the years. I was the youngest and the only boy in the family. I always hung around the old folks when I was young; they'd forget I was there and tell all those old stories about the family. Before my mother died, she said she guessed I'd have to hold onto the stories. She knew I was the only one she could trust to get things right. Afterwards, when I'd visit my sisters and their families, I'd tell some of our stories; but they were full of secrets and didn't want younger family members to know about the old family. But I could tell some of the young ones were interested. I didn't have any kids of my own; that was my only regret in life, so I figured the stories would die with me if I couldn't pass them on. I noticed one of my nieces began to write down some of the stories and family information I talked about. After a few years, she even taped some of my holiday visits when we talked about the family stories. I could see she was a good listener and asked questions, like the family was important to her too. Over the years, I talked about our family stories a lot, but as I got older, sometimes I talked about my life as a musician on the road; about some of my experiences and the characters I'd met. I asked her once what she planned on doing with my stories. She told me she'd decided to research our family genealogy; may be write it up so the whole family could read it. I told her it was a deal—I'd keep telling her stories and she could tell me what she was finding out. I wanted her to know up front she might run into family members who wanted to keep their secrets, but she could count on me to run interference, like I'd learned from my mother. It got so whenever she found out something new or unexpected in her research, I'd be the first one she'd call.

Example of an Implicit Life Narrative Historian and Mentoring Role: 68-year-old Catherine Spano. I'm not sure how I ended up as the family reunion organizer. I was a surgical nurse before I retired. When I tried to get my sisters, brothers, and cousins to start the family reunion, they all had excuses about why they couldn't do it. So I fell into it. Over the years, as the family grew I started keeping better track of old and new family members and their relationships; that meant after a while I knew almost as much as the older family members. Then I started writing down their stories when I noticed some of them were dying off; it seemed the thing to do so we wouldn't lose their voices. Now more and more family members are helping to plan our reunions, but somehow I'm still the one with all the family stories and I've added a few. I don't have a clue what to do with these family jewels before my generation starts to die out. My granddaughter is showing some interest—she did a family project in school this year—but I'll just have to see what happens with her.

The Role of Service Providers Regarding Intergenerational Mentoring

Service providers can assist older adults such as Everett and Catherine who seek services in both traditional and nontraditional settings. They can help such clients identify roles assumed within their family regarding its history and stories, and help them to clarify how their roles may be related to the concerns that led to their involvement in services (see Table 9.1: #IV-C-3). Examples of such concerns are the quality of their present lives, their current identity, and how to manage the aging and/or chronic illness process. Table 9.1 includes additional life narrative coaching questions that providers can use as part of their social assessments and services with this population.

For instance, Everett, from the first example above was being seen in a community health clinic for chronic leukemia. During their initial session, the social worker explored Everett's family roles and individual interests: The family role he assumed (see Table 9d: #IV-B) and how that role helped him to cope in the past and currently (#IV-C-1). This provider also assessed and encouraged him to continue to utilize his intergenerational support from the niece that he was mentoring (#IV-C-2).

In the second previous example, Catherine lived in an assisted living facility in her own apartment, which provided her with independence as well as support. A community psychologist from a near-by family service agency, co-located in the building where she lived, helped her to assess whether she needed to involve other family members more in planning their reunions. This strategy helped Catherine to improve her quality of life (less stress). It also increased her life narrative mentoring opportunities by including her granddaughter and other younger family members in their family reunion planning.

A recent trend has been increased funding for intergenerational storytelling, historian development, and mentoring projects by private foundations and state or federal agencies (Brown, 1995). Although such projects may be structured or operated differently, they often have common purposes and interventions which are provided by social workers, psychologists, recreation therapists, community outreach workers, and other professionals. These projects generally involve intergenerational mentoring of youths by older adults; including storytelling, social skill development (collaboration and communication), and relationship building.

Stewardship is another common aspect of these projects, often accomplished through community building activities, such as political activism and cultural maintenance, which are designed to improve conditions in the participants' communities. Other activities have included vegetable gardening and landscaping in housing developments, quilting in churches and temples, and mentoring circles in community or cultural centers. In some projects, these stewardship activities include youths becoming family or community historians so that family and community history and stories are preserved and passed down to younger generations (Brown, 1995).

Discussion

This chapter summarizes and applies some of the basic life narrative continuity questions introduced in Chapter 4, as well as advanced life narrative review skills. Therefore, the chapter demonstrates how practitioners can use basic and advanced life narrative skills in an integrated manner with older adults, in both traditional and nontraditional settings. The discussion normalizes the aging process and unique developmental tasks older adults are confronted with, such as integrity and identity, coming to terms with their lives, and managing the stigma often associated with this life stage. In addition, the chapter clarifies how service providers can decrease individual and institutional stigma by providing preventive services such as psycho-education groups on the life review and aging, as well as providing other services in non-traditional settings. Finally, the chapter highlights intergenerational partnerships, which involve family stories, community stories, and personal life narratives to increase social supports for older adults and their opportunities to mentor future generations.

References

Allen, K. R., & Walker, A. J. (2009). Theorizing about families and aging from a feminist perspective. In V. L. Bengtson, M. Silverstein, N. M. Putney, & D. Gans (Eds.), *Handbook of theories of aging* (pp. 517–528). New York: Springer.

Andereck, P., & Pence, R. (1991). *Computer genealogy: A guide to research through high technology*. Salt Lake City, UT: Ancestry.

Anderson, R. (Retrieved 6/20/10). College Degrees in Genealogy and Family History. www.ehow.com/agout_6305213_college-degrees-genealogh-family-history.html.

Brown, J. G. (1995). Co-located intergenerational activities in the Department of Health and Human Services. Washington, DC: U.S. Government Document #A-05-94-0009.

Bruner, J. (1999). Narratives of aging. *Journal of Aging Studies, 13*, 7–9,

Burroughs, T. (2001). *A beginners' guide to tracing the African American family tree*. New York: Fireside.

Caldwell, R. L. (2005). At the confluence of memory and meaning-life review with older adults and families: Using narrative therapy and the expressive arts to remember and reauthor stories of resilience. *Family Journal of Counseling and Therapy for Couples and Families, 13*, 172–175.

Clark, P. G. (2001). Narrative gerontology in clinical practice: Current applications and future prospects. P. G. Clark & G. M. Kenyon (Eds.), *Narrative gerontology: Theory, research, and practice* (pp. 193–214). New York: Springer.

Diaz de Chumaceiro, C. L. (2000). A note on poetry therapy in health care training programs. *Journal of Poetry Therapy, 13*, 219–223.

Dorfman, L. T., Murty, S. A., Evans, J. J., Ingram, J. G., & Power, J. R. (2004). History and identity in the narratives of rural elders. *Journal of Aging Studies, 18*, 187–203.

Erikson, E. H. (1994). *Identity and the life cycle*. New York: W. W. Norton.

Haley, A. (1976). *Roots: The saga of an American family*. New York: Doubleday.

Howells, M. (2004). Google for genealogy. *Ancestry Magazine*, pp. 59–61.

Jarvinen, M. (2004). Life histories and the perspective of the present. *Narrative Inquiry, 14*, 45–68.

Osher Life Long Learning Institutes (Retrieved 6/20/10). Wikipedia encyclopedia. en.wikipedia.org/wiki/osher_Lifelong_Learning_Institutes.

Pals, J. L. (2006). Authoring a second chance in life: Emotion and transformational processing in narrative identity. *Research into Human Development, 3*, 101–120.

Peck, M. D. (2001). Looking back at life and its influence on subjective well-being. *Journal of Gerontological Social Work, 35*, 3–17.

Shenk, D. (2002). Narratives and self-identity in later life: Two rural American older women. *Journal of Aging Studies, 16*, 401–413.

Taylor, J. A. (1985). Haiku: A form to air feelings about aging. *Geriatric Nursing, 6*, 81–82.

U.S. Surgeon General (Retrieved on June 15, 2010). The United States Surgeon General's Family History Initiative. http://www.surgeongeneral.gov/familyhistory/.

Webster, J. D. (1999). World views and narrative gerontology: Situating reminiscence behavior within a lifespan perspective. *Journal of Aging Studies, 13*, 29–42.

Chapter 10

HELPING FAMILIES AND COUPLES TO MANAGE CONFLICTS THROUGH RESOLUTION-BASED METAPHORS AND OTHER NARRATIVE RITUALS

> The most embarrassing part of this whole thing was when Child Welfare rang my door bell and accused me of abusing my son Todd. I had no idea they were coming or why they were there. All our neighbors and congregation know what happened! Just think what that was like for me, a pastor and well-known community leader. The Bible warns us not to spare the rod and spoil the child, so I just did what I was supposed to do. I'm a good parent *and* a good Christian!
>
> -Rev. Bobby Jansen

When parents such as the Reverend and Ms. Jansen are confronted with conflicts, or the need for family rule changes, they may become stuck from relying on past parental, family, religious, cultural, or value injunctions (Hardy & Laszloffy, 1995; Killian, 2001; Marks, 2004) (see Chapter 4 regarding meaning making based on world views and values). Those injunctions may involve inherent conflicts, or conflicts can surface because of how the injunctions are applied by families or by particular members. Often those conflicts surface during transitions in a family's life, such as when a special needs child is diagnosed with a chronic disability or the oldest child reaches adolescence. (Bermudez & Bermudez, 2002; Dollahite, 2003; Thomson, Bell, Holland, Henderson, McGrellis, & Sharpe, 2002).

Schwartz (1999) indicates that while stresses from a transition may precipitate a family crisis, there may be other underlying and equally significant family conflicts that need to be addressed simultaneously. As the practitioner recognized from the Jansen family's presenting narrative, listening closely to those narratives can reveal how a family has become stuck, for example, due to a religious injunction. This type of critical listening and thinking is an essential aspect of narrative practice with families and couples (Killian, 2001; McLeod, 1997).

This chapter addresses typical practice questions raised by service providers about how to help couples and families to manage conflicts, and how to facilitate change when religious, cultural, and other issues are keeping them stuck. Three narrative skills are included in the discussion to illustrate how providers can facilitate changes related to those questions: Helping families to analyze their existing conflict-based metaphors, develop and practice new redecision skills, and establish and celebrate new resolution-based metaphors and other positive family rituals.

Practice Skills: Listening to and Analyzing Families' Existing Metaphors And Helping Them to Develop and Practice New Redecision Skills

Practice Overview

One of the goals in the first session, after listening to the family's presenting narrative, is to help the members diffuse their conflicts sufficiently so some beginning work can take place. This diffusion process involves facilitating the family's understanding and acknowledgement that getting stuck is a normal part of family life (Doherty, 2001). It helps families also to understand how normalizing getting stuck or reaching an impasse can provide an opportunity for positive change, even in small steps.

It is equally important for providers to point out to families that certain issues need to be addressed directly. Examples include injunctions and beliefs that have contributed to the presenting problem or are dangerous for various members (Wendell, 2003). The Jansen family, in this chapter's introduction, illustrates how members can reveal such injunctions in their presenting narratives. Families such as the Jansens often have difficulty acknowledging initially that old decisions such as using physical punishment are not adaptive although they may seem to be; or that they have serious consequences. However, the goal is to help the members reach those conclusions as a foundation for redecision making (Brabender, Smolar, & Fallon, 2004).

Some practitioners can inadvertently reinforce family conflicts and impasses. Carlson, Kirkpatrick, Hecker, and Killmer (2002) documented the reluctance of some family therapists to address religion and spirituality even when those issues are a source of injunctions that have contributed to a family's impasse (see Chapter 1 on spirituality). Discussing concepts such as normalizing family impasses, and identifying injunctions that contribute to impasses, early adaptive decisions, later consequences of those decisions, and redecision making sets the stage for a family's initial and ongoing work.

Practice Example: Background Information

Bobby and Lillie Jansen are a Caucasian couple who live in a small town in the southeastern state where they grew up. They have been married for 15 years. The couple was referred by Protective Services for court-mandated counseling with a Family Service Agency (FSA) in a nearby city after their 13-year-old son, Todd, called the Protective Services hot line. A subsequent investigation revealed Reverend Jansen regularly used corporal punishment to discipline all of their children, including 11-year-old Simone, six-year-old Bobby Jr., and Todd.

The hotline call occurred after his father beat Todd for sneaking out of the house at 10:00 o'clock one night to smoke cigarettes with his friends. Reverend Jansen punished Todd by locking him in his room at night for a week. When he discovered Todd was continuing to sneak out, according to Todd, his father beat him with a large belt and his fists. Reverend Jensen admitted beating Todd with a large belt, but said he only hit him once with his fist accidentally when Todd pulled away from him. The parents preferred counseling at the FSA instead of a Christian counseling agency in the same city, when given a choice, because they thought church members might find out about the counseling from staff at the latter agency. Reverend Jansen requested a male counselor at the FSA because he did not think he could work well with a female counselor.

Practice Analysis: Cognitive Behavioral and Narrative Interventions

INITIAL WORK. During the first session, the practitioner, Ben Caruthers, met with the unit to identify the family's strengths and the members' individual concerns about the family. He also had each member talk about the father's use of corporal punishment with Todd and the other children, the hotline call, and how the members had been affected during and after the incident. Ben reminded the family that the Court had stipulated that no physical punishment should be used with any of the children and that the goal was to help the parents find other more acceptable ways to discipline. Meanwhile, Todd was expected to follow the family's curfew and other rules with the support of family counseling.

Ben then scheduled the next five sessions with the parents, while also checking in with the entire family at the beginning of each session about their issues and concerns. The plan included several subsequent sessions with the family as a unit to address family issues, after the first three sessions were completed with the couple alone to address parenting issues. Ben also continued the couple work after he began the family sessions.

COUPLE COUNSELING. During their couple sessions, it became clear that Ms. Jansen did not always agree with her husband's use of physical punishment. But she did not intervene because of a parental injunction she had been taught as a child. This injunction meant: "The husband is the head of the household and the wife should obey him."

As noted previously, her husband was following what they called a conservative religious belief that they quoted from the Book of Proverbs in the Old Testament: "Foolishness is bound in the heart of a child, but the rod of correction shall drive it far from him." Interestingly, Reverend Jansen found the above verse after he discovered the one he had paraphrased in their presenting narrative, "Spare the rod and spoil the child," was not actually in the Bible (Ontario Consultants on Religious Tolerance, retrieved October 24, 2010). Although the parents characterized their beliefs as strong, they admitted they sometimes wavered and experienced conflicts about them and about their identities as well (White, 2001). Ms. Jansen wondered why she had to be "a silent ghost" about her husband's use of physical punishment in order to show respect for him. Similarly, Mr. Jansen said he thought about himself as "an avenging angel" when he was beating his children.

Ben helped to reinforce and expand on the couple's insights about family conflicts related to the metaphors they had each identified: "Being a silent ghost" meant not having any power according to Ms. Jansen, once she thought about the issue for a while (see Chapter 2 and Table 2.1: "Clients' Found Narratives," public domain narrative forms) (Ewing & Allen, 2008). "Being an avenging angel with a rod," rather than a loving father, made Reverend Jansen feel like a bully. He had been bullied a lot by larger boys when he was growing up. Table 10.1 points out that family redecision making begins when practitioners use the skill of listening to and helping families to analyze their rule- and conflict-based metaphors (Skill I-A) (Zimmerman & Dickerson, 1994), as Ben did in this case.

Ben normalized the family's impasse and the interventions used by internal and external agents (see Table 10.1: Skill I-B). He said Todd's Protective Services HotLine call provided necessary help to the family (internal), and the court's stipulation about participating in mandated counseling and not using corporal punishment provided them with the resources they needed to change (external). Moreover, the latter intervention led to the parents' agreement with the moratorium on their existing corporal punishment rule (see Table 10.1: Skill I-C). To reinforce the moratorium, the internal and external agent interventions, and the parents' identification of the conflict-based metaphors that were keeping them stuck, Ben wrote those issues on a flip chart he kept in his office. He referred to those issues frequently during counseling sessions to remind the couple and family about their progress and their agreements.

The counseling included working within the couple's existing belief system or metaphors, without judging them, to initiate change (see Table 10.1: Skill I-D) (Hodge, 2004; Keller-Cohen & Gordon, 2003). For example, not blaming Ms. Jansen for silently supporting her husband's use of corporal punishment was important. The process included not stigmatizing Mr. Jansen for using this form of punishment. Ben's nonblaming response made it possible to help the couple recognize the consequences of their belief systems for themselves as parents and individuals, which helped them to begin to challenge those beliefs (see Table 10.1: Skill II-A).

In addition, Ben encouraged the parents to identify some of the consequences for their children, to encourage additional changes on their part. The children had discussed a number of consequences related to

Table 10.1
HELPING FAMILIES TO CLARIFY OLD CONFLICT-BASED METAPHORS
AND TO DEVELOP NEW RESOLUTION-BASED METAPHORS AND
OTHER NARRATIVE RITUALS

Family Redecision Making: A Narrative and Cognitive Behavioral Change Process		
I. Listen to-Analyze Families' Existing Metaphor(s)	II. Help Families Develop-Practice Redecision Skills	III. Help Families Develop-Celebrate New Metaphor(s)

(A) Listen to and help families identify their system's rule-based conflict metaphors (from their presenting narratives)
 	
(B) Normalize intervention efforts of internal and external agents
 	
(C) Agree on existing rule moratorium
 	
(D) Begin initial change strategy by working within families' belief system or existing metaphor
	(A) Help identify consequences of existing rule- and conflict-based metaphors
	
	(B) Explore desired short- and long-term goals and effects of existing consequences on those goals
	
	(C) Explore alternative rules or rituals that can help the unit reach its goals and newly desired consequences
	
	(D) Practice redecision making and modify as needed within the parental subsystem first
		(A) Spread redecision making practice to whole family system and external systems, including tasks
		
		(B) Develop and practice new resolution-based metaphor(s)
		
		(C) Celebrate those new metaphor(s):
		
		  1. by monitoring and revising change process over time as needed
		
		  2. by establishing other new narrative rituals to support family changes

corporal punishment in their presenting sibling narrative during the initial family session. The parents remembered their children had described feeling unloved, scared, hurt, and treated unfairly. The children had talked about sometimes feeling more defiant about breaking rules after being beaten, rather than wanting to follow the rules, and wanting to kick the walls or hurt someone else.

Although the parents heard their children describe those consequences in the initial family session, it was only during the couple sessions where they identified the consequences for themselves as parents that they actually understood the consequences for their children. Ben included the consequences for the parents and children on the Jansen family flip chart, which listed the family's previous progress such as what they had learned and their agreements. Reviewing this information and the change process with the couple helped them to see they were now working together as an empowered collaborative parent subsystem (Marks, 2003), rather than as a powerful husband-powerless wife dyad.

Continuing to work within the couple's belief system (see Table 10.1: Skill I-D), Ben asked them during one session if they knew the origin of the word "rod," that they had mentioned from the Bible. Ben had consulted a nondenominational minister and then researched this information in the Bible and on several websites (Ontario Consultants on Religious Tolerance, retrieved October 24, 2010 and November 11, 2010). The couple said they did not know the origin of the word.

Therefore Ben explained that a rod was an ancient tool that shepherds used to herd sheep. The rod helped them to guide, protect, and care for the sheep, and to prevent them from becoming lost from the herd or being attacked by coyotes or wolves. Ben described the rod or staff as an educational tool rather than something used to hit or punish the sheep; consistent with the Psalms twenty-third verse, "Thy rod and thy staff comfort me." Ben asked the couple how they could apply this ancient definition of a rod to how they raised their children. He suggested that they work together on their response to this question as a homework assignment.

During their next session, the couple reported they agreed a rod could help them to be shepherds in raising their children (a new metaphor). They said that meant rethinking their use of physical punishment. If the Bible did not say they should use physical punishment, Reverend Jansen concluded, they should not use it; although he admitted that changing would be difficult for him. Ms. Jansen wondered if using a rod to educate and guide their children might mean helping them to understand why the family's rules were important. But what discipline should they use if the children did not obey the rules, Reverend Jansen asked?

FAMILY COUNSELING. The Jansen's work in their couple sessions created a space for the practitioner to explore alternative forms of discipline to use with their children, and to facilitate the process of redecision making. Redecision making is the heart of Cognitive Behavioral Therapy (CBT) (Mathe, 2005) and the narrative process (Thomson et al., 2002), as shown in Table 10.1. The redecision making process is designed to help clients develop new resolution-based narratives and metaphors. To this end, the Jansens were asked to write out two or more goals they could agree on for raising their children, and to bring those goals to a planning session with the whole family unit. As the parents read their goals, Ben wrote them on the flip chart. He then asked the parents to point out which of the consequences on the flip chart that the children had identified helped to achieve the parents' goals for raising their children (see Table 10.1: Skill II-B).

The parents were quiet initially, and it became clear that they were concentrating on this task. Then they slowly pointed out one by one that their goals for raising children who were obedient, independent, good decision makers, and liked themselves were not consistent with the consequences their children had reported. The flip chart indicated that instead of achieving those goals, the children reported wanting to break the rules, feeling scared, thinking about striking out against something or someone, and seeing themselves as unloved. Ben pointed out that obviously the goals identified by the parents were important to them, but that family's interactions were taking them away from those goals. He asked the parents and the children to think about other types of discipline that could help to achieve those goals, since corporal punishment was not working. Ben also encouraged the parents to clarify their rules with the children, for example, to identify how the goal of obedience was related to particular rules, including not leaving the house without permission and completing their chores. Future family sessions included continuing to clarify the rules and child-rearing goals for the children, as well as redecision making and developing other resolution-based metaphors and narrative rituals.

Practice Skill: Helping Families to Develop and Celebrate New Resolution-Based Metaphors and Rituals

Practicing New Resolution-Based Metaphors/Rituals within the Family

NEW FAMILY RULES AND OTHER FORMS OF DISCIPLINE. Once the Jansens' redefined their rules such as the children returning home at the agreed curfew times, the family unit brainstormed a number of different forms of discipline. The parents were surprised when the children suggested grounding, extra chores at home, service to church members such as cutting grass and helping with household repairs, and writing "think sheets" like the ones students had to do at school when they broke the rules. Those sheets included a clear description of the rules that were broken and how they were broken, the consequences, an explanation of what the student had learned, and how he or she could handle future decisions to improve the outcomes. Think sheets are an example of age-related redecision-making narratives that are consistent with the Jansens' goal of helping their children learn to make good decisions.

NEW FAMILY RITUALS AND RESOLUTION-BASED METAPHORS. As the family implemented its new rules and other forms of discipline, the members used their new family meeting ritual at home and the family counseling sessions to monitor and improve the change process (see Table 10.1: Skills III-C-2 and III-C-1) (Doherty, 2001). The parents talked about their family as a "brainstorming or problem-solving machine," indicating they had developed a more resolution-based metaphor to describe themselves. Table 10.1 indicates the family was moving toward developing and celebrating new metaphors and family rituals within the whole family system (Skill III-A) (Muntigl, 2004; Thomson et al; 2002; White, 2000 and 2001; Zimmerman & Dickerson, 1994).

In one family counseling session, Reverend Jansen shared the following redecision making narrative, which highlighted his changed identity and family role (see Chapter 4: Figure 4.1: Cluster 1: The Core Narrated Self: Source of self-discovery, meaning making, and continuity):

> I remember telling you (Ben) in our first session, that "I'm a good parent and a good Christian. That was what I was trying to be, not what I was. I talked about being embarrassed about Child Welfare coming to our house. But now I see that God must have sent them to open my eyes, although it hurt at the time. But it helped us in the end. I was repeating my family upbringing and being bullied by bigger boys in my school. My father used beating to punish me mostly, and sometimes my brothers, like his father probably punished him. And that's how I learned to raise our children. I'm not making excuses. It was hearing them talk about how the whippings made them feel unloved and scared that made me see our family in their eyes. Now we have our family meetings where we talk about what's happening in the family and we include our children's ideas and my wife's too. We've become a problem-solving machine by working together. And my eyes have been opened. I'm a shepherd now and that means I use my rod to educate, guide, and protect our children!"

Practicing New Resolution-Based Metaphors in External Areas

THE PARENTS' PLANS. Ben's goal prior to terminating services to the family was to help the members anticipate and address challenges they were likely to encounter as they continued to practice their new skills. Consequently, he asked the two parents to develop separate plans for practicing their new resolution-based family metaphors and skills in a situation outside of the family (see Table 10.1: Skills III-A and B, and Skill C-1). Reverend Jansen decided he would discuss the use of what he now called healthy forms of discipline during a future meeting of his Ministerial Alliance.

Ben encouraged him to consider whether it would be more helpful to share his redecision-making narrative, sermon, or speech with his fellow ministers or with his congregation first. Reverend Jansen decided to begin with the ministers first. He planned to focus on his roles as a parent and shepherd in his personal life, especially regarding the use of corporal punishment. He also planned to broaden his shepherd metaphor by applying it to his role with his congregation. The discussion would involve his colleagues in assessing and sharing about their own experiences regarding their personal and professional roles. It would also help him to decide how to handle a future sermon on this topic with his congregation.

Ms. Jansen decided to talk to her quilting group, which included some ministers' wives, about how to change from being a "waiting heart attack" to a "stress buffer." One of her silent friends had died during the past year from a stress-related heart attack. Ms. Jansen made the connection between her friend's silent nature and her own "silent ghost" metaphor by explaining that keeping stress inside allows it to kill you (Flemke & Allen, 2008). Her adoption of the stress buffer metaphor introduced another new resolution-based metaphor in the Jansen family, and provided her quilting group with a tool for examining their own family and spousal roles.

TODD'S PLAN. Todd decided he would write a prevention letter or narrative that he then volunteered to read to a middle school class. In preparing for his counterattitudinal narrative (Campos, 2000), Todd revealed he and his friends had actually been smoking cigarettes *and* marijuana. His letter narrative was designed to help him convince younger students, including his younger siblings, to refrain from smoking both substances. This process requires the speaker to adopt a perspective that is incompatible with the future use of tobacco and other drugs based on cognitive dissonance (Campos, 2000).

Discussion

The Jansens' change process continued with some challenges and hurdles due to the strong injunctions that had guided their past family life. The members learned how to handle conflict effectively during the counseling and the period of supervision by Child Welfare and the Court. They became more supportive and helpful to one another. This discussion not only clarifies how they changed, but also how providers can facilitate change by identifying and exploring conflict-related metaphors from families' presenting narratives. Some of those metaphors may be explicit while others are implicit.

In addition, the discussion illustrates how practitioners can facilitate a family's search for resolution-based metaphors in the counseling process by working within the family's belief system, whether that system is religious-, cultural-, racial/ethnic-, location-, sexual orientation-, or social class-based. It is equally important for practitioners to use resources outside the client family system to clarify those belief systems, whether or not providers are members of those groups or belief systems.

In this chapter's case example, the family's religious-based belief system was the source of some of the family's strengths and challenges (Dollahite, Marks, & Goodman, 2004). Consequently, the practitioner utilized a nondenominational religious consultant and information from online websites to understand and work effectively within the family's belief and value systems. Chapter 1 described the role of spirituality in facilitating the emergence of narratives, and therefore, it is related to this chapter's discussion about the emergence of the family's presenting narrative and Reverend Jansen's redecision-making narrative. The discussion drew upon Chapter 4's analysis of Cluster 1 World Views and Related Main Belief Systems, along with value injunctions related to individuals and families (see Figure 4.1). Finally, this chapter builds upon Chapter 2 regarding the use of metaphors as a narrative form for understanding and helping families' address aspects of their belief systems that contribute to conflicts.

References

Bardill, D. R. (2001). Nonverbal poetry: Family life-space diagrams. *Journal of Poetry Therapy, 14*, 159–167.

Bermudez, J., & Bermudez, S. (2002). Altar-making with Latino families: A narrative therapy perspective. *Journal of Family Psychotherapy, 13*, 329–347.

Brabender, V., Smolar, A., & Fallon, A. E. (2004). *Essentials of group therapy.* New York: John Wiley & Sons.

Campos, L. (2000). It's OK to belong: A developmental view of redecision therapy with juvenile offenders. *Journal of Redecision Therapy, 2*, 43–66.

Carlson, T. D., & Erickson, M. J. (Eds.). (2002). *Spirituality and family therapy.* New York: Haworth.

Carlson, T. D., Kirkpatrick, D., Hecker, L., & Killmer, M. (2002). Religion, spirituality, and marriage and family therapy: A study of family therapists' beliefs about the appropriateness of addressing religious and spiritual issues in therapy. *Journal of Family Therapy, 30*, 157–171.

Doherty, W. J. (2001). *The intentional family: Simple rituals to strengthen families.* New York: Quill.

Dollahite, D. C. (2003). Fathering for eternity: Generative spirituality in Latter-Day Saint fathers of children with special needs. *Review of Religious Research, 44*, 339–351.

Dollahite, D. C., Marks, L. D., & Goodman, M. (2004). Religiosity and families: Relational and spiritual linkages in a diverse and dynamic cultural context. In M. J. Coleman & L. H. Ganong (Eds.), *The handbook of contemporary families: Considering the past, contemplating the future.* Thousand Oaks, CA: Sage.

Ewing, J., & Allen, K. R. (2008). Women's narratives about God and gender: Agency, tension, and change. *Journal of Systemic Therapies, 27*, 90–107.

Flemke, K., & Allen, K. R. (2008). Women's experience of rage: A critical feminist analysis. *Journal of Marital and Family Therapy, 34*, 92–110.

Grabe, W. (2002). Narrative and expository macro-genres. In A. Johns (Ed.), *Genre in the classroom: Multiple perspectives* (pp. 249–267). Mahwah, NJ: Lawrence Erlbaum Associates.

Hardy, K. V., & Laszloffy, T. A. (1995). The cultural genogram: Key to training culturally competent family therapists. *Journal of Marital and Family Therapy, 21*, 227–237.

Hodge, D. R. (2004). Developing cultural competency with Evangelical Christians. *Families in Society, 85*, 251–260.

Keller-Cohen, D., & Gordon, C. (2003). "On Trial": Metaphor in telling the life Story. *Narrative Inquiry, 17*, 1–40.

Killian, K. D. (2001). Reconstituting racial histories *and* identities: The narratives of interracial couples. *Journal of Marital and Family Therapy, 27*, 27–42.

Marks, L. (2004). Sacred practices in highly religious families: Christian, Jewish, Mormon, and Muslim perspectives. *Family Process, 43*, 217–231.

Marks, L. D. (2003). The effects of religious beliefs in marriage and family. *Marriage and Family, 12*, 2–10.

Mathe, C. (2005). *The Redecision Approach to Transformative Change.* In house publication by Authentic Leadership Center: Cold River, CA.

Mazza, N. (2001). The place of the poetic in dealing with death and loss. *Journal of Poetry Therapy, 15,* 29–35.

Mazza, N. (1999). *Poetry therapy: Interface of the arts and psychology.* Boca Raton, FL: CRC Press.

McLeod, J. (1997). *Narrative and psychotherapy.* London: Sage.

Mathe, C. (2005). Approach to transformative change. Training Materials, 1–16. Gold Rush, CA: Authentic Leadership Center.

Monk, G., Winsdale, J., Crocket, K., & Epston, D. (Eds.). (1997). Narrative therapy in practice: The archaeology of hope (pp. 8–15). San Francisco: Jossey-Bass.

Muntigl, P. (2004). Ontogenesis in narrative therapy: A linguistic semiotic examination of client change. *Family Process, 43,* 109–129.

Ontario Consultants on Religious Tolerance (retrieved 11/9/2010). http://www.religioustolerance.org/spankin13.htm.

Ontario Consultants on Religious Tolerance: Corporal Punishment (retrieved 10/24/2010). http://www.religioustolerance.org/spankin8.htm.

Schwartz, R. C. (1999). Narrative therapy expands and contracts family therapy's horizons. *Journal of Marital and Family Therapy, 25,* 263–267.

Thomson, R., Bell, R., Holland, J., Henderson, S., McGrellis, S., & Sharpe, S. (2002). Critical moments: Choice, chance, and opportunity in young people's narratives of transition. *Sociology, 36,* 335–354.

Wendell, R. (2003). Lived religion and family therapy: What does spirituality have to do with it? *Family Process, 42,* 165–179.

White, M. (2001). Narrative practice and the unpacking of idenity conclusions. *Gecko: A Journal of Deconstruction and Narrative Practice,* 1–3.

White, M. (2000). Reflections on narrative practice. Adelaide, South Australia: Dulwich Centre Publications.

White, M., & Epston, D. (1990). *Narrative means to therapeutic ends.* New York: W. W. Norton.

Zimmerman, J. L., & Dickerson, V. C. (1994). Using a narrative metaphor: Implications for theory *and* clinical practice. *Family Process, 33,* 223–245.

Chapter 11

UTILIZING COMMON MARGINALIZED AND EXCEPTION NARRATIVES WITH MULTIPLE CLIENT SYSTEMS TO FACILITATE INDIVIDUAL AND STRUCTURAL CHANGES

> When you (the therapist) asked Cheryl if she remembers a time when she kept a cool head, I thought—Me? Never! But I remember a time when I didn't get promoted at work. I told a coworker I was upset. She said I was always expecting to be discriminated against because I'm gay—that I'm too sensitive. It made me feel small. My grandfather said, "If somebody says something bad about you, say something good to yourself." So I said, Shawn, you worked hard for that promotion, but you're okay whether you got it or not. The anger I felt caught a ride on a thunder cloud and flew away.
>
> —Shawn Riley

Individuals have rich opportunities to learn from one another through their involvement in multiple client modalities. Those modalities can help them to heal themselves based on the universal and unique experiences they reveal during narrative rituals in small groups, organizations or institutions, and communities (Carley, 2005; Jones, 2004; Barton, 2000). In one support group, Shawn shared the above narrative segment after another group member did not respond to the facilitator's effort to elicit an exception narrative from her. Shawn's "Me? Never"! response demonstrates how clients often deny the existence of such narrative experiences initially even though, like him, they then demonstrate the capacity to share and learn from their exception narratives (Gilbert & Beidler, 2001).

Moreover, one individual's exception or transformative narrative (see Table 5.2: Skill I-B) often leads to a narrative flooding process, when other participants suddenly recall and begin sharing similar narratives (Adler, Wagner, & McAdams, 2007; Carley, 2005; Hiersteiner, 2004). This chapter describes how practitioners can build on Chapter 5's discussion of basic social justice-related narrative skills, including advocacy by storytelling (involving exception narratives), and power transfer narratives. The chapter also presents advanced narrative skills for facilitating changes in the members of small groups, in institutional policies, and in communities. Those advanced skills consist of questions practitioners can ask to clarify narrative gaps and expand narrative openings, and to elicit and analyze social change narratives.

Practice Skills: Using Narrative Gaps and Openings Questions to Facilitate Movement from Marginalization to Exception Narratives

Practice Overview

BACKGROUND INFORMATION ON THE PRACTICE SETTING. The Samuel Parker Health Center is located in the northwestern region of the United States. The Center is a Federally Qualified Health Center (FQHC) and therefore, like other such centers, it provides free medical home services for under-and uninsured clients (Chandler, 2006). Primary care and mental health services are integrated in the Center. Staff members who provide those services are colocated onsite and they work collaboratively on the same treatment teams and units. The Center's catchment area includes two large counties, one urban and the other rural. The latter county has many remote and sparsely populated impoverished areas, including two Native American Reservations.

Primary care and mental health staff in the urban county provide their integrated clinic services in the Center, along with integrated outreach services in two satellite offices in other parts the county. One of the Center's current initiatives is to improve the integration of its substance abuse support group services and Diabetes Education groups. Integrated services are a priority because many adults served by the Center have long-term substance addictions and they are also diabetic or prediabetic. Some of them have related renal and high blood pressure complications.

GROUP STRUCTURE, FACILITATORS, AND COMPOSITION. Consequently, primary care and Integrated Dual Diagnosis Treatment staff members cofacilitate both types of group sessions. The groups are scheduled for one hour each, back to back, with the education groups following immediately after the support groups once per week. Although the main focus of the two types of groups is on either substance abuse recovery or diabetes education, staff encourages the members to connect the two topics in both groups. Staff members also help clients to explore cultural factors in their backgrounds that support or challenge efforts to enhance their physical and mental health. To emphasize connections between the two groups, as well as cultural effects, the facilitators use discussion questions focused on those topics, and related exercises and written handouts. They encourage guest speakers to integrate the topic areas in their presentations to the groups.

The group facilitators are 47-year-old Michael who has a degree in Counseling Psychology and is trained in substance abuse treatment; and 29-year-old Carla who is an Advanced Practice Registered Nurse (APRN) with a certification in diabetes education. Michael is of Hispanic background and speaks Spanish, while Carla's family immigrated to the United States from Bulgaria when she was ten years old. Both are experienced group facilitators, and they have cofacilitated the integrated groups over the past year. They have also collaborated on implementing narrative strategies in the groups.

The support group presented in this chapter's introduction has seven members, but during the identified session, only five members were in attendance. The members included:

1. 26-year-old Cheryl, a single Caucasian woman who has bulimia and is pre-diabetic. She is addicted to crack cocaine and has bipolar depression. Cheryl is a library technician, and has support from her concerned parents. Because of her low self-esteem; she only shares information when she is directly encouraged to by the facilitators.

2. 32-year-old Alicia is Puerto Rican; but she speaks very little Spanish. She just returned to the group after a two-month relapse. Her drugs of choice are powder cocaine and alcohol. Alicia has few social contacts outside of her family; she and her three children live with ex-husband's parents and siblings.

3. Shawn is a 24-year-old single man who was raised by his Irish Catholic grandfather and older sister. Since entering treatment for methamphetamine abuse and drug sales, Shawn has started a course in computer programming to upgrade his skills. He earned his GED within the last three months. He has Type I diabetes.

4. Bob is a 48-year-old African American Gulf War veteran who is married and has two stepchildren. He became addicted to alcohol after his discharge and he also has PTSD and Type II diabetes. Bob has not been able to obtain disability benefits from the Veterans Administration, although he has a mental health diagnosis and has worked only sporadically. His wife supports his group participation.

5. Ross is a 40-year-old Italian American married man who works as a plumber. He is in a court diversion program for a driving under the influence (DUI) conviction so his participation in alcohol treatment is mandatory. Ross has high blood pressure. His wife has been patient with his getting treatment, but now wants him to "hurry up and get a normal life."

Narrative Practice in the Integrated Small Groups

THE ADDICTION RECOVERY SUPPORT GROUP. Although the discussion in the following section focuses on only one of the integrated recovery support-diabetes education groups, it is representative of the other integrated groups provided by the Center. Shawn's narrative segment in this chapter's introduction begins as a marginalized narrative. Such narratives are defined in Chapter 5 as being invisible to privileged groups because they have low currency or value to those groups. Low currency narratives exist in the margins of dominant society since they contain experiences and perspectives that document institutionalized power discrepancies and they can challenge the status quo if they are acknowledged as reality (see Figure 5.1) (Barton, 2000; Williams, Labonte, & O'Brien, 2003). Those narratives are also embedded with social justice issues (Dessel, Rogge, & Garlington, 2006). Although Shawn's narrative begins as a marginalized narrative, it ends as an exception narrative, of which he seems unaware, perhaps because he is narrating it for the first time.

The exception segment of his narrative was elicited by Carla's question to Cheryl, "Do you remember a time when you kept a cool head?" Carla's strategic use of this question encouraged Shawn and other group members to think of a narrative experience in which the usual negative outcome, such as "losing their heads," or getting angry did not occur (see Table 5.2: Skill I-B). Such questions are designed to elicit a survival or exception narrative which involves advocacy by storytelling, whether the advocacy is designed to accomplish self-change or institutional change (Dessel et al., 2005; Greene, Lee, & Hoffpauir, 2005). In response to Carla's question, Shawn began to share a narrative that revealed how he was stuck in the marginalized aspects of that experience. He said, for example, the experience ". . . made me feel small." When clients like Shawn have not narrated such experiences previously, or even after narrating them, they may continue to feel devalued and powerless.

The narrative gap questions in Table 11.1 are designed to help Shawn and other clients to explore the sources of such feelings, and also to identify hidden narrative resources they are unaware of (Jones, 2004). Those questions are important because feeling devalued, powerless, angry, or abandoned are often triggers for addicted clients to relapse (become active addicts again), or to binge on unhealthy foods (raise their blood sugar or blood pressure ratings to dangerous levels). Therefore, after Shawn shared his narrative, Carla and Michael helped him to fill in some of the gaps by asking gap questions such as those included in Table 11.1. For example, Carla asked him to describe his coworker's facial expression and voice tone when she said Shawn was too sensitive (Narrative Gap Question/Skill I-A). Shawn said she had one hand on her hip, suddenly raised her voice, rolled her eyes, and then leaned toward him and flipped her other hand in the air.

Ross said, "That sounds like she really meant, here we go again, same old sob story from Shawn." Michael turned to Shawn and asked, "Is that how you read the situation, Shawn?" Shawn nodded his head saying, "Yea, and when she said I was always expecting to be discriminated against because I'm gay, I think she mighta' meant I was playing the 'gay card.'" Based on input from Ross and Michael, Shawn had answered an unasked gap question from Table 11.1, that is, "What he thought his coworker meant or was implying by what she said?" (Narrative Gap Question/Skill I-B). Bob said, "Well Shawn, it coulda' been worse, she coulda said you weren't really passed over, that it was

Table 11.1
ADVANCED NARRATIVE PRACTICE SKILLS WITH CLIENTS IN GROUPS,
INSTITUTIONS, AND COMMUNITIES TO ADDRESS SOCIAL-JUSTICE ISSUES

Narrative Questions About Clients' Marginalized Experiences	Narrative Questions About Clients' Marginalized Experiences
I) Narrative Gap Questions/Skills (Clarify Gaps):	II) Narrative Opening Questions/Skills (Expand Openings)
(A) What did the person in your narrative or listening to your narrative say and do specifically regarding what happened?	(A) What was the experience like when you narrated what happened?
(B) What do you think he/she meant or implied about what happened based on what was said (it didn't happen at all, it didn't happen as described, or it happened for a different reason than the narrator indicated)?	(B) Based on narrating this experience and answering gap questions, what lessons have you learned about: (1) Your strengths, including your talents, resources, skills, qualities, and supports? (2) Potential allies or who you identify with or have common experiences with?
(C) What value or importance did the person place on the experience you described (stated or implied?), based on a scale from 1(= not important) to 10 (=extremely important)	(3) Lessons learned about problem solving, coping, values, identity, or prevention?
(D) What effects, outcomes, or consequences did you experience based on what the person said or implied?	(4) Strategic reframing of your situation or alternative ways of thinking?
(E) What did the person say or imply about what needs to be addressed, improved, or remain the same in the situation? Who is the hero/heroine, the villain, powerful, powerless?	(5) Strategic next steps such as advocacy with allies, decision-makers, or others? (6) Strategic life narrative work or renaming the life book?

all in your mind, like you imagined what happened." Carla said to Bob, "Good point, sometimes when someone says a person is too sensitive, they're implying, yes it happened as you described it (they didn't notify you before announcing someone else was being promoted), but you shouldn't take it so personally."

Michael summed up their discussion by saying, "So someone like Shawn's coworker can imply a situation someone described didn't really happen at all, or it happened as it was described, but the person is really overreacting or taking it too personally? What else could Shawn's coworker have been implying, Cheryl"? After thinking for a few seconds, Cheryl responded, "Well, she could have meant Shawn didn't deserve a promotion." "Or that he wasn't promoted for some other reason, like he wasn't there long enough," Ross suggested.

Carla asked the group how important Shawn's coworker thought his being passed over was from her perspective, looking directly at Alicia (see Table 11.1: Narrative Gap Question/Skill I-C). "Maybe not important at all," Alicia responded. Shawn said again, "Our talk that day made me feel small, like I was being petty and unfair. It put a big hard knot in the pit of my stomach, and I felt my face get rigid and surprised at what she said. I thought to myself, don't tell her anything else, you can't trust her with your feelings."

Shawn's response clarified the effects of what his coworker said and did, including her implied lack of empathy about his disappointment over not being promoted and his concerns about possibly being discriminated against. His comment about the gay card implies he believes his coworker saw him as the villain in the situation (see Narrative Gap Question/Skill I-E). Shawn said his coworker implied that "He should suck it up"! To him, her response meant that nothing else needed to be done about the situation or that the employers' promotion policies did not need to be changed because they were all powerful (see Narrative Gap Question/Skill I-E).

The rest of the group session was used by the facilitators to discuss how stress such as what Shawn described, a big knot in the pit of his stomach, affected the members' physical and mental health. They did an exercise in which the members identified a stressful situation from the previous week, and then discussed the effects on each member's health. Their examples included Cheryl's blood sugar readings which spiked after her car stopped running and she was unable to pay for needed repairs. The facilitators announced they would begin the Diabetes Education Group after a brief break.

THE DIABETES EDUCATION (DE) GROUP. The facilitators began the DE group session by saying they reviewed the recovery support group session during the break. They had decided to begin the session by having the members identify strategies they could use to manage the stress they had described in their examples, in order to prevent a relapse to active addiction or high blood sugar ratings (Arroyo, Miller, & Tonigan, 2003; Brown, Kouzekanani, Garcia, & Craig, 2002). They asked the members to talk about what strategies worked for them, beginning with Shawn. "How had he managed the stress he experienced while talking with his coworker about not being promoted?"

Shawn said the discussion with her happened right after he entered his first drug treatment program the previous year. He explained that when he talked about the situation for the first time during the recovery support group they had just finished, it was as though he was back in the middle of the discussion with his co-worker again and feeling the same physical reactions (see Table 11.1: Narrative Opening Question/Skill II-A). Shawn remembered thinking if he could only get high, he would be able to smother or medicate the stress and bad feelings he was experiencing.

Michael asked Shawn how he had survived the effects of that stress during his prior treatment program and what he had learned from that experience. The goal of this narrative opening question is to help clients identify and expand on the lessons they have learned from their survival or exception narratives (see Table 11.1: Narrative Opening Question/Skill II-B-1) (Williams et al., 2003). Shawn said, "I think it was remembering what my grandfather always told me, 'You're better off taking care of yourself when you're in hard times. If somebody says something bad about you, instead of feeling worried or sad, say something good to yourself.' Remembering his words got me through the early days of my treatment back then, when I was feeling helpless and probably scared too." Shawn added, "It was like my grandfather was there with me, and watching over me."

Michael said, "It sounds like your grandfather was a support for you, a real ally." Shawn nodded his head saying, "He kept me from leaving the program AMA (against medical advice), and he helped me to cope with all the treatment rules I had to follow. So I survived!" Here Shawn pointed out another lesson he learned from the experience, how to cope with stress by staying connected with someone he viewed as a strong person and an ally (see Table 11.1: Narrative Opening Question/Skill II-B-2 and II-B-3).

Carla said, "Your grandfather actually reframed your situation to make it work for you. Basically he said when someone tries to rob you of your power by making you feel bad about yourself, you can take that power and use it to help heal yourself" (see Table 11.1: Narrative Opening Question/Skill II-B-4) (Freeman & Couchonnal, 2006; White, 2000). Shawn said he felt less stress because, "I realize now how I managed to keep from relapsing during my first treatment program. But I think I kept some of the stress from that disagreement with my coworker until now. The group helped me see what I learned today so I can use what my grandfather taught me in the future. I can see he's had an important effect on me all of my life, even today" (see Table 11.1: Narrative Openings/Skill II-B-6).

Michael then asked Cheryl if she would talk about her stress example involving her car breaking down, and the strategies she has used or could use to manage her stress. Cheryl shared the following narrative segment with the group:

> Yesterday when I left the car repair shop I got a ride to my neighborhood with someone who worked there. I was too agitated to go to work so I called in sick. The man that owned the shop said he wasn't running no charity shop-that I had to pay for my car like everybody else did.

Carla then asked Cheryl how she felt or reacted when the man said that to her. Carla explained it would help the other group members to understand the situation if she, Cheryl, could explain what happened next (Table 11.1: Narrative Gap Question/Skill I-D). Cheryl then continued with an additional segment of her narrative:

> Well, I was upset. I knew if I binged on food that wasn't in my diet I'd make my situation worse, like donuts and fast food, but I couldn't stop myself. So that's what I ate the rest of the day. I just didn't care at the time, 'cause I didn't have the money to fix my car. I was feeling bad because I can't get to work without a car. If I'd made myself vomit that would have been worse, but making my blood sugar readings shoot up didn't help either. No matter what I did, it was a problem. I just didn't know what to do! By then, the more I ate the worse I felt. I knew I was stressed out because I had a real bad headache and I was feeling heavy and bloated by then.

Carla asked Alicia, "What would you have done in Cheryl's situation; what stress management strategies have you tried that worked for you?" (see Table 11.1: Narrative Openings Question/Skill II-B-3 and II-B-4). Alicia said she tried not to miss the group sessions when she was having problems; that she always learned from the other members' situations. She also mentioned that she sometimes talked over problems with her mother-in-law or her minister, especially when she was stressed out about raising her children or about money. Michael asked Cheryl if any of Alicia's strategies could be helpful to her.

Cheryl responded, "I guess I could have gone to my OA (Over-Eaters Anonymous) group and talked about my situation. Or I could have come here to Samuel Parker for the Crisis Clinic. I don't know why, but at the time, I wasn't thinking about the support I could get from my OA peers or the Crisis Clinic." Michael said it was clear that Cheryl and the other group members had a better understanding of the connections between their physical and mental health issues based on the discussion during the two group sessions. He said those sessions were reinforcing for he and Carla as the group facilitators, because they reinforced the importance of helping the members identify sources of power to manage their addiction recovery, diabetes education, or PTSD (Beach, 2005; DeCoster & Cummings, 2005; Norman, 2000).

Practice Skills: Using Advocacy by Storytelling, Power Transfer Narratives, And Organizational and Community Social Change Narratives

Background on the Practice Organization and the Community

INITIAL STRATEGIC PLANNING AND COMMUNITY INVOLVEMENT EFFORTS. The cofacilitators of the Samuel Parker Health Center's integrated small groups made regular reports to the Chief Executive Officer about evaluation outcomes for those groups. Doe and Lowery (2004) recommend such evaluations for general practice, and for developing community interventions in particular. The CEO requested evaluation reports on the groups' effectiveness in order to plan how to enhance the quality and quantity of services to residents in the rural communities within the Center's catchment area, called the Great Neck Township. As part of the Center's strategic planning for the current year, administrators decided to convene a community meeting to discuss the type of group and other culturally appropriate services residents in Great Neck believed they needed. The administrators were especially concerned about making the Center's services more accessible to residents from the two Native American Reservations as well as residents living in a nearby Hmong community (Beach, 2005; Bernal & Saez-Santiago, 2006; Hyde, 2004; Whitbeck, 2006). Those residents were extremely underrepresented among the clients and family members that the Center served currently.

Through its informal coordination partnerships with the Indian Health Service, the Housing Authority, and the Asian American Alliance in Great Neck, the Center's administrators compiled a list of community leaders and residents to participate in their strategic planning meeting. The afternoon meeting was held in the Center's large meeting hall to accommodate the number of expected participants and a meal was served to welcome them. Center staff included the administrators, the cofacilitators of the integrated groups, and other members of the integrated primary care and mental health teams. Participants from outside the Center included staff and members of the Center's three Great Neck coordination partners, and a small number of the township's Native American and Hmong community members.

The Center's administrators welcomed the communities' input regarding the strategic plan, but they were surprised by the members' recommendations to: (1) establish two separate outreach strategies for the Native American and Hmong communities' involvement; (2) canvas the reservation residents with a Native American key informant to solicit their input about who should be included in the next planning meeting, the site of the meeting, and how it should be conducted; and (3) schedule a meeting with the recommended participants to identify services they prefer, prioritize the services, and then plan how to provide those priority services with culturally appropriate interventions and modalities.

THE REVISED COMMUNITY INVOLVEMENT AND PLANNING PROCESS. The Center administrators decided to follow the recommendations of the initial planning group because those recommendations had the potential for creating new partnerships with individuals at the grass roots and leadership levels on the two reservations (Wertheimer, Beck, Brooks, & Wolk, 2004; Whitbeck, 2006; Williams et al., 2003). Two potential key informants were identified by the reservations' Tribal or General Councils, and those individuals agreed to participate in helping to identify and encourage residents to participate in the second planning meeting, and in helping to facilitate that meeting. One of the key informants was Peter Redbird, a tribal elder and Tribal Council member who was recognized by reservation residents for his strong community leadership and storytelling abilities. The second key informant was Thomas Sixkiller, a 35-year-old traditional healer who was also a certified family mediator.

Based on information that the two key informants helped to collect during the canvass of residents on the two reservations, the second community planning meeting was held in a community hall on one of the reservations. Feedback from the potential participants indicated they preferred a Friday or Saturday evening meeting on the reservation rather than a morning or afternoon meeting at the Center. The planners agreed that the Center administrators and Peter Redbird would facilitate the meeting. Peter was asked to first welcome the participants and the Center staff and administrators, while also providing some opening remarks about the meeting's purpose and process, and then handling the introductions.

The Practice Organization and Community Social Change Process

SETTING THE STAGE FOR SOCIAL CHANGES WITH A CULTURAL NARRATIVE. As part of Peter's opening remarks, he told the following Native American narrative about power and social change, which was entitled "How the Fly Saved the River":

> Many years ago when the world was new, there was a beautiful river. Fish in great numbers lived in this river, and its water was so pure and sweet that all the animals came there to drink. A giant moose heard about the river and he too came there to drink. But he was so big, and he drank so much, that soon the water began to sink lower and lower. The beavers were worried. The water around their lodges was disappearing. Soon their homes would be destroyed. The muskrats were worried too. What would they do if the water vanished? How could they live? The fish were very worried. The other animals could live on land if the water dried up, but they couldn't. All the animals tried to think of a way to drive the moose from the river, but he was so big that they were too afraid to try. Even the bear was afraid of him. At last the fly said he would try to drive the moose away. All the animals laughed and jeered. How could a tiny fly frighten a giant moose? The fly said nothing, but that day, as soon as the moose appeared, he went into action. He landed on the moose's foreleg and bit sharply. The moose stamped his foot harder, and each time he stamped,

the ground sank and the water rushed in to fill it up. Then the fly jumped about all over the moose, biting and biting and biting until the moose was in a frenzy. He dashed madly about the banks of the river, shaking his head, stamping his feet, snorting and blowing, but he couldn't get rid of that pesky fly. At last the moose fled from the river, and didn't come back. The fly boasted to the other animals, "Even the small can fight the strong if they use their brains to think.

Peter Redbird concluded his narrative with a lesson he had learned from it: He said, "No matter how small and unimportant people seem to be, they have the power to create change, but only if they believe in change!" Peter's narrative set the stage with the participants by indicating the process was expected to lead to major changes, if the participants believed in change as the fly did. Consequently, the results of this second community meeting and subsequent meetings included a number of social changes that were implemented within the Center and within the Native American community.

CREATING SOCIAL CHANGES WITHIN THE INSTITUTION AND COMMUNITY. First, social changes occurred in the Center's institutionalized policies and practices related to planning and providing services to Native American residents. Some of those social changes included strategies recommended by authors and researchers in terms of culturally competent services and effective community development (Brown et al., 2002; Carpenter, 2002; Feinberg, Greenberg, & Osgood, 2004; Freeman, 2004; Tsui, Cheung, & Gellis, 2004; Wertheimer, Beck, Brooks, & Wolk, 2004; Whitbeck, 2006):

1. A Memorandum of Agreement was developed between the Center and the two Tribal Councils related to the latter's continued active involvement in planning, monitoring, and revising as needed culturally competent and integrated services to the Great Neck Native American communities;

2. The planning group designated two of the Center's 30 member Executive Board seats for Native American representation;

3. The Center hired a Native American outreach worker/case manager to increase the services provided to that community and to help organize and provide culturally competent services and evidence-based practices for that purpose; and

4. The planners recommended the development of integrated group services as the first priority among the recommended social changes.

This last recommendation was based on feedback from the planning participants that many Native American consumers would prefer group over individual services based on the cultural stigma they associate with individual mental health services. That earnest feedback signaled the beginning of a working relationship between the Center and the Native American planning participants. The feedback was also evidence of an intracommunity social change process among those participants. However, some community members' ambivalence about collaborating with the Center, and in other instances their unwillingness to do so, created challenges to the planning process. As Peter Redbird's rendition of the "Fly and Moose Narrative" suggests, there were community members who believed the destructive and self-involved moose could represent the Center and its administration. However, over time, the trust that had been gradually established within the Center-community planning group participants, spread to more of the community members who were not directly involved in the planning process.

Perhaps community members began to see themselves as the fly that took back or acknowledged and then used its own power to bring about meaningful social change. The narrative might also have represented an opportunity for community members who had experienced a lost or distorted cultural identity to gain a sense of wholeness. Carley (2005) and Lowery (1998) allude to the critical effects of spirituality and hope respectively on community and individual change. In fact, this entire description of the Center's initial and follow up efforts to involve the Great Neck Native American community in a strategic planning process is essentially a power transfer narrative. Table 5.2 indicates that such narratives involve groups that "Join forces to expand power and to influence those who can achieve or block systems change" (see Systems Change Skill II-B).

Discussion

This chapter's discussion of power transfer narratives, advocacy by storytelling, narrative gaps and opening questions, and social change narratives builds on the principles and skills introduced in Chapters 4 (the life narrative) and 5 (systems change). The present discussion connects the use of lessons learned from expanding narrative openings to how the life narrative can be revised (see Table 11.1: Narrative Opening Question/Skill II-B-6). The present discussion also links how understanding social change narratives can enhance the effective implementation of systems change strategies at micro, mezzo, and macro levels.

Chapter 11 provides additional examples of the close relationship between narrative and culturally competent practice. For example, the integrated small group services that were developed tor Native American clients were different from those provided for clients in the urban county. Thomas Sixkiller was hired to do outreach and recruitment to the Native American community and to encourage them to participate in primary health care or mental health services if they chose to do so. There was more emphasis on addressing alcohol and methamphetamine abuse based on the drugs of choice reported by participants, as well as an emphasis on education and management of diabetes and obesity in the integrated urban groups

Thomas developed and cofacilitated the integrated groups for Native Americans in one of the reservation meeting halls. The primary group strategies involved Native American music and group dancing, the acting out of Native American narratives and folklore in the form of brief plays, and artwork that included the members completing paintings of subject areas selected by them. They were free to relate the paintings and stories to their lives or to other factors that seemed unrelated to them. The members told stories or narratives about their paintings that turned out to be helpful to them in terms of coping and problem solving, and they described the process as culturally satisfying as part of the Center's ongoing evaluation.

References

Adler, J. M., Wagner, J. W., & McAdams, D. P. (2007). Personality and the coherence of psychotherapy narratives. *Journal of Research in Personality, 41,* 1179–1198.

Arroyo, J. A., Miller, W. R., & Tonigan, J. S. (2003). The influence of Hispanic ethnicity on long-term outcome in three alcohol-treatment modalities. *Journal of Studies in Alcohol, 64,* 98–105.

Barton, E. (2000). Sanctioned and non-sanctioned narratives in institutional discourse. *Narrative Inquiry, 20,* 341–375.

Beach, M. C. (2005). Cultural competence: A systematic review of health care provider educational interventions. *Medical Care, 43*, 356–373.

Bernal, G., & Saez-Santiago, E. (2006). Culturally centered psychosocial interventions. *Journal of Community Psychology, 34*, 121–132.

Brown, S. A., Kouzekanani, K., Garcia, A. A., & Craig, L. H. (2002). Culturallly-competent diabetes self-management education for Mexicans Americans. *Diabetes Care, 25*, 259–268.

Carley, C. (2005). An influence of spiritual narrative in community work. *Canadian Social Work, 7*, 81–94.

Carpenter, J. (2002). Mental health recovery paradigm: Implications for social work. *Health & Social Work, 27*, 86–94.

Chandler, M. (2006). The rights of the medically uninsured: An analysis of social justice and disparate health outcomes. *Journal of Health and Social Policy, 21*, 17–36.

DeCoster, V. A., & Cummings, S. M. (2005). Helping adults with diabetes: A review of evidence-based interventions. *Health & Social Work, 30*, 259–263.

Dessel, A., Rogge, M. E., & Garlington, S. B. (2006). Using intergroup dialogue to promote social justice and change. *Social Work, 51*, 303–315.

Doe, S. S., & Lowery, D. (2004). The role of evaluation in developing community-based Interventions: A COPC project. *Journal of Community Practice, 12*, 71–88.

Feinberg, M. E., Greenberg, M. T., & Osgood, D. W. (2004). Readiness, functioning, and perceived effectiveness in community prevention coalitions: A study of communities that care. *American Journal of Community Psychology, 33*, 163–175.

Freeman, E. M. (2004). Economic and social development within Black families and communities. In E. M Freeman & S. L. Logan (Eds.), *Reconceptualizing the strengths and common heritage of Black families: Practice, research, and policy issues* (pp. 281–305). Springfield, IL: Charles C Thomas.

Freeman, E. M., & Couchonnal, G. (2006). Narrative and culturally based approaches in practice with families. *Families in Society, 87*, 198–208.

Gilbert, M. C., & Beidler, A. E. (2001). Using the narrative approach in groups for chemically dependent mothers. *Social Work with Groups, 24*, 101–115.

Greene, G. J., Lee, M. Y., & Hoffpauir, S. (2005). The languages of empowerment and strengths in clinical social work: A constructivist perspective. *Families in Society, 86*, 267–277.

Hiersteiner, C. (2004). Narratives of low income mothers in addiction recovery centers: Motherhood and treatment experience. *Journal of Social Work Practice and the Addictions, 4*, 51–64.

Hyde, C. A. (2004). Multicultural development in human service agencies: Challenges and solutions. *Social Work, 49*, 7–15.

Jones, A. C. (2004). Transforming the story: Narrative applications to a stepmother support group. *Families in Society, 85*, 129–138.

Lowery, C. T. (1998). American Indian narratives: ". . . my spirit is starting to come back." *Reflections, 4*, 26–35.

Norman, J. (2000). Constructive narrative in arresting post-traumatic stress disorder. *Clinical Social Work Journal, 28*, 303–319.

Reamer, F.G. (2006). Nontraditional and unorthodox interventions in social work: Ethical and legal implications. *Families in Society, 87*, 191–197.

Tsui, M., Cheung, F.C.H., & Gellis, M. (2004). In search of an optimal model for board-executive relationships in voluntary human service organizations. *International Social Work, 47,* 169–186.

Wertheimer, M. R., Beck, E. L., Brooks, F., & Wolk, J. L. (2004). Community partnerships: An innovative model of social work education and research. *Journal of Community Practice, 12,* 123–140.

Whitbeck, L. B. (2006). Some guiding assumptions and a theoretical model for developing culturally specific preventions with Native American people. *Journal of Community Psychology, 34,* 183–192.

White, M. (2000). *Reflections on narrative practice.* Adelaide, South Australia: Dulwich Centre Publications.

Williams, L., Labonte, R., & O'Brien, M. (2003). Empowering social action through narratives of identity and culture. *Health Promotion International, 18,* 33–40.

Epilogue

LESSONS LEARNED AND FUTURE DIRECTIONS FOR NARRATIVE PRACTICE

> Every road has two directions.
> —Spanish Proverb

This book begins with the letter narrative of a young child in the Midwest from an immigrant German family, and it ends with the cultural narrative of a Native American elder who lives in the Pacific Northwest area of the United States. The two narratives help to clarify the effects of the cultural contexts of clients on their narratives and the importance of their locations and developmental transitions as well (Bermudez & Bermudez, 2002; Caldwell, 2005; Freeman & Couchonnal, 2006; O'Connor, 2005). Those narratives reveal also clients' strengths along with some of the challenges involved in their past and current circumstances.

The two narratives serve as anchors for many other clients' narratives that are recounted in this book, as a reminder of what social workers and other helping professionals know and understand about the effective use of narrative approaches. It is important to pause in order to clarify the lessons practitioners, administrators, policy makers, researchers, and educators have learned about narrative practice. This assessment process can enhance future narrative-related services to clients. The above Spanish proverb points out the importance of understanding the road that has already been traveled or the lessons learned, along with the impact of those lessons on the road that goes forward into the future.

Lessons Learned About Narrative Practice

Narrative Approaches and Effective Social Work Practice

An important lesson learned is that the use of narrative approaches is good social work practice. This is especially the case when those approaches are integrated with other practice theories that are appropriate for clients' situations, such as Multidimensional Family Therapy, and systems, task-centered, and cognitive behavioral approaches (Freeman, 2008). In addition, narrative approaches involve creative and practical strategies for addressing clients' needs in ways that are consistent with social work values and methods. Examples of critical needs include social justice issues in clients' situations that require assessment and problem-solving, supports for maintaining their strengths and resources for addressing their challenges, and frameworks for celebrating the positive role of culture in their lives (Bernal & Saez-Santiago, 2006; Chadiha, Adams, Phorano, Ong, & Byers, 2002; Chan, 2003; Dessel, Regge, & Garlington, 2006; Greene, Lee, & Hoffpanuir, 2005).

The Importance of Narrative Learning Communities

Another lesson is that the use of narrative approaches is enhanced when clinical and administrative learning communities are established in social work and other practice and education settings. Learning communities require a system-wide network of professionals and peer helpers who are committed to the use of narrative approaches at the individual practitioner, administrator, researcher, and educator level (Freeman, 2004). Such commitment is necessary also in order to achieve important structural changes in the relevant settings related to institutional policies and practices (Finn & Jacobson, 2003; Stuart, 1999). Commitment is required as well for the related process of planning, implementing, and monitoring the effects of narrative practice over time (Barton, 2000).

The learning community process can help practitioners and others to change their perspectives about clients as passive individuals without power to clients as vital to a practitioner-client partnership. The process helps practitioners to shift from only asking questions that reveal clients' presenting problems to listening for and eliciting narratives that reveal lived experiences that are relevant to their current concerns (Freeman, 2004; Saleebey, 1994), It can also help administrators, researchers, policy developers, and educators to understand and analyze clients' narratives when it is appropriate. Freeman (2008) indicates that those individuals can use such approaches effectively themselves, including narrative inquiry (researchers), advocacy by storytelling (administrators and policy developers), and curriculum development on deconstruction and externalization skills (educators).

The Role of Clients' Narratives

It is now clear that clients' narratives are primary sources of information about the nature and context of their valuable lived experiences (Freedman & Combs, 1996), whether those experiences have or have not been narrated previously. Clients attempt to share their narratives with service providers and to learn from them even when providers are not aware of the value and importance of those narratives to clients and to effective practice. Clients share their narratives with family members, friends, coworkers, mentors and coaches, and peers as well to gain support and feedback about those narratives (Freeman & Couchonnal, 2006).

The Role of Service Providers' Narratives

Service providers and administrators narrate their own personal experiences and lives, as well as significant professional experiences related to life in their practice settings. Saleebey (1994) assumes those narratives can reveal important lessons providers and administrators have learned about effective narrative practice and how it can be enhanced within practice settings. A resource for helping providers to understand, value, and trust the narrative process of clients is their understanding of their own narratives and the role those narratives play in professionals' lives.

Narrative-Related Aids and Tools

Lessons learned include integrating narrative approaches with the use of cognitive maps, location and spatial maps, games, toys, artwork, music, dance, plays, literature, poetry, and other visual- and auditory-related tools to enhance the positive effects of those approaches (Freeman, 2004; Hinman, 2003; Leukefeld, Godlaski, Clark, Brown, & Hays, 2002; Smith, 2000; Tyson, 2002). Such tools help to concretize important aspects of clients' oral narratives, and in some instances, they serve as a client's narrative itself. These nonverbal or multimedia narratives may be required when developmental, linguistic, physical, Post-Traumatic Stress Disorder, or other inhibiting factors make it impossible for clients to narrate their lived experiences orally.

Basic Narrative Principles and Practice Skills

The fact that narrative approaches can be understood in terms of five basic principles is another lesson learned along the narrative practice road that has already been traveled. However, Freeman (2004) notes this lesson clarifies that basic principles are not a cook book, follow-the-dots, or linear process. Those five principles provide a systematic process for helping providers to learn about and apply narrative practice in a grounded theory and organic manner. They encourage providers to involve themselves in a self monitoring, analytic, and self-correcting process that is the foundation for formally evaluating and improving their practice over time (Brocklehurst & Liabo, 2004).

Advanced Narrative Practice Skills

The previous lesson about self-monitoring and self-correction can help practitioners to build on and enhance their basic narrative practice skills. Advanced skills can be applied differentially to clients' situations based on life span, cultural, gender, disabling, and other conditions (Freeman, 2004). The lessons learned have helped to clarify how practitioners can analyze the specific effects of such factors and conditions on clients' situations and clarify which advanced skills should be used at the micro, mezzo, and macro levels. Advanced skills and interventions include those that target individual clients, small groups, couples, families, the community, and/or large institutions. Examples of advanced skills include using or facilitating coconstructed narratives, improvisation, short novel development, structured social skills stories, the life review process, redecision skills, solution-focused narrative questions, deconstruction, and advocacy by storytelling.

Future Directions for Narrative Practice

The lessons about narrative practice that were discussed in the previous section raise questions about the future of narrative practice. How can those lessons be used to improve such practice in the future? What future conditions and factors do social workers and other helping professionals need to anticipate and prepare to address in ways that can advance those professions and the field of narrative practice?

Improving Narrative Practice

First, based on the lessons discussed in the previous section, what other lessons need to be identified? For example, do the five basic principles in this book address the range of basic skills practitioners and administrators need for effective practice? Or do intermediate narrative skills need to be identified and analyzed as additional lessons learned? The basic principles summarized in Part One of this book are actually five interrelated and but different lessons about how to understand and implement narrative practice at a beginning level. Freeman (2004) indicates those principles apply across practice fields (mental health and child welfare), intervention modalities (small groups and family services), and life span transitions (young childhood and middle adulthood). The five principles can be considered the first generation lessons about basic narrative practice. A future step for improving narrative practice is to monitor and evaluate to what extent those basic principles or lessons are useful and accurately describe the range of basic narrative practice.

Second, in terms of advanced narrative practice skills, is grouping them according to how they can be used with clients across the life span the best way to clarify their use and effectiveness? Are there other equally or more useful ways to group and illustrate those advanced practice skills? Freeman (2004) also assumes those skills can be useful not only to service providers, but also to administrators, policy practitioners, researchers, and educators in professional training programs. Are there other organized ways of implementing narrative practice approaches that are more useful than this learning community and systems orientation, and how can other organizational rubrics be used to improve narrative practice in the future?

Anticipating and Addressing Relevant Future Conditions

ADVANCED TECHNOLOGY AND OTHER TRENDS. A number of future trends and conditions can affect the cross-discipline use of narrative and related practice approaches such as solution-focused questions and improvisation strategies. Two major fields of practice, mental health and primary care, are currently moving toward integrated co-located services in many parts of the country. The two practice fields are at different points currently in terms of their use of narrative approaches. Those different points will have to be considered as providers in the two mostly separate fields begin a more integrated service delivery and collaborative relationship (Borkan, Reis, & Medalie, 2001; Holmes, 2003; Launer, 2002). In addition, future uses of an integrated electronic client record in mental health and primary care settings could affect to what extent narrative practice can be incorporated into this new form of record keeping.

The coordination of services by helping professionals in new nontraditional settings is another trend that is occurring nation-wide that can affect narrative practice. For example, Drug Courts and Mental Health Courts for diverting clients of all ages from the corrections and legal systems are new practice settings for social workers and other helping professionals. Narratives could be powerful tools for those professionals to assess clients' needs and make recommendations to the courts. However, future efforts will need to address how to demonstrate the value of narrative approaches in those legal settings while achieving the institutional diversion goals of those programs (Freeman, 2004; 2008).

SOCIAL CHANGES. Other future changes that need to be anticipated and addressed include the use of online social media by individuals, including clients, and the use of computerized treatment planning by some practice settings. Individuals are posting their narratives and other personal information on social media sites and they are reading and texting other individuals about their narratives on those sites. How should and will providers who use narrative approaches relate to such sites as part of their service delivery in the future? Are those sites potential resources for practitioners to use for community education about narrative practice and services? What will be the pros and cons related to the use of these sites by providers? In some family service agencies and mental health centers, clients are encouraged and supported in writing periodic summaries of their progress in treatment. Can those decision-support computerized programs be used by practitioners to encourage clients to write their information in narrative form? And to what extent could such narratives help in monitoring and evaluating narrative practice with clients in the future?

SOCIAL WORK RESEARCH AND EVALUATION. Social workers and other helping professionals who conduct research and evaluations are currently using narrative strategies to conduct their work. For example, they are using narrative inquiry to study the effectiveness of narrative approaches (Hanninen & Koski-Jannes, 1999; Muntigl, 2004), as well as the effectiveness of other practice approaches (Brocklehurst & Liabo, 2004; Grafanaki; 1999). Many of those researchers and evaluators believe narrative inquiry and other narrative qualitative research methods are more consistent with how social workers provide services to clients and work in a partnership relationship with them (Freeman, 2008).

Social work researchers may need to take a leadership role in the future in demonstrating the viability of narrative-related research methods as they conduct collaborative research with professionals in other fields. This leadership role should also include social workers' research on the strengths perspective and other narrative-related approaches to document those approaches as evidence-based practices (Brocklehurst & Liabo, 2004; Freeman, 2008; Grey & Hastings, 2005).

SOCIAL WORK EDUCATION. Similarly, social work educators can increase their integration of narrative approaches into their curricula in the future. This is an important future step, because there is a danger that such approaches can become the approach or flavor of the year without sustaining longevity in social work practice and graduate education settings. It is equally important to infuse those approaches across the curricula, in direct practice, community, human behavior, research, and policy courses and in the field practica. This systemic integration will be necessary to provide students with an integrated narrative curriculum for future practice, administration, and research (Freeman, 2008).

Conclusion

It is true that every road has two directions. The ultimate goal is to use the road just traveled to understand the lessons that are available from that experience, and to use those lessons to improve the future journey in the other direction. Hence social work and other helping professions are at an important turning point in their use of narrative approaches. They are compelled to do what they encourage clients to do, to narrate their lived experiences with those approaches in order to enhance their future practice and the lives of the clients they serve.

References

Barton, E. (2000). Sanctioned and non-sanctioned narratives in institutional discourse. *Narrative Inquiry, 20*, 341–375.

Bermudez, J., & Bermudez, S. (2002). Altar-making with Latino families: A narrative therapy perspective. *Journal of Family Psychotherapy, 13*(3-4), 329–347.

Bernal, B. & Saez-Santiago, E. (2006). Culturally centered psychosocial interventions. *Journal of Community Psychology, 34*, 121–132.

Borkan, J., Reis, S., & Medalie, J. (2001). Narratives in family medicine: Tales of Transformation: Points in breakthrough for family physicians. *Families, Systems, & Health, 19*, 121–134.

Brocklehurst, N., & Liabo, K. (2004). Evidence nuggets: Promoting evidence-based practice. *Community Practitioner, 77*, 371–376.

Caldwell, R. L. (2005). At the confluence of memory and meaning-life review with older adults and families: Using narrative therapy and the expressive arts to remember and re-author stories of resilience. *Family Journal of Counseling and Therapy for Couples and Families, 13*(2), 172–175.

Chadiha, L. A., Adams, P., Phorano, O., Ong, S. L., & Byers, L. (2002). Stories told and lessons learned from African American female caregivers' vignettes for empowerment practice. *Journal of Gerontological Social Work, 40* (1/2), 135–144.

Chan, D. W. (2003). Multicultural considerations in counseling Chinese clients: Introducing the narrative alternative. *Asian Journal of Counseling, 10*(2), 169–172.

Dessel, A., Regge, M. E., & Garlington, S. B. (2006). Using intergroup dialogue to promote social justice and change. *Social Work, 51*, 303–315.

Finn, J. L., & Jacobson, M. (2003). Just practice: Steps toward a new social work paradigm. *Journal of Social Work Education, 39*, 57–78.

Freeman, E. M. (2008). Methods of practice overview. *Encyclopedia of social work* (20th ed.). Washington, DC: National Association of Social Workers.

Freeman, E. M. & Couchonnal, G. (2006). Narrative and culturally based approaches in practice with families. *Families in Society, 87*(2), 198–208.

Grafanaki, S. (1999). Narrative processes in the construction of helpful and hindering events in experiential psychotherapy. *Psychotherapy Research, 9*, 289–303.

Grey, I. M. & Hastings, R. P. (2005). Evidence-based practices in intellectual disability and behavior disorders. *Current Opinion in Psychiatry, 18,* 469–475.

Greene, G. J., Lee, M. Y., & Hoffpanuir, S. (2005). The languages of empowerment and strengths in clinical social work: A constructivist perspective. *Families in Society, 86,* 267–277.

Hanninen, V., & Koski-Jannes, A. (1999). Narratives of recovery from addictive behaviors. *Addiction, 94,* 1837–1848.

Hinman, C. (2003). Multicultural considerations in the delivery of play therapy services. *International Journal of Play Therapy, 12,* 107–122.

Holmes, J. (2003). Narrative in psychiatry and psychotherapy: The evidence? *Journal of Medical Ethics: Medical Humanities, 26,* 92–96.

Launer, J. (2002). *Narrative-based primary care: A practical guide.* London: Radcliffe Medical Press.

Leukefeld, C. G., Godlaski, T., Clark, J., Brown, C., & Hays, L. (2002). Structured stories: Reinforcing social skills in rural substance abusers. *Health and Social Work, 27,* 213–218.

Muntigl, P. (2004). Ontogenesis in narrative therapy: A linguistic-semiotic examination of client change. *Family Process, 43,* 109–129.

O'Connor, K. (2005). Addressing diversity issues in play therapy. *Professional Psychology: Research and Practice, 36,* 566–573.

Saleebey, D. (1994). Culture, theory, and narrative: The intersection of meanings in practice. *Social Work, 39*(4), 351–359.

Smith, M. A. (2000). The use of poetry therapy in the treatment of an adolescent borderline personality disorder: A case study. *Journal of Poetry Therapy, 14,* 3–14.

Stuart, P. H. (1999). Linking clients and policy: Social work's distinctive contribution. *Social Work, 44,* 335–347.

Tyson, E. H. (2002). Hip hop therapy: An exploratory study of a rap music intervention with at-risk and delinquent youth. *Journal of Poetry Therapy, 15,* 131–143.

AUTHOR INDEX

A

Adams, P., 18, 33, 43, 226
Adler, J. M., 209
Allen, K. R., 165, 167, 169, 185, 199, 204
Alschuler, M., 170
Andereck, P., 178
Anderson, R., 178
Ardila-Rey, A. E., 125
Arroyo, J. A., 215
Asbring, P., 172, 173
Azzara, C., 49

B

Bahyham, M., 5
Bamberg, M., 71, 73, 75
Barton, E., 97, 108, 208, 211, 226
Beach, M. C., 217, 218
Beck, E. L., 117, 218, 220
Beidler, A. E., 25, 32, 44, 112, 208
Belavich, T., 15
Bell, R., 69, 71, 72, 146, 147, 148, 152, 157, 164, 167, 195, 201, 203
Bermudez, J., 18, 195, 225
Bermudez, S., 18, 195, 225
Bernal, B., 132, 226
Bernal, G., 218
Boehm, A., 27, 43
Boje, D. M., 99
Borden, W., 36
Borkan, J., 173, 230
Brabender, V., 197
Brandell, J. R., 21
Brocklehurst, N., 228, 231
Brooks, F., 117, 218, 220
Brown, C., 125, 153, 228
Brown, J. G., 178, 192

Brown, S. A., 215, 220
Bruner, J., 183
Bulow, P. H., 165
Burroughs, T., 178
Buteau, E., 132
Butter, E., 15
Byers, L., 18, 33, 43, 226

C

Caldwell, R. L., 18, 178, 225
Camilleri, P., 146, 164
Campos, L., 204, 205
Carley, C., 208, 209, 220
Carley, G., 33, 161
Carlson, T. D., 197
Carpenter, J., 220
Chadiha, L. A., 18, 33, 43, 165, 226
Chambers, H. D., 125
Chan, D. W., 18, 226
Chandler, M., 209
Chappell, K., 153
Chen, S., 149
Chenfield, M. B., 125
Cheung, F. C. H., 220
Cicchetti, D., 126
Clark, J., 125, 153, 228
Clark, P. G., 178
Clement, J., 117
Coady, N. F., 48
Coates, J., 173
Cole, B., 15
Colton, M. 100
Combs, G., x, 6, 46, 48, 168, 227
Couchonnal, G., 5, 35, 49, 101, 216, 225, 227
Coulter, S. J., 146
Craig, L. H., 215, 220
Crossley, M. L., 14

Csak, N. L. B., 126, 140
Cummings, S. M., 217

D

Daiute, C., 132
Dart, J., 10
Davenport, D. S., 149
Davies, R., 10
Dean, R., 41
DeCoster, V. A., 217
Del Valle, P. R., 125
Dessel, A., 101, 108, 211, 212, 226
Diaz de Chumaceiro, C. L., 187
Dickerson, V. C., 199, 203
Dimaggio, G., 49
Diriye, R. O., 141
Dixon, R. A., 9, 13
Docherty, D., 34, 41, 49, 112, 168
Doherty, W. J., 203
Dollahite, D. C., 195, 205
Donegan, P., 150
Dorfman, L. T., 89, 177
Dorr, C., 173

E

Eisengart, S., 48
Emde, R. N., 126
Erikson, E. H., 177
Evans, J. J., 89, 177
Ewing, J., 167, 199
Ezzy, D., 172

F

Fallon, A. E., 197
Fein, G. G., 125
Feinberg, M. E., 220
Finn, J. L., 110, 226
Fitzpatrick, D., 47
Flemke, K., 167, 169, 204
Freedman, J., x, 6, 46, 48, 168, 227
Freeman, E. M., 5, 6. 9, 13, 17, 19, 25, 26, 28, 32, 33, 35, 38, 47, 49, 57, 68, 71, 72, 74, 86, 97, 101, 126, 135, 147, 148, 153, 157, 161, 173, 187, 216, 220, 225, 226, 227, 228, 229, 230, 231
Freeman, M., 70, 71, 74, 86
Fried, C. B., 153

G

Gair, S., 146, 164
Gale, D. D., 49
Garand, I., 49
Garcia, A. A., 215, 220
Garlington, S. B., 101, 108, 211, 212, 226
Gatania, D., 49
Gellis, M., 220
Gilbert, M. C., 25, 32, 44, 112, 208
Gillispie, C., 169
Gingerich, W. J., 48
Godlaski, T., 125, 153, 228
Golden, K. M., 167, 169, 170
Goodman, M., 195, 205
Gordon, C., 169, 199
Gordon, H., 130
Gould, O. N., 9, 13
Grafanaki, S., 231
Greenbaum, L., 32
Greenberg, M. T., 220
Greene, G. J., 114, 117, 212, 226
Grey, I. M., 141, 231
Groth, L. A., 125
Guerin, B., 141
Guerin, P., 141
Gusdorf, C., 74, 83

H

Habermas, T., 69, 71, 73, 75
Haley, A., 179
Hall, M. E., 165, 170
Hannan, E., 97
Hanninen, V., 231
Hardy, K. V., 193
Hastings, R. P., 141, 231
Hays, L., 125, 153, 228
Hecker, L., 197
Henderson, S., 69, 71, 72, 146, 147, 148, 152, 157, 164, 167, 195, 201, 203
Hermans, H. J. M., 49
Hiersteiner, C., 32, 36, 43, 209
Hinman, C., 125, 142, 228
Hipp, K., 15
Hodge, D. R., 199
Hoffpanuir, S., 114, 212, 226
Holland, J., 69, 71, 72, 146, 147, 148, 152, 157, 164, 167, 195, 201, 203
Holmes, J., 230

Holmes, I. H., 33
Howarth, E., 130
Howells, M., 178
Huenefeld, N. E., 165, 170
Husser, E. K., 165
Hyde, C. A., 218
Hyden, L., 165

I

Ingram, J. G., 89, 177

J

Jacobson, M., 110, 226
Jarvinen, M., 178
Jones, A. C., 208, 212
Jordan, C. E., 165

K

Kadar, J., 15
Keller-Cohen, D., 169, 199
Kelley, P., 47, 49, 54, 114, 169, 173
Kempton, W., 97
Keyton, J., 99
Killian, K. D., 195, 196
Killmer, M., 197
Kirkpatrick, D., 197
Kitchell, A., 97
Kondrat, D. C., 117
Koski-Jannes, A., 231
Kouzekanani, K., 215, 220

L

Labonte, R., 211, 215, 218
Laird, J., 149
Lang, C., 149
Laszloffy, T. A., 195
Launer, J., 172, 230
Leber, D., 165
Lee, J. A. B., 27
Lee, M. Y., 114, 117, 173, 212, 226
Leukefeld, C. G., 125, 153, 228
Levene, L. E., 48
Levine, R., 34
Liabo, K., 228, 231
Linhorst, D. M., 101

Lowery, C. T., 18, 220
Luborsky, M. R., 68, 70

M

Macfie, J., 126
Marks, L. D., 195, 201, 205
Mathe, C., 201
Mattis, J. S., 15, 16
McAdams, D. P., 70, 71, 209
McCabe, A., 127
McCarthy, M., 167, 169
McColl, M. A., 34, 41, 49, 112, 168
McEachern, A. G., 125
McGill, D. W., 17, 18
McGrellis, S., 69, 71, 72, 146, 147, 148, 152, 157, 164, 167, 195, 201, 203
McLeod, J., 14, 196
McQuaide, S., 60
Medalie, J., 173, 230
Meichenbaum, D., 47
Mentzer, R. A., 117
Miller, W. R., 215
Mitchell, A. M., 49
Murty, S. A., 89, 177
Muntigl, P., 203, 231

N

Nishimoto, K., 150
Nevo, M., 42, 43
Norman, J., 47, 217

O

O'Brien, M., 211, 215, 218
O'Connor, K., 141, 225
Ong, S.L., 18, 23, 43, 226
Ontario Consultants on Religious Tolerance, 198, 201
Osgood, D. W., 220
Osher Life Long Learning Institutes, 178, 179, 185, 186

P

Paha, C., 69, 71, 73, 75
Pals, J. S., 93, 178
Pargament, K., 15

Peck, M. D., 89, 178
Pellegrini, R. J., 173
Pence, R., 178
Phorano, O., 18, 33, 43, 226
Pierret, K. 165, 173
Pinnell, S. R., 117
Pipher, M., 62
Polo, M., 70
Potts, R., 15
Power, J. R., 89, 177

R

Rasmussen, B. M., 63
Rawlins, C., 132
Regge, M. E., 101, 108, 211, 212, 226
Reis, S., 173, 230
Rivett, M., 130
Roche, S. E., 65
Rosen, L. V., 149
Rye, M., 15

S

Saez-Santiago, E., 132, 218, 226
Saleebey, D., 17, 21, 31, 34, 36, 47, 227
Salvatore, G., 49
Sarbin, T. R., 173
Sawyer, R. K., 125, 126, 142
Schultz, K., 164
Schwartz, R. C., 196
Scott, A., 15
Semerari, A., 49
Sharpe, S., 69, 71, 72, 146, 147, 148, 152, 157, 164, 167, 195, 201, 203
Shenk, D., 89, 178, 183
Shimizo, K., 150
Siebert, H., 117
Smith, F. L., 99
Smith, M.A., 228
Smolar, A., 197
Stalker, C. A., 48
Staples, L. H., 27, 43
Stone, D. J., 165
Stuart, P. H., 100, 101, 226
St. Amour, M. J., 125, 126, 141

T

Taylor, J. A., 187

Thomson, R., 69, 71, 72, 146, 147, 148, 152, 157, 164, 167, 195, 201, 203
Thornton, J. E., 5, 8, 13, 26, 38
Tonigan, J. S., 215
Toth, S. I., 126
Tsui, M., 220
Tyson, E. H., 153, 228

U

Ucko, L. G., 33
U.S. Surgeon General, 178

V

Veroff, J., 165

W

Wagner, J. W., 209
Walker, A. J., 185
Weber, Z., 167, 169
Webster, J. D., 177
Wendell, R., 196
Wertheimer, M. R., 117, 218, 220
Wesner, S., 49
Whitbeck, L. B., 218, 220
White, M., 198, 203, 216
Williams, L., 211, 215, 218
Woike, B., 70
Wolk, J. L., 117, 218, 220
Wood, G. G., 65
Wortham, S., 70

Y

Yates, S., 141
Yeich, S., 34
Yellow Bird, M. J., 26

Z

Zimmerman, J. L., 199, 203
Zinnbauer, G., 15

SUBJECT INDEX

A

Assessment and intervention, integration of, 49, 51–56
Asymetrical power relationships, definition of, 98

B

Bibliotherapy, with adolescent clients,
  examples related to transition narratives, table 7.1, 151;
  practice applications, poetry therapy, 148–152,
  short novel development, 154–162,
  structured social skills stories, 153
Boot strap narratives,
  form of privileged narratives, definition of, 100;
  function of, 100;
  related to marginalization of non privileged groups, 100

C

Change,
  related to use of narrative questions, 47–48
Cognitive behavioral therapy,
  example of a related
  redecision making narrative, 203;
  integrated with narrative approaches, 198–205
Cognitive maps,
  instructions for and examples of, 56–58, figure 3.1, 57 (adults); 129–131, figure 6.1, 131,133–134, figure 6.2, 133 (children); 158-159, figure 7.1, 159 (teenagers)
Community and social change narratives,
  example of, 219–220;
  related to planning and implementing macro system changes, 217–222
Couple counseling and narrative approaches,
  inconjunction with family counseling, 197–201
Cultural analysis of an organization,
  example of, 102–103
Cultural competence,
  definition of, viii;
  examples involving narrative approaches, 126–139, 139–143, 147–153, 154–162; 196–205
Cultural factors, addressed in narrative practice, related to,
  age (children), 18–19, 125–134, 139–143
  age (older adults), 50–58, 80–94
  age (teenagers), 146–162
  disabilities, 170–175
  gender, 32–40, 64–66,164–175
  location, 12–22, 154–162, 217–221
  race and ethnicity, 50–58, 80–94, 139–143, 147–153, 177–193, 217–222
  spirituality and religion, 139–143, 179–185, 195–205, 221–222
  sexual orientation, 154–162, 209–212
Cultural narratives,
  analysis of, 32, 220–223;
  definition of, 32;
  examples of, 219–220
Cultural theory,
  application to narrative practice, 10, table 1.2, 11, 12, 17–19
  related to the meaning of cultural moments, 18

D

Dream narratives,
  example of, 59–60
  narrative intervention based on, 60–66

E

Early intervention services for children, using narrative approaches with, 134–139
Entitling narratives,
  purpose of, 43–44;
    examples of, involving children, 139–131, 133–134
    involving teenagers, table 7.1, 151, 160–161
Exception narratives,
  analysis of, 112–115, 119–120;
    distinguishing between experience-gathering and information gathering, 37–38
    examples of, 111–112, 117–119
    providers' difficulties in eliciting, 35
    related to identifying clients' strengths and competence, 35

F

Family counseling and narrative approaches, 201-205
  focus on nuclear family changes, 202–203
  focus on family changes in external areas, 204–205
Found narratives, forms and examples of, 30
  practice applications involving, 32–33
Future directions for narrative practice, regarding, anticipating and addressing future conditions,
    such as, advanced technology and other trends, 230,
    practice improvements, 229– 230
    social changes, 230– 231
    social work education, 231
    social work research and evaluation, 231

G

Gender development narratives,
  examples of, regarding females 164– 167
  examples of, regarding males 170–171
  narrative practice and analysis of, regarding females, 167–170
  narrative practice and analysis of, regarding males, 171–174
Group work and narrative approaches, related to,
  addiction recovery support groups, 209–214
  diabetes education groups, 214–217
  gender related development, 165–174
  HIV/AIDS support groups, 170–175
  life review groups, 179–185
  medication management, 89–94
  social skills training, 131–132
  substance abuse treatment, 28–44
  gender related development, 165–174

I

Imposed narratives,
  cultural groups affected by, 35–36
  example of, 36–37
  function of, 35–36
  methods for counter-acting the effects, 37
Individual narratives,
  examples of, 13, 29, 77, 171

L

Lessons learned from narrative practice related to,
  advanced narrative practice skills, 228–229
  basic narrative principles and practice skills, 228
  narrative approaches and effective social practice, 226
  narrative learning communities, 226–227
  narrative-related maps and tools, 227–228
  role of clients' narratives, viii-ix, 8–9, 26–27, 70–71, 227;
  role of service providers' narratives, 25–26, 40–42, 227
Letter narratives,
  examples of, 12-13, 188-189
Life narratives,
  components related to, 72-74,
    figure 4.1, 72;
    construction of adolescents' life narratives; 83, 87, 88
    definitions of, table 2.1, 31, 32, 69-70

Subject Index

effects of biographical gaps on adolescents' life narratives, 75
examples of, 82-89; 91-92, 93-94 (adolescents), 181, 187-189, 190-191 (older adults)
related to adolescents' short novel development, 160-161
related to older adults' identity and coming to terms with life, 177, 179-185
resources for older adults' life narrative work, 178-179

Life span development theory,
application to narrative practice, 10, table 1.2, 11, 12-14
as explanation for change or growth, 13-14

Life span transitions,
examples of life span developmental transitions related to narratives, 14, 27-28, 125-127, 146-148, 164-165, 177-179, 195-196
purpose of, vii

Life story writing process, with older adults, 185-189
examples of, 187-189
practitioners' roles regarding, 186-189
related to Osher Life Learning Institutes, 179, 185-186

Lived narratives,
examples of, 29

Loss and grief approaches,
integrated with narrative work, 56-58

M

Metaphors,
related to family and couples' conflicts and resolutions, 195-205
related to transition narratives, 156, 160

Marginalized narratives,
definitions and examples of, 100-101, 104, 208, 216
effects from using marginalization analysis (externalization and deconstruction) to create change, 98-109;
from using advocacy by storytelling for power transfers, 110-115
from using narrative gaps and opening questions to identify exceptions and facilitate change, 209-219

N

Narrative approaches, used across the life span
with adolescents, 36-37, 75-89, 146-162, 201-205
with children, 10-23, 125-143
with middle adults, 170-175, 195-205
with older adults, 50-58, 89-94; 177-193
with young adults, 28-35, 37-44, 58-66, 165-170
with young and middle adults, 208-217

Narrative forms
types and examples of, table 2.1, 31
practice applications related to, 31-32

Narrative functions,
types and examples of, table 2.1, 31

Narrative impasses,
consequences of, 5-6
resolution of, 6

Narrative indicators, related to the
emergence of narratives, for narrators, 38-40
for listeners who enter the narratives, 40-42

Narrative mentoring,
example of explicit life narrative mentoring, 190
example of implicit life narrative mentoring, 191
related to intergenerational life narrative historians, 189-193
related to service providers' roles, 191-192

Narrative practice
applied to specific need areas/practice settings, caregivers' support group services (policy reforms), 115-119
diabetes education/primary care, 214-217
drop in center life review group, 179-185;
eating disorders, 148-153
family violence, 58-66, 73-89, 126-134; 195-205
organizational and community change, 217-222
out of home placements, 75-89, 152-153
school-related issues/community settings 134-139
school related issues/education settings, 36-37, 126-134, 154-162
substance abuse treatment/mental health, 27-37, 209-214

work-related problems/EAPs, 50–58
youth mentoring services, 110–115
youth prevention programs, 134–138
Narrative principle 1
   main elements of, table 1.1, 7, 8–9;
   significance to practice, table 1.1, 7, 9
   theories related to, 10, table 1.2, 11, 12–19
Narrative principle 2,
   main elements based on strengths perspective, 26–27
   related to narrative forms and functions, table 2.1, 31
   significance to practice, 27, table 1.1, 7, 31
Narrative principle 3
   main elements of, 47–48
   related to focus and purpose of naming questions, table 3.1, 52
   significance to practice, 48–49
Narrative principle 4
   main elements of, 70–71
   meaning making components, 71–74 figure 4.1, 72
   significance to practice, 71
   themes of meaning related to, 77–82, table 4.1, 79–80
Narrative principle 5
   main elements of, 98–100, figure 5.1, 99
   related to stigma and social justice issues, 100–101
   significance to practice, 100–101
Narrative principles,
   characteristics of, table 1.1, 7–8;
   overview of, 6, 8
Narrative skills, advanced level,
   coaching intergenerational narrative mentoring, 189–193, table 9.1, 184
   evaluation of outcomes, 129–134, 135–139
   facilitating life narrative review process with older adults, 179–185, table 9.1, 184
   facilitating the life story writing process with older adults, 185–189; table 9.1, 184
   helping families to celebrate new resolution based metaphors and rituals, 202–205, table 10.1, 200
   helping families to develop and practice new redecision skills, 199–202, table 10.1, 200
   helping middle adults use solution-focused questions to address important life course changes, 170–175, table 8.2, 174
   helping young adults to reauthor narratives and poems, 165–170, table 8.1, 168
   integrating individual, group, and systems strategies for transition and life narrative work with adolescents, 154–162, figure 7.1, 159
   listening to and analyzing families' existing metaphors, 196–199, table 10.1, 200
   providing developmentally-sensitive transition narrative services to adolescents, 147–153, table 7.1, 151
   using advocacy by storytelling, power transfer narratives, and community social change narratives, 217–222
   using narrative gap questions to facilitate change, 209–214, table 11.1, 213
   using narrative opening questions to facilitate change, 214–217, table 11.1, 213
   using power sharing narrative strategies in education settings, 127–134, table 6.1, 128, figure 6.1, 131, figure 6.2, 133
   using power sharing narrative strategies in community settings, 134–139
   using power sharing narrative strategies with pre-school children, 139–143
Narrative skills, basic level,
   asking timing and context questions, 19–22, table 1.2, 20
   applying the knowledge base, 10–19;
   conducting marginalization analyses (externalization and deconstruction) with helping professionals, 101–109, figure 5.1, 105, table 5.1, 107
   identifying narrative forms and functions, 27–37
   listening for/acknowledging spontaneous narratives, 37–41, table 2.2, 39, 42–44
   using advocacy by storytelling and power transfers with marginalized clients, 110–115, 107
   using advocacy by storytelling and power transfers with privileged clients, 115–119;
   using life narrative coherence questions, 75–82, table 4.2, 81

using life narrative continuity questions, 82–94, table 4.3, 84–85
using solution-focused naming questions, 49–58, table 3.1, 52
using solution-focused unpacking questions, 58–66, table 3.2, 61

Narratives,
definition of, vii, 9–10
definition related to a letter narratives, 13
knowledge components of, 10, table 1.2, 11, 13–18
source of clients' strengths, viii
used in conjunction with other theories, ix;
including solution-focused approaches, 47–57,
systems theory, 56–58,
task-centered approach, 56–58

O

Organization narratives,
as the basis for organizational analysis and planned change, 101–119
cultural analysis of, 102–104
related to social justice issues, 103–109
types of, sanctioned/privileged narratives, 102,
types of, nonsanctioned/low currency narratives, 103–104;
Other people's narratives,
definition and examples of, table 2.1, 31;
sources of, 33

P

Parables, public domain narrative forms, definition of, table 2.1, 31
Play strategies with children,
examples of, Table 6.1, 28
general practice applications of, 125–144
integrated with graphic art and computer technology methods, 134–139
Poetry
as an aspect of bibliotherapy, table 7.1, 151;
example of haiku as a narrative form, 150;
practice application of haiku and the related practice analysis, 149–152

Power sharing narrative strategies,
definition of, 125
developmental relevance to services for children, 126–127
examples of, table 6.1, 128
methods for evaluating outcomes from using as pre/post strategies, 127–134
practice advantages for providers, 126
practice applications of, 139–144
Practitioners'/administrators' narratives,
examples of and relevance to practice, 102, 104, 118–119
Prevention services for children,
using narrative approaches, 126–134
Problem saturated narratives
definition and examples of, 173
practice analysis of, 171–174
Progressive narratives
definition and examples of, table 2.1, 31, 35
functions of, 35
Proverbs, narrative forms,
examples of, 5, 25, 30, 46 68, 97, 225
practice applications related to, 5–6, 25–26, 33, 46–47, 68–69, 101
roles related to narrative practice in general, 225
Public domain narrative forms,
definition and examples of, table 2.1, 31

R

Regressive narratives
definition and examples of, table 2.1, 31
effects on narrators and listeners, 33–34
function of, 34–35
related to acknowledging clients' strengths, 34

S

Shared storytelling strategy
example of, 76–81;
themes of meaning related to, 77–82, table 4.1, 79–80
Single event narratives
definition of, table 2.1, 31, 32, 69–70
examples of, 29, 50-51, 150

types of, table 2.1, 31
Social construction theory
    application to narrative practice, 10, table 1.1, 11, 12, 14–15
    foundation for reconstructed identities, 14–15
    relevance to the cultural context of narratives, viii
Social justice issues
    examples of, 110–120, table 5.2, 113–114
    integrating individual, group, and systems strategies for transition and life narrative work with adolescents, 154–162, figure 7.1, 159
    related to life story writing by older adults, 187–188
    related to marginalized narratives, 101–109, figure 5.2, 105, table 5.1, 107, 210–217
    relevant narrative skills, conducting marginalization analyses (externalization and deconstruction), 101–09; figure 5.1, 105, table 5.1, 107
    using advocacy by storytelling, power transfer narratives, and community social change narratives, 217–222
    using advocacy by storytelling and power transfers with marginalized clients, 110–115, 107
Solution-focused approaches,
    related to narrative practice in general, 47–48
    specific practice applications, 49–56, 170–175
Spirituality (theory)
    application to narrative practice, 10, table 1.1, 11, 12, 15–17
    as an aspect of narrative practice, 139-143
    as compared to religion, 15–16
    related to organizational and community change, 221
    role of spiritual crises in the emergence of narratives, 16

Stability narratives
    definition and examples of, table 2.1, 31
    function of, 35–36
Strengths perspective
    as main element of principle 2, 26–27
    compatibility with narrative approaches, vii–viii
    related to affirming clients' narration of their experiences, 43–44
    related to clients' expertise and local knowledge, 47–48
    related to regressive narratives, 34
Systems theory,
    as the basis for planning systems changes, 101
    examples of ecomaps and other cognitive maps, figure 3.1, 57, figure 6.1, 131, figure 6.2, 133, figure 7.1, 159
    integrated with narrative approaches, 56–58, 156–162
    related to an example of organizational and community change, 217–222
    related to marginalization analysis and organizational policy changes, 101–109

T

Task-centered approach,
    integrated with narrative approaches, 56–58
Transition narratives
    examples of, 156
    definition of, 147;
    related to clients' epiphanies/critical moments, 151-152, 157–159
    relationship to life narratives, 147–148

U

Unnarrated experiences
    effects on narrators and listeners, 30, 32
    role of dominant society regarding, 32

Charles C Thomas
PUBLISHER • LTD.

P.O. Box 19265
Springfield, IL 62794-9265

- Freeman, Edith M.—**NARRATIVE APPROACHES IN SOCIAL WORK PRACTICE: A Life Span, Culturally Centered, Strengths Perspective.** '11, 218 pp. (7 x 10), 7 il., 19 tables.

- Payne, Brian K.—**CRIME AND ELDER ABUSE: An Integrated Perspective. (3rd Ed.)** '11, 374 pp. (7 x 10), 7 il., 18 tables, $68.95, hard, $48.95, paper.

- Henderson, George & Willlie V. Bryan—**PSYCHOSOCIAL ASPECTS OF DISABILITY. (4th Ed.)** '11, 254 pp. (7 x 10).

- Palmo, Artis J., William J. Weikel & David P. Borsos—**FOUNDATIONS OF MENTAL HEALTH COUNSELING. (4th Ed.).** '11, 486 pp. (7 x 10), 6 il., 3 tables.

- Storey, Keith & Craig Miner—**SYSTEMATIC INSTRUCTION OF FUNCTIONAL SKILLS FOR STUDENTS AND ADULTS WITH DISABILITIES.** '11, 272 pp. (7 x 10), 14 il., 31 tables.

- Bernet, William—**PARENTAL ALIENATION, DSM-5, AND ICD-11.** '10, 264 pp. (7 x 10), 15 il., 4 tables, $63.95, hard, $43.95, paper.

- Bryan, Willie V.—**SOCIOPOLITICAL ASPECTS OF DISABILITIES: The Social Perspectives and Political History of Disabilities and Rehabilitation in the United States. (2nd Ed.).** '10, 284 pp. (7 x 10), 12 il., $61.95, hard, $41.95, paper.

- Ensminger, John J.—**SERVICE AND THERAPY DOGS IN AMERICAN SOCIETY: Science, Law and the Evolution of Canine Caregivers.** '10, 340 pp. (7 x 10), 25 il., 1 table, $69.95, hard, $47.95, paper.

- Jones, Carroll J.—**CURRICULUM DEVELOPMENT FOR STUDENTS WITH MILD DISABILITIES: Academic and Social Skills for RTI Planning and Inclusion IEPs. (2nd Ed.)** '09, 454 pp. (8 1/2 x 11), 50 tables, $63.95, (spiral).

- Rhoades, Ellen A. & Jill Duncan—**AUDITORY-VERBAL PRACTICE: Toward a Family-Centered Approach.** '10, 420 pp. (7 x 10), 19 il., 5 tables, $79.95, hard, $59.95, paper.

- Thyer, Bruce A., John S. Wodarski, Laura L. Myers, & Dianne F. Harrison—**CULTURAL DIVERSITY AND SOCIAL WORK PRACTICE. (3rd Ed.)** '10, 370 pp. (7 x 10), 14 tables, $74.95, hard, $54.95, paper.

- Blomquist, Barbara Taylor—**INSIGHT INTO ADOPTION: Uncovering and Understanding the Heart of Adoption. (2nd Ed.)** '09, 212 pp. (6 x 9), $27.95, paper.

- Bryan, Willie V.—**THE PROFESSIONAL HELP-ER: The Fundamentals of Being a Helping Professional.** '09, 220 pp. (7 x 10), $51.95, hard, $31.95, paper.

- Emener, William G., Michael A. Richard & John J. Bosworth—**A GUIDEBOOK TO HUMAN SERVICE PROFESSIONS: Helping College Students Explore Opportunities in the Human Services Field. (2nd Ed.)** '09, 286 pp. (7 x 10), 2 il., 4 tables, $44.95, paper.

- Li, Yushi (Boni)—**EMIGRATING FROM CHINA TO THE UNITED STATES: A Comparison of Different Social Experiences.** '09, 250 pp. (7 x 10), $52.95, hard, $34.95, paper.

- Stepney, Stella A.—**ART THERAPY WITH STUDENTS AT RISK: Fostering Resilience and Growth Through Self-Expression. (2nd Ed.)** '09, 222 pp. (7 x 10), 16 il., (14 in color), 19 tables, $56.95, hard, $38.95, paper.

- Thompson, Richard H.—**THE HANDBOOK OF CHILD LIFE: A Guide for Pediatric Psychosocial Care.** '09, 378 pp. (7 x 10), 5 il., 15 tables, $79.95, hard, $55.95, paper.

- Wilkes, Jane K.—**THE ROLE OF COMPANION ANIMALS IN COUNSELING AND PSYCHOLOGY: Discovering Their Use in the Therapeutic Process.** '09, 168 pp. (7 x 10), 2 tables, $29.95, paper.

- Wodarski, John S. & Marvin D. Feit—**EVIDENCE-BASED INTERVENTIONS IN SOC-IAL WORK: A Practitioner's Manual.** '09, 318 pp. (7 x 10), $62.95, hard, $42.95, paper.

5 easy ways to order!

PHONE: 1-800-258-8980 or (217) 789-8980
FAX: (217) 789-9130
EMAIL: books@ccthomas.com
Web: www.ccthomas.com
MAIL: Charles C Thomas • Publisher, Ltd. P.O. Box 19265 Springfield, IL 62794-9265

Complete catalog available at ccthomas.com • books@ccthomas.com

Books sent on approval • Shipping charges: $7.75 min. U.S. / Outside U.S., actual shipping fees will be charged • Prices subject to change without notice

HV 41 .F66 2011
Freeman, Edith M.
Narrative approaches in
social work practice